AN EIGHT DAYS' RETREAT

FOR

RELIGIOUS

BY

HENRY A. GABRIEL, S.J.

IMPRIMI POTEST

J. A. Rockliff, S. J.,
Praep. Prov. Calif.

NIHIL OBSTAT

Sti. Ludovici, die 7. Sept. 1914

F. G. Holweck,
Censor Librorum.

IMPRIMATUR

Sti. Ludovici, die 8. Sept. 1914

✠Joannes J. Glennon,
Archiepiscopus
Sti. Ludovici.

PREFATORY NOTE

To claim much originality for a work like this, which is little more than an adaptation of the Spiritual Exercises of St. Ignatius, would be obviously unwarranted, while to mention in detail all the sources from which it has been derived in the course of a score of years would be next to impossible. However, I gladly acknowledge that, besides being under great obligation to many members of the Society who have labored successfully to explain and illustrate the wonderful little book of our Holy Founder, particularly to Fathers Roothaan, Meschler, Denis, Verbeke, von Hummelauer, and Nonell, I am largely indebted to the well-known work of Rev. M. J. Ollivier, O. P., for the descriptive portion of several meditations on the Passion. The text of the Spiritual Exercises has, of course, been extensively quoted throughout the work.

The Author.

Santa Clara, Cal.
Feast of the Annunciation, 1914.

PRAYERS

Before the Points.

Come, O Holy Ghost, fill the hearts of Thy faithful and enkindle in them the fire of Thy love.

V. Pour forth Thy Spirit, and they shall be created.

R. And Thou shalt renew the face of the earth.

Let us pray.— O God, Who by the light of the Holy Spirit didst instruct the hearts of the faithful, grant that by the same Holy Spirit we may relish what is right and may ever rejoice in His consolations. Through Christ our Lord. Amen.

Hail Mary.

O Sweetest Heart of Jesus, we implore,
That we may love Thee daily more and more.

After the Points.

We give Thee thanks, O Almighty God, for all Thy benefits, Who livest and reignest world without end. Amen.

Hail Mary.

Sweet Heart of Jesus, be my love.
Sweet Heart of Mary, be my salvation.

ANIMA CHRISTI.

Soul of Christ, sanctify me!
Body of Christ, save me!
Blood of Christ, inebriate me!
Water from the side of Christ, wash me!
Passion of Christ, strengthen me!
O Good Jesus, hear me!
Within Thy wounds, hide me!
Suffer me not to be separated from Thee!
From the malicious enemy defend me!
In the hour of my death, call me!
And bid me come to Thee;
That with Thy Saints I may praise Thee
For ever and ever. Amen.

CONTENTS

CONTENTS

AN EIGHT DAYS' RETREAT

DURING THIS HOLY RETREAT, CONSIDER FREQUENTLY THE ADORABLE PERSON OF JESUS CHRIST, PRESENTING HIMSELF BEFORE YOU IN HIS INCOMPARABLE MAJESTY AND SHOWING TO YOU HIS WOUNDED HEART, WHOLLY INFLAMED WITH LOVE, WHILST ADDRESSING TO YOU IMPLORINGLY THESE TENDER WORDS: "MY CHILD, GIVE ME THY HEART."

"MY CHILD, GIVE ME THY HEART."

FIRST DAY

SPECIAL PATRON: St. Michael.

MOTTO: "Lord, who is like to Thee?"— Ps. 34:10.

SPIRIT: Humility on account of my Nothingness.

READING: Imitation; Bk. I, C. 1, 2, 3, 10, 11, 20.
Bk. II, C. 5, 6.
Bk. III, C. 1, 9, 10, 25, 40.

Begin the Retreat with great earnestness, thorough recollection, and humble confidence, generously offering yourself to God that He may dispose of you according to His most Holy Will.

THE RIGHT DISPOSITION

Introductory Remarks.— In St. Luke 19:41-44, we read: "And when Jesus drew near, seeing the city, He wept over it saying; 'If thou also [like my true disciples] hadst known, and that [even] in this thy day [on which I, thy Lord and Savior have come to teach, convert, and save thee,] the things that are for thy peace; but now they are hidden from thy eyes. For the days shall come upon thee, when thy enemies shall cast a trench about thee, and compass thee round, and straiten thee on every side, and beat thee flat to the ground, and they shall not leave a stone upon a stone, because thou hadst not known the time of thy visitation!'" God Almighty is towards each individual soul, towards every single human being, more loving than the most devoted father, mother, or friend, infinitely more so. He is ceaselessly watching over each one of us with the most tender care, the most patient solicitude, intending and arranging even the smallest details of our lives, for our temporal happiness no less than for our eternal bliss. Oh! let us not resist His unspeakable love, let us not disappoint His mysterious longing, let us not compel Him by our ingratitude to withdraw from us the outward protection of His Admirable Providence or the inward guidance of His Holy Spirit.

The Retreat is a time of rest from study and care, but also a time of exertion and prayer. Yes, especially a time of prayer, of earnest, whole-

souled, humble, confident supplication for light and
strength, crying out to our Lord, like the blind man
of Jericho, "Jesus, Son of David, have mercy on
me." Yet we should avoid nervous strain, not work
ourselves up into an unnatural or hysteric condition.
We should not take it for granted that every fault
and every defect, mentioned in the course of this
Retreat, must necessarily be ours. Reason and reflection are never to be discarded. It would be well,
with due permission, to take some extra repose if
really needed in order to keep awake during the Meditations, but by all means we should take plenty of
fresh air during free time and sufficient nourishment
at our meals.

The Retreat, when made in the old and approved
way, consists chiefly of a series of Spiritual Exercises, arranged by St. Ignatius Loyola; exercises that
will teach us how to conquer ourselves and to regulate our lives for the greater glory of God, in other
words, how to rid ourselves of all sin and inordination in order to accomplish perfectly the Divine
Will. The Meditations form the main work of the
Retreat. Even while preparing the Points we should
raise our heart to God in humble aspirations, but
afterwards we should put forth all our energy to secure the desired fruit by fervent supplication. Next
in importance to the Meditations come the daily
Examens of Conscience, which may very profitably
be devoted to a thorough review of our past lives and
especially of the last year. The other exercises,
Holy Mass, Communion, Visits, Office, Rosary,
should all be directed to the immediate object of the
Retreat, which is our thorough self-conquest, our lasting amendment, our complete conversion. But we
should not tire ourselves with a multiplicity of vocal

prayers. The spiritual reading indicated for each
day is left entirely free, except the study of our Rules
and Customs. As to Holy Communion, all can receive every day; and this will certainly prove very
helpful to stir up in our heart a sincere desire of
correcting our faults and of advancing in virtue, provided we strive to make a better preparation than
usual as well as a more fervent thanksgiving.
Indeed, Holy Communion is one of the best means to
profit by the Retreat, and hence is to be recommended most emphatically. Yet, at the same time,
any one is free not to receive from motives of humility or for reasons of convenience. While each one
should pray for his own special needs, he should
nevertheless remember also those of others, that the
entire Community may reap the most abundant fruit
from these Exercises.

Subject of this Meditation.—The Disposition with
which we should enter upon this Retreat.

Composition of Place.— To see myself kneeling or
prostrate in the presence of the Blessed Sacrament
and hearing these words issue from the tabernacle:
"Come to Me all ye that labor and are heavy burdened, and I will refresh you."

**Petition for the Grace which I do actually Need
and should ardently Implore.**— That I may enter upon
this Retreat, that I may accept this most loving in-
invitation of the Sacred Heart of Jesus, with the best
possible Disposition, so as to make it better than any
previous Retreat, and thus to render it the beginning
of a life of real Holiness.

**First Point. I should Look Forward to the Re-
treat with Desire and Longing.**

This Desire ought to be Sincere and Earnest, in

view of the great and manifold dangers arising from the Flesh, the World, and the Devil: — my natural habits of thoughtlessness, precipitation, restlessness; and still worse, my deep-rooted passions, pride, sensuality, selfishness: the contagious atmosphere, the downward influence, the continual allurements of the World: the past victories, the present temptations, and the future assaults of the Devil. Perhaps I have already had a sad experience of my weakness, perhaps even yielded to doubts about my Vocation; but in any case I must not be deluded by a false security. I should, then, welcome this Retreat, with great earnestness at least from this moment. "Remember," says our Adorable Savior, " that Satan has asked to sift you like wheat, and that the Devil is going about like a roaring lion, seeking whom he may devour. Yes, you especially, Religious, that have consecrated your lives entirely to My holy Service; you most especially, who left the world before knowing its corruption and entered the convent with souls unsullied by mortal sin." Briefly, as I have to save my soul at any cost and in spite of every obstacle, my Desire of the Retreat ought to be most Sincere and Earnest.

But this Desire should also be Intense and Ardent. For the Retreat is an extraordinary Divine Favor: singular inasmuch as it is granted to relatively very few; entirely unmerited by me but rather very much demerited; and most precious, being productive of true peace of soul on earth and conducive to my eternal bliss in heaven. If made properly, these Spiritual Exercises will enlighten me on the motives that should animate me and the principles that are to guide me in the Service of God; they will arm me against the enemies by which I am surrounded and the hindrances which I have to overcome. These same Exercises have filled the Church with fervent members, the convents with holy Religious, and Heaven with blissful Souls. Witness their effect in Bl. Peter Faber, in St. Francis Xavier, in Bl. Edmund Campion, and hundreds of other Jesuits; in thousands of Confessors and Martyrs, Priests, Religious, and Laymen. Did I myself not experience something similar in my first Retreat well made? Every time I go through these Exercises, they should cause also in me a thorough transformation of mind, a real conversion of heart. Who knows but this may be for me the last time.

My Desire should nevertheless be Joyous and Gladsome. As a matter of fact, the Retreat imposes no special burden; after the mental work is done, nothing remains but to pour out my soul in prayer; and even as to this, God Himself will do by far the greater part, if only I let Him, if only I open my mind to His light, if only I yield my heart to His grace. Besides, if I strive to do my little share generously from the start, His Divine consolations will abundantly compensate me for the extra fatigue, self-restraint, and seclusion. But even if I should not be favored with any sensible fervor, yet all is to be done in the spirit of sweetness, that is, with Humility and Confidence. For I am not alone, I am not fighting single-handed; however unworthy, I am a member of a numerous Religious Institute; more than this, I am a child of the Holy Catholic Church, militant on earth, suffering in purgatory, and triumphant in Heaven. They are all praying and interceding for me; the fervent faithful, the Holy Souls, the Blessed Saints and Angels, and what is specially comforting, the Immaculate Virgin Mary herself, the Great Mother of God.

Second Point. Dispositions to be Avoided on Entering upon the Retreat.

Among the Dispositions to be Avoided because they would hamper the efficacy and destroy the object of the work on which we are entering, we should particularly guard against the following.

Discouragement with the Results of our past Retreats and Disappointment at the Failure of our good Resolutions.—" What is the use? " we may be tempted to exclaim: " I have made already so many Retreats, and I am still as imperfect as ever, if indeed not worse, while the Religious Life instead of becoming easier seems to be getting harder every year." One might just as well argue with himself after this manner: " What is the use of eating and drinking? After so many thousands of meals I am still no stronger than when I was in my twenties, in fact, I am growing weaker and more sickly every day." Life is a race for Heaven. When we set out on a long excursion, everything is easy and pleasant in the coolness and brightness of the early morning; but how different things appear, when we plod along weary, thirsty, and footsore, in the hot and dusty afternoon. So it has been ordained by our Heavenly Father, that, as we grow older in years, sincerer in humility, and stronger in love, our difficulties, our sufferings, and even our temptations should increase in the same proportion, in order that thus we may always be able to increase our merits and to advance towards Perfection. There is no progress without hindrance, just as there is no life without death. As to our former Resolutions, we should bear in mind that we took them, not to be kept unfailingly, nor to be broken constantly, but in order that we might learn, pray, and labor to carry them out. Hence we have no reason to be discouraged on account of the past, only we should profit by our experience. Let us combine the buoyant energy and generous enthusiasm of earlier years with the sincere self-distrust and sturdy determination of riper age.

Listlessness and Routinism.— Just as we are all subject to Discouragement, so we are all inclined towards Stagnation. Some Religious do not seem to take the Retreat seriously till the third or fourth day. Their mind and heart are so engrossed with pet creatures, recreation, study, classwork, business-matters, that they lose the first and most important part of the Retreat in Listlessness, Frivolity, and Distraction. "This is the hour for us to rise from sleep." We must shake off this spiritual sloth, this baneful lethargy, and get to work at once. We must by all means make a good start and give ourselves wholly to solitude, silence, recollection, application, and punctuality. To lose our time is silly, to despise the grace of God is sinful. Other Religious, again, lead an existence that is largely mechanical and almost purely natural, in one word, Routinary. They perform their duties, either because they have to, or because they like to, superficially, without any desire of perfection. To practise some extra penance, to make an extra visit to the Blessed Sacrament, seldom or never enters their head. Such as these are likely to pass the entire eight days of the Retreat without making the least exertion. Unless we resolutely cast off this fatal Routinism, we cannot hope either for consolation in these Spiritual Exercises or for perseverance in our Vocation. "Because thou art neither hot nor cold, I will begin to vomit thee out of my mouth."

Selfishness, Worldliness, and Pride.— There are

also found Religious who enter upon the annual Retreat with a somewhat uneasy conscience, and their main object is to recover peace of soul by means of a general confession at the end of the second or third day. Once that is over, they flag in their exertions and the rest of the Retreat possesses little or no interest for them. Their Selfishness renders them spiritually short-sighted. These persons forget that the only way to insure permanent peace of conscience is to work with might and main at their sanctification, at the mortification of their unruly passions, at the imitation of Christ our Lord and His Saints. Again, though their number is small, one may sometimes meet Religious infected with Worldliness, who entertain a more or less definite notion that sanctity is not for them, that holiness is somewhat out of place in our modern business-world. But the worst Disposition of all would be a spirit of Pride prompting a Religious to think that he has no need of so much prayer, or to take it for granted that he cannot learn anything from this Retreat, or even to criticise, reject, and condemn the exhortations, counsels, and warnings of the Director. Without making much account of his natural qualifications, we should listen to his words with humble docility and great eagerness. Unless we entertain a supernatural regard for the Priest appointed to guide us through this Retreat, we shall derive from it but little fruit, even if he were as learned and holy as St. Alphonsus Liguori or St. Ignatius Loyola.

In conclusion, then, discouragement and disappointment; listlessness and routinism; selfishness, worldliness, and pride; — these are the Evil Dispositions I must Guard Against, by vivid realization of my Spiritual Needs and by fervent prayer for the

Divine Assistance, if I wish to make a really good Retreat. How should I wish to have made this Retreat, if it were to be my last? That is the way I will strive to make it, with the grace of God.

Third Point. The One Essential Disposition Required to Begin the Retreat Perfectly.

This most Desirable Disposition is within the reach of all. It consists in the Firm Determination to make during these few days all possible progress, to reap from these Spiritual Exercises the greatest possible benefit. The Holy Founder of Clairvaux, in the early period of his Religious Life, used to spur himself on with this question: "Bernard, for what purpose did you come here?" Of all occasions none surely can be more appropriate than the present one to ask myself after the same manner: "Why did I forsake the world, my relatives, my home, my earthly prospects? Why did I become a Religious?" All I need just now is the manly resolve to enter upon the Retreat this very instant, with my whole heart and soul, with all my energy of body and mind, occupied with nothing else but the work of my salvation and sanctification, and embracing generously whatever inconvenience or weariness it may entail. If, however, I fear the opposition of Nature and the molestation of Satan, it would be well to forestall these difficulties by performing this evening a little act of penance. For I must remember, this Determination is Absolutely Required to make the Retreat. Without it, indeed, it were useless to begin.

But if I am really determined to make the greatest possible progress, to reap from this Retreat all the fruit I can, I must be ready for any sacrifice that God in His Wisdom and Love may demand. Hence this Firm Determination conceived in my inmost heart, should find its natural expression in a Sincere Act of Self-Oblation to God my Lord, that, especially during this Retreat, He may deign to dispose of me entirely as He pleases;— a humble and fervent offering of my body and my soul, but particularly of my own will, so apt to go astray to my own injury and misery, while God can will only what is good, my peace here and my bliss hereafter. All the advantages, therefore, will be for myself; though not for myself alone. No. For on this Retreat will depend not only my own sanctification and salvation, but also, according to the inscrutable designs of God, the sanctification and salvation of many others.

I ought, then, to make this offering with great Alacrity, considering that, in spite of my many infidelities, He should allow me, invite me, nay, even command me to make this holy Retreat; with boundless Confidence, for though "I can do nothing of myself," especially nothing that is hard to human nature, "yet I can do all things in Him that strengthens me;" with the utmost Generosity, knowing that the more liberal one shows himself towards the Divine Majesty, so much the more liberal he shall also find God towards himself. Since God has been so Good, so Loving, so Merciful towards me all along, while I was so niggardly, so ungrateful, so faithless towards Him, what favors will He not shower down upon me, if I really give myself to Him by this Firm Determination and Total Self-Oblation?

Colloquy with our Dear Lord in the Adorable Sacrament, saying to each of us; "Come to Me all ye that labor and are heavy burdened, and I will refresh you," and adding with Infinite Condescension and

Incomprehensible Love; "My child, give Me thy heart." I will beg, beseech, implore, conjure Him, by the sufferings of His Immaculate Mother and also my Heavenly Mother, Mary, that during this Retreat, every day, every hour, every moment, I may live wholly with Him and for Him, after her most admirable and perfect example, in silence, solitude, and application. I will conclude with the Our Father.

THE FOUNDATION, FIRST PART

Introductory Remarks.— If our past Retreats have sometimes failed to produce any lasting fruit, this was probably owing to one or other of two causes. Either we applied ourselves during the first two or three days only, or else we began to apply ourselves only after the first two or three days. In any case such failure has presumably been due to our neglecting and resisting, to some extent, the grace of God. This time let us enter upon the Retreat with the Right Disposition; namely, an Earnest Desire, or rather a Firm Determination to derive from these Spiritual Exercises the Greatest Possible Benefit, to get out of them All the Good we Can.

Subject of this Meditation.—" The Principle and Foundation; " namely, that principle, that simple and evident truth, which forms the foundation of the whole spiritual life, of all asceticism: a supreme maxim for the intellect and at the same time a solid basis for the will. " Man was created to praise, reverence, and serve God our Lord, and by this means to save his soul; and the other things on the face of the earth were created for man's sake, in order to aid him in the prosecution of the end for which he was created."

Composition of Place.— To see heaven opened above me and hell yawning under my feet, and myself placed on this earth halfway between heaven and hell, saying to myself: " For all eternity I shall either be in heaven enjoying the bliss of God, or else in hell suffering the torments of the damned; and it depends on me alone, which of these two conditions will be my lot within a few years, perhaps within a few months, weeks, or days; it depends on me alone whether I am to gain so great a good or to incur so great an evil."— How true! How certain! How appalling!

Petition.— What is the particular need of my soul with regard to this awful alternative? Light to know clearly, to realize intimately the supreme importance of this affair — my salvation and sanctification — as well as strength to adopt resolutely all the means that will most surely bring it to a successful issue. This, then, I must implore with all the energy of my being, with the utmost earnestness and fervor.

First Point. The End of Man in This Life.

God Created Me.— Let me briefly recall the Existence of God, His Infinite Perfection, His Absolute Sovereignty. By a free act of His Will, guided by Supreme Wisdom, He made me out of nothing; my body, indirectly, through my parents and ancestors back to Adam and Eve and even to the beginning of the physical universe; my soul, directly, only a few years ago. Without God I should not exist. Of myself I am sheer nothingness. He created me to His own image and likeness, which is found especially in my soul: a spiritual and immortal being, endowed with a mind capable of knowing truth, of having certainty, and under the necessity of accepting truth as soon as sufficiently manifested; and endowed with a

will capable of loving goodness, free to determine its
own action, yet under the necessity of ever striving
after happiness.

My whole soul, consequently, is created capable
of making progress, of being more and more perfected
while here on earth. This present existence, therefore, is, as it were, but the first day of my creation,
it is only the dawn of my life; and actually, at every
moment, I am preserved and sustained by the same
creative act of Almighty God. Evidently, by the
very origin and essence of my being, I entirely belong to God, much more, incomparably more than a
vessel belongs to the potter who made it; I completely depend on God, incomparably more than any
slave could depend on his master. God is the Sovereign Lord and Absolute Master of my life, of my
body, of my soul, of my senses, of my faculties, of
everything that in any sense can be called mine. I
am His servant, His possession. How noble, then, is
my origin! What an immense elevation! For of
myself I am nothing, and without God I should still
be nothing.

God's Motive in Creating Me.— God created me by
an infinitely wise and absolutely free choice. Not having the slightest need of me, He created me out of
pure love. Yet, though God created me freely, He
did so, of course, for a definite purpose. He created
me for Himself. In what sense? As the infinitely
Skilful Artist, He could not create me except for His
own Extrinsic Glory to be attained in the perfection
of my mind by knowledge, of my will by love, and of
my whole being by happiness. He created me necessarily for Himself, not because of any deficiency in
Himself, but because of His Supreme Excellence, His
Ineffable Goodness, that I might reflect and manifest

His own Unlimited Perfection, in my mind, in my will, and in my whole being. This, then, is my Ultimate End.

God also supplied me with all the means to work out this sublime purpose, and the use of these means constitutes my Proximate End in this life. In other words, I have been placed in this world, that I might more and more perfect in myself the Image and Likeness of God: that with my mind I might Praise Him; acknowledge Him, study His Divine Attributes, investigate His Gracious Designs, and at the same time realize my manifold limitations, my own nothingness: that with my will I might Revere Him; love His Transcendent Beauty and Infinite Holiness, submit and conform myself in all things to His Fatherly Providence, and especially worship Him by faith, hope, and charity: that with my whole being I might Serve Him; accomplish His Adorable Will in all things, at all times, under all circumstances, as intelligently and affectionately as possible, whether it be expressed by way of Commandment, or Counsel, or Example.

I am, then, on earth to fulfil the office of a Heavenly Spirit; I am even now to exercise what is afterwards to constitute my eternal bliss. My entire existence is to be one of loving adoration, of unreserved dedication and irrevocable consecration of my mind, my will, and my whole being to God.— Here we may note how Prayer combines Praise, Reverence, and Service. We cannot do more for the Glory of God than by Prayer, and all the rest is useless, except it be preceded, accompanied, and followed by Prayer. Prayer should prompt, animate, and fructify all we do. It is often only when through sickness or old age we are incapacitated for other duties, that we begin to lead really useful lives by Prayer. With this in mind, St. Paul says: " Pray without ceasing."

A Matter of Paramount Importance.— Praise, Reverence, and Service,— this alone can make me truly great and noble; this is to be my only occupation, my only care, my only joy, my one absorbing thought. This is the only thing I am made for, namely, to know, to love, and to serve God. No nobler End can be conceived for the creature, it is common to men and Angels, it is the End of the Blessed Virgin Mary, " the Handmaid of the Lord," the End of Christ our Savior " the Servant of God." Again, this End is essential and supreme, to which everything else in man ought to be subordinated. Whatever, therefore, is done in keeping with this End, is wise, good, and honorable; whatever is done apart from this End, is foolish, bad, and disgraceful. Everybody knows how sacred a thing it is to be under a moral obligation. What should we think of a perfidious man, of a husband, a soldier, a servant that proves false to his main duties? What then should we think of one who, repudiating the essential allegiance he owes to God his Creator, says, " I will not serve "? What duty can there be more sacred than this one, which is the sole foundation of every other duty?

Hence, no wealth or health, no exterior or interior endowment, except in some way furthering the service I owe to God, has for me any real value; it would only contribute to my greater misery. No thought however sublime, no desire however noble, no work however brilliant, no action however efficient, no enterprise however grand, should ever occupy me even for one instant, unless positively according with the Divine Will and actually tending to the Divine

Glory. How diligently, therefore, I should strive to eliminate all trashy thoughts, all worldly desires, all disorderly words and actions, which flow inevitably from a vagrant mind, an unstable will, and an undisciplined body.

Such, then, is Direct Praise, Reverence, and Service. But there is also a Praise, Reverence, and Service that may be called Indirect, which consists in acknowledging God, loving God, and serving God, in our neighbor as His representative by Charity, and especially in our Superiors as His vicegerents by Obedience. In a certain sense this Indirect Praise, Reverence, and Service is more practical, because we do not see God, but we do see our fellow men. In fact, no one can fail to observe that Obedience, demanding as it does the complete sacrifice, the continual consecration of our mind, our will, and our whole being, truly combines the loftiest Praise, the deepest Reverence, and the best Service. On the other hand, if instead of esteeming, cherishing, and assisting our neighbor, if instead of revering, loving, and obeying our Superior, we have been contemptuous, hateful, and rebellious, have thought, spoken, and done evil against these special representatives and actual vicegerents of Almighty God; we can readily infer from this what has been our Direct Praise, Reverence, and Service.

As a Religious, I may consider, besides, that I owe Praise, Reverence, and Service, in the spirit of my holy Institute, that I should practise Prayer, Charity, and Obedience in accordance with my Rules. To this well-defined Praise, Reverence, and Service, I have bound myself by the Vows; which is certainly a great grace, enabling me to work unceasingly at my own sanctification, at my own perfection, at God's

Greater Glory. Hence how highly I should esteem my Vocation.

In conclusion, I am not created to have my own way, to follow my whims, to do as I please, to be my own master. To do anything apart from or without regard to the Holy Will of God is inordinate, because it is beside my one only purpose in life; but to do something against the Adorable Will of God is sinful. Evidently, I must shun and hate not only sin, but also inordination, which leads to sin. If an object does not answer its purpose, we call it useless and throw it aside or else destroy it. Similarly, if a man does not fulfil the End for which God made him,— the only End for which God could make him,— that man will be cast out as useless into utter darkness, into everlasting fire. Here, let me stir up sincere regret and confusion for the past, make a generous resolve for the future, and renew my self-dedication.

Second Point. My Proximate End in the Next Life.

My Service is to Benefit Myself.— Among men the service rendered by an employee or an inferior is for the benefit of the employer or the superior. The contrary happens when we serve God. No creature, in fact, can by its exertion afford Him any intrinsic utility, for in Himself He is infinitely rich and good and happy. But God desires us to labor in His service that He may reward us, that He may bestow upon us as a merited recompense the Eternal Felicity of Heaven. And the more excellent our Service, the greater also will be our Recompense. There are, we may say, three degrees in the Divine Service. Ordinary Service goes only so far as not to break any

Commandment that is binding under pain of mortal sin. Better Service, of course, would be given by avoiding also venial sin. But the Best Service that can be rendered to God consists in accomplishing His Adorable Will, even when not to do so would involve no sin, even when no strict Precept or Prohibition is laid upon us, but when He simply manifests to us His Good Pleasure by way of Counsel or Example. Amongst men, the first and second kinds of service would not be accounted such at all. What employer would think that his workmen are fulfilling their duty, merely because they do not kill him or any other member of his family, or do not rob him of all his money, or do not set fire to his house and shops? What master would consider his servant to be entitled to any wages, simply because he has not done any injury to the children, nor stolen anything from the storeroom, nor quarreled with his fellow servants? Yet God, the Lord of Infinite Majesty, rewards, as if it were a great and signal service, the very avoidance of sin, mortal and venial. How liberally, then, will He not reward those who would offer themselves to accomplish His most Holy Will, however hard may be the task, at the merest intimation, without any positive command; those who strive to give Him the very Best and most Perfect Service?

How God Intends to Reward my Service.— Reason tells us that service calls for reward, just as neglect of service merits punishment. God created us in order that after praising, revering, and serving Him in this world, He might make us eternally happy with Him in Heaven. Hence, no earthly good,— no wealth, nor learning, nor enjoyment, nor prominence,— nor all earthly goods together, can completely satisfy man's desire for happiness. God

alone can fill our heart; in God alone our soul can
rest. The highest reward, however, we could naturally expect would consist in the perpetual contemplation and enjoyment of God, the Supreme Goodness and Beauty, through some created image of the
Divine Essence. But, as we know by revelation,
God in His Wonderful Love has gone much further.
Not satisfied with bestowing on us this natural bliss,
He has designed to render us capable of seeing Him
directly, "face to face," and to make us drink of the
torrents of His own Measureless Felicity. "Behold
what manner of charity the Father hath bestowed
upon us that we should be called, and should be the
sons of God." (1 John 3 :1.) By Sanctifying Grace
we have actually been adopted into the Divine
Family. This is Supernatural Salvation, a reward
such as no eye has seen, no ear has heard, and no
human heart has ever conceived; yet most certain,
because promised us by Him who is infinitely Faithful, Liberal, and Powerful. An Everlasting, Unspeakable, Divine Good. All the labors, and even
all the sufferings of this life, would be nothing in
comparison with this unfading crown of glory. But
I must merit it by my voluntary Service.

How Earnestly God Desires to Save Me.— To protect me against my own weakness, He threatens me
with everlasting punishment, if I should despise so
inconceivable a favor, if I should refuse my cooperation to merit so magnificent a reward. Hence there
is no other course open to me: I must either be
eternally blissful with God, the Saints, and the
Angels in Heaven, or else be eternally wretched with
Satan, the Demons, and the Reprobate in Hell.
There the soul, irresistibly drawn towards perfect
happiness, will remain completely isolated from the

Sovereign Good, filled with sadness, devoured with remorse, and overwhelmed with despair. This pain of loss will be accompanied by a corresponding pain of sense, both afflictions to be unchangeable and endless. Again, God desires my Supernatural Salvation so vehemently that He has deigned to become Man, to labor, to suffer, and to die for me on the Cross, in the deepest ignominy, in the most frightful torments. And to attain His loving purpose still more surely, He has bestowed on me the special grace of a Religious Vocation. In view of all this, my confidence should simply know no bounds.

The Supreme Importance of Salvation.— This is the plain truth I must strive by all means to bring home to myself: Supernatural Salvation is "unum necessarium," the one thing necessary. If I save my soul, my life is a splendid and everlasting success; if not, a total and irreparable failure. "For what does it profit a man if he gain the whole world and suffer the loss of his own soul?" And how am I to save my soul? By praising, revering, and serving God; by doing God's Holy Will. To this, then, I must apply myself with all my energy. I must keep the Commandments; I must observe my Rules; I must practise prayer, humility, charity, and obedience; I must follow the inspirations of grace, the promptings of the Holy Ghost. Yet how easy it is to save my soul, in comparison with the difficulty of acquiring earthly goods, perishable wealth, and empty honors! How easy especially with the abundant helps placed at my disposal in the Religious State!

Third Point. End or Purpose of Other Creatures. All things Outside my own Personality are In-

tended to be Helps.— They were all created for my
sake, in order to aid me in reaching my End, in fulfilling my purpose, namely, the praise, reverence, and
service of God in this life, and the salvation of my
immortal soul in the next. How can they help me?
By contemplation, by use, and by abstinence. Of
these three ways the first is most noble, the second
most common, and the third most necessary, inasmuch as neglect of the third means excess in the second and unfitness for the first. How admirable God's
Goodness is, considering that every one of these
countless creatures is a token of His personal love
and tender solicitude for me, His possession, His
servant, His child. They were created for me, not
I for them; none, in fact, could satisfy the boundless
cravings of my heart made for God, Who alone can
fill its capacity.

To Help me is their Only Purpose.— I am not the
absolute master of these creatures, of my senses, my
faculties, my time, or my talents. They are given
me by God, not for my selfish enjoyment, but for my
rational use. I am not to usurp them or to discard
them just as I please, according to my momentary
impulses. But I am under strict obligation to avail
myself of them for the purpose which God has in bestowing them upon me, namely, to praise Him,
to revere Him, to serve Him, and thus to merit
Supernatural Salvation. If I use creatures aright
I shall be rewarded, if not, I shall be punished.
God being an All-Wise Administrator, observes most
carefully what use I am making of His creatures; He
will soon call me to a minute account, and then either
admit me to everlasting happiness in Heaven, or else
condemn me to unending affliction in Hell. Practically, therefore, everything depends on whether or

not I use creatures according to God's Adorable
Will. Merely not to use a gift, to hide it as the sloth-
ful servant of the Gospel hid his talent, would be ungrateful. So I was, every time I did not avail myself of an actual grace, every time I neglected to follow an inspiration of the Holy Ghost. Another in-
ference I should draw is, that I must never blame anything, any person, or any circumstance, for my failings and my sins. All this is sheer self-deception.
The cause of my faults lies wholly and solely in my
own perverse will.

Three Categories of Men.— We may note, in conclusion, that, with regard to this First Principle and
Foundation, responsible men may be divided into
three categories. First, those who have wilfully
turned their minds away from the knowledge of their
Creator and of their own End; secondly, those who
still know God and their duties but deliberately
make a bad use of creatures; thirdly, those who intimately relish these fundamental truths and shape
their whole conduct in perfect accordance with the
Divine Will: Infidels, Worldlings, and Saints; but
among the latter incomparably more holy than all
others, the Blessed Virgin Mary.

Colloquy with God, my Heavenly Father, giving
expression to my intense gratitude for all His favors, to my profound regret for my numberless shortcomings, and to my firm purpose, henceforth to live,
think, speak, and labor only for the praise, reverence,
and service of His Infinite Majesty, using everything
that is intended to help me strictly in accordance with
His Holy Will, but never usurping any creature for
my own selfish satisfaction. At the end I will recite the Our Father.

OUR SPIRITUAL DUTIES

In this first Conference we shall briefly consider the best way of performing our principal Spiritual Duties; namely, Meditation, General Examen, Particular Examen, Confession, and Holy Communion.

Meditation.

We should always prepare the Subject overnight. It ought to be suitable, that is, adapted to our actual needs and trials. If we find the matter proposed unsuitable or inapplicable, if we cannot see in it anything that will help us to pray, we might prepare our own points, taking as the subject of our Meditation some event from the Life or the Passion of our Lord. However, we should not deem a subject unsuitable or inapplicable simply because it does not appeal to us forcibly from the start. A manly effort to meditate on what has been proposed will often, with the help of grace, make us discover a rich gold-mine where before we saw but an arid waste. This much is certain: our morning Meditation will never succeed unless we make a practical and thorough Preparation for it overnight.

The " additions " are recommendations or directions given by St. Ignatius, which we should diligently comply with, if we desire to make a good Meditation. While seemingly trivial, it would be difficult to overestimate their importance. Before falling asleep, we should think, for the space of a Hail Mary, of the hour when we have to rise and of the object for which we intend to do so, briefly re-capitulating the Meditation we are to make; namely, the Three Preludes,— the subject-matter or the historical fact, the composition of place, and the petition,— together with the Points. In the morning, we should get up instantly at the first sound of the bell, say some fervent prayer — if possible after kneeling down and kissing the floor — being determined not to lose one moment of the precious time granted us for the exercise of Divine Love, in thought and desire, in labor and suffering. Immediately after this, while dressing, we should resolve to attend to our Particular Examen during the forenoon, and then once more recall the Meditation we are about to make, as we did overnight, but now also striving to stir up in our soul appropriate sentiments and dispositions.

These directions are simple and easy enough; but the unfortunate fact is that we are all very much hampered in their observance by laziness, sensuality, and worldliness. Why should we have to accuse ourselves so frequently of being distracted during Meditation and other Spiritual Duties? Why can we not begin each Exercise of Prayer with earnestness and give to it our whole mind and heart, like sensible, wide-awake men of business? It is because our lives are not sufficiently real, sincere, consistent, and thorough. It is because we forget that, what makes us Religious is not the habit of serge but the habit of self-crucifixion.

Next comes the "ingress," or the entrance upon our Meditation, and this too is a matter of great importance. We must by all means strive to make an energetic start, with the firm determination not only to pray but also to succeed in prayer. The ingress

comprises the following acts; Presence of God,
Preparatory Prayer, Composition of Place, and Petition. As to placing ourselves in the Presence of
God, St. Ignatius recommends that, one or two steps
from the place of kneeling, we should stand for about
the space of an Our Father, lifting our mind and
heart up to God and considering how He looks down
on us as about to meditate. The following prayer
may be helpful to fix our attention: "I will speak
to the Lord, though I am but dust and ashes. O my
God, I believe that Thou art everywhere present.
All things are naked and open to Thy eyes. Thou
seest my weakness, my nothingness, my manifold
sinfulness. Thou lookest down upon me with pity
and with love." Then we should make an act of inward adoration and outward humiliation, saying for
instance, "I bow down before Thee with my body
and soul and worship Thee. Oh! teach me to pray."

The Preparatory Prayer may be worded more or
less like this: "O Lord my God, look graciously
down upon Thy creature, the work of Thy hands, and
grant me grace, that all my thoughts, desires, and
actions, particularly during this Meditation, may
be purely directed to the praise and glory of Thy
Infinite Majesty." It might be well now and then to
vary the form of the Preparatory Prayer, especially
if this would help us to recite it more thoughtfully
and fervently. The Composition of Place consists
in seeing with the eyes of the imagination the spot
where what we are going to meditate on was enacted.
Sometimes this is to be taken in a metaphorical
sense, as in the Exercises on Sin, where sin is considered to reside in our own soul. The Petition,
finally, consists in asking of God our Lord, with all
the intensity of our will, the particular grace sug-

gested by the subject-matter. St. Ignatius constantly takes care to remind us that the grace we beg for in the Petition should be the actual object of our earnest desires.

We are now ready to begin the Meditation proper. The one purpose of Mental Prayer, we must remember, is converse with the Most High, union of our soul with the Infinite Goodness. The labor of the mind in discussing the subject is intended to lead up to this converse, this union; but if the Holy Ghost should move our heart at once to pray, so much the better. For spiritual union is consummated, not in sublime knowledge, but in supernatural love. Hence we must be careful not to neglect the end for the means. Meditation should consist mainly of ardent emotions prompted by the consideration of the matter proposed in the Points, and of fervent petitions arising from the remembrance of our past shortcomings or the realization of our present needs, both of which — emotions and petitions — we should express in Colloquies, or conversations, with God and the Saints, at any time during our Meditation but particularly towards the end. It is imperative that we do not look for novelty or excitement, for something on which to feed our natural curiosity or morbid sentimentality. Pious selfishness is just as much a hindrance to Prayer as spiritual apathy.

But what if dry and distracted? Of course, we must suppose that these distractions are not wilful; for if they were, our Meditation would be only a pretense, and we had much better read a useful book or sweep a staircase. But we entered Religion to become Saints and for nothing else. We resolved long ago to live for this one purpose; and hence, unless we want to take back our offering and to cheat ourselves of our reward, we ought to make the best possible use of all the means that will enable us to reach Sanctity, the first and chiefest of which is Prayer. Yet, even though we are really anxious to make a good Meditation, our mind may sometimes persist in wandering. What are we to do? We may fall back on the Sacred Passion or the Holy Eucharist; or else we may make acts of faith, hope, love, humility, contrition, according to the Second Method of Prayer, dwelling on each thought and reflecting upon the meaning of the words as long as this affords us some spiritual relish; or again we may recite the Our Father, the Hail Mary, a psalm, a hymn, an invocation, slowly and meditatively, according to the Third Method of Prayer. But the main thing is not to give up, and even if we cannot pray at all, to keep at least in the Divine Presence, patiently waiting for a heavenly favor, in the spirit of the Syrophenician woman who, when our Savior told her, "It is not good to take the bread of the children and to cast it to the dogs;" humbly remonstrated, "Yea, Lord, for the whelps also eat of the crumbs that fall from the table of their masters." (Matt. 15:26-27.) As to drowsiness, if habitual, the cause should be investigated and removed; if occasional, we should try to rouse ourselves thoroughly, not only spiritually but also physically. But whatever difficulties we may have to contend with during our Meditation, in any case towards the end, we should renew our petition for the desired fruit, making a special effort to pray intently and concluding our Colloquy, if simple, with the Lord's Prayer, but if triple, with the Hail Mary, the Anima Christi, and the Our Father.

A Review of our Meditation is indispensable, if we desire to secure its full benefit. By investigating our

failures it teaches us also how to overcome our difficulties and correct our shortcomings. If we find
that we have been at fault, we should impose on ourselves some suitable penalty. This Review can be
made at any hour in the morning — though breakfast time would generally seem the most convenient — for about ten or fifteen minutes, and may
be very appropriately concluded with a visit to the
Blessed Sacrament.

Besides Common Mental Prayer, or Ordinary
Meditation, there is Affective Prayer and the Prayer
of Simplicity. In Affective Prayer the reasoning is
done more easily and rapidly and excites affections
proportionately more ardent and efficacious, which
consequently take up the greater part of our Meditation. The Repetition of previous Meditations affords a good opportunity to practise Affective
Prayer. But when these affections become more simple, that is, less varied and less interrupted or im-
peded by mental considerations, they constitute
what is usually termed the Prayer of Simplicity.
The Exercises of the Second Week, especially after
having been repeated frequently, are well adapted
to the practice of the Prayer of Simplicity, which is
the same as Ordinary or Acquired Contemplation.
From this highest degree of apparently natural Mental Prayer, Divine Grace alone, and not our own efforts, may raise us to some elementary form of manifestly Supernatural Prayer or Mystic Union. These
two kinds of Prayer are differentiated by this, that in
Ordinary Contemplation God is satisfied with helping
us to conceive and to recall His Presence, while in
Extraordinary Contemplation He deigns to give us
an experimental knowledge and a spiritual sensation
of His Presence. Just as there are successive steps

in what has sometimes been called Natural Prayer, so there are several stages in what is commonly styled Supernatural Prayer, namely, Incomplete, Complete, Ecstatic, and Transforming Union, this last favor approaching most closely to the crowning grace of Heaven, the perfect participation of the Divine Nature by Beatific Vision. There can be no doubt that, if we are faithful in the performance of our daily Meditation, God will, in His own good time, make us advance to something more profitable, more arduous, and also more sublime.

The General Examen.

The General Examen is an exercise of Prayer chiefly bearing on our sins and imperfections and commonly made twice a day, about noon and before retiring, for the space of fifteen minutes. After placing ourselves, as usual, in the Presence of God, we should first give Him Thanks for all His favors, but particularly for those received during the previous part of the day.

Secondly, we should beg earnestly for Light and Grace that we may know and detest our sins. This petition, to be sure, is not always made with sufficient fervor. Yet precisely here we are facing one great obstacle to progress; we do not know ourselves, we do not recognize our faults, we do not want to see them in their real malice and baseness, we shut our eyes to them, we connive at them, we excuse and palliate them, we lay the blame for them on accidental circumstances, the conduct of others, our own fatigue, illness, and what not, and even we pride ourselves on them as if they were acts of virtue. Our mind is darkened and our will is hardened. Hence we do need much light and grace, and should make this petition with great humility and confidence.

Now, thirdly, comes the Examination proper, which should not require more than three or four minutes. A very convenient way is to take up the main obligations of the Religious Life: Prayer, mental and vocal; Self-Denial, in suffering and contempt; Charity, in thought, speech, and action; our Vows; our Rules; our Resolutions. Or else we may go through the successive hours and occupations of the preceding portion of the day, but this procedure is more open to distractions.— Here we may also make our Particular Examen.

Fourthly, we should make acts of sincere Contrition, including all the sins of our past life, especially those which were more grievous or more deliberate. We should also lament with deep confusion the ugly and dangerous dispositions of our soul, of which our faults are but so many symptons — self-esteem, self-love, sensuality, impatience, ingratitude towards God, unkindness towards our neighbor,— in other words, our actual and manifold leaning towards rebellion, our pride. After all, in this lies the only evil, the only sin: in the foolish turning away of our heart from God, in our feeble volition departing from His most Holy Will. And to humble Contrition we should join suitable Satisfaction. After resolving on what we ourselves can shortly do in expiation for our numerous offenses, we may for this same end also offer up the prayers, penances, and sufferings of all fervent Religious on earth, the merits of the Saints and Angels in heaven, especially those of the Blessed Virgin Mary, and above all the infinite atonement made by Christ our Lord.

Lastly, we should renew our Determination to correct our faults, to keep our Rules, to perform our

Duties, to practise our Particular Examen, with special regard to present circumstances and positive difficulties; and then conclude this General Examen with the Our Father.

The Particular Examen.

Some Religious fancy that they could never acquire a virtue by the method of the Particular Examen, that is, by a gradually increasing number of acts. They fear it would break their head to try to make daily, say a hundred acts of humility, or of charity, or of union with God. But their apprehension is entirely groundless. Worldlings surely do not break their head by making daily, not hundreds, but even thousands of useless and sinful acts in thought, word, and deed. All habits, and especially good ones, are formed slowly; but once formed they enable us to make a large number of acts with comparative ease. What we need is dogged perseverance in applying ourselves to the subject chosen, and the very fact that we have not as yet fully succeeded should suffice to keep the matter fresh and interesting.

The first thing to do, therefore, is to select a Suitable Subject, some defect we desire to overcome or some virtue we wish to acquire. In deliberating about this choice we should implore the Divine guidance and avail ourselves of the counsels and admonitions of our Superiors. But this is not enough. In the next place, we must firmly make up our mind that, with the help of grace, we are going to conquer ourselves in the matter decided upon, by a diligent use of the Particular Examen; and, especially when there is question of some outward fault, we must not hesitate to set a limited time for its correction. Besides, we should carefully study our duties, occupations, and surroundings, with a view to the opportunities they may offer for carrying our resolution into practice. So much for the preparation.

The real work consists in this: never to allow the subject of our Particular Examen to be entirely absent from our mind; daily to pray earnestly for energy and perseverance, particularly during Mass, Communion, and Visits; to renew our resolve twice a day, namely, after arising and about noon; to ascertain our progress likewise twice a day, namely, about noon and before retiring, or practically during the two General Examens of Conscience; lastly, if in this Particular Examen we discover that instead of making progress we have fallen back or been guilty of negligence, to impose on ourselves some penance for the faults committed or the acts of virtue omitted, in proportion to their number. Fidelity and generosity in complying with these simple directions will infallibly insure success.

Confession.

What to do before Confession.— While it is most commendable to manifest our doubts of conscience with childlike candor to our Confessor, yet we should never accuse ourselves of anything unless we are convinced that it is our own fault, never as long as in our inmost heart we excuse ourselves and lay the blame on something outside our own perverse will, never as long as we are not determined to overcome and correct ourselves at any cost. We cannot keep it too vividly before our mind that Confession without Contrition is of no avail and that it is not enough to be merely impatient or disappointed at our weakness and misery. Though it is not necessary that we should shed tears of compunction, still we must be really sorry for the sins we confess and detest them with our whole soul from supernatural motives. Before Confession, therefore, in addition to a diligent Examination of our Conscience and a thorough Realization of our Guilt we need an earnest Consideration of these Supernatural Motives; namely, the foulness of sin, the danger of perdition, the goodness of God. Through the neglect of these preliminaries our Confessions will necessarily become somewhat insincere, and such insincerity can never be productive of any good but, on the contrary, is certain to do harm. We must strive, then, to be Sincere: the statement of our sins should be a Real Self-Accusation, made with true Shame and Confusion at our ingratitude, our selfishness, our sensuality, our infidelity, our rebellion. In proportion to this sense of Shame and Confusion will be our Contrition, and the more intense our Contrition the more rapid and thorough will be our Amendment. We shall never correct a single fault of which we are not heartily ashamed.

How to Confess.— In making our Confession we should strive to be Brief and state as a rule only three or four sins; the other venial faults, if we are guilty of any more, will be canceled also by the absolution, provided we are truly sorry for them. Whenever we have to confess only venial sins, or none at all as far as we can distinctly remember — in which case we should state so in all simplicity — it is advisable to add a General Accusation of the sins of our past life, mentioning that particular sin or kind of sins which fills us with deeper Confusion and is, consequently, more likely to be confessed with true and fervent Contrition. We can say, for instance,

"I accuse myself also of the sins of my past life and especially of sins of disobedience," "anger," "gluttony," "lying." In other words, unless we have good reason for acting differently, we should emphasize those sins which humble us more and confess them in the manner we find more humiliating. Thus we shall prevent this general accusation from degenerating into a mere formula. As for the Method of making our Confession, it is very desirable that all should follow the one taught in some standard Catechism approved by the entire Hierarchy of the country in which we are living.

What to do after Confession.— When the Priest tells us to renew the Act of Contrition, a good plan is to recite it in an audible whisper, somewhat after the Third Method of Prayer, that is, dwelling on the important words and realizing their meaning. Many people say the Act of Contrition, like their other vocal prayers, too quickly, and some do not say it at all but keep thinking of their Confession. For the rest, let us be simple, open, obedient, and fervent. Questions relating to Spiritual Guidance, imperfections, scruples, or similar matters, had better be asked after the Absolution. Otherwise the Priest might meanwhile forget of what we accused ourselves and be obliged to make us repeat. Lastly, as to the Penance, we should bear in mind that we satisfy it as soon as we perform what has been enjoined, even though at the time we may not be thinking of our obligation. There is no harm in adding some Additional Penance, acts of outward humiliation or bodily chastisement. On the contrary, such Austerities are very beneficial and in many cases indispensable. Not age or occupation, but only weakness or disease, should make us give up these Penitential Exercises so highly recommended by the Masters of the Spiritual Life to all who are in real earnest about their Sanctification. It is difficult to understand how any Religious training can give satisfactory results when these Corporal Afflictions are either not known or not permitted. But, on the other hand, they should not be imposed or practised indiscriminately.

General Confession.— It is customary for Religious during the early part of the annual Retreat to make a General Confession, "a review," from the time of their last Retreat. Provided it be made with real earnestness, this is certainly a very salutary custom. A General Confession of our entire life is to be recommended at our entrance into Religion; also at any subsequent conversion to greater fervor, owing to some extraordinary visitation of God, or to some remarkable grace of more ardent contrition; and at our admission to the final Vows. But what has been said of ordinary confessions applies likewise to General Confessions; their effect will be exactly proportionate to the depth of our Confusion, that is, to the sincerity of our Self-Accusation. One should never think of making a General Confession simply because he does not remember any longer whether he ever confessed some sin of the past, or merely because he does not feel quite satisfied about his former confessions for lack of sensible contrition and subsequent amendment.

Spiritual Direction is practically indispensable for making progress. If we should have a Confessor that is both able and willing to guide us to higher perfection, we should practise towards him childlike openness and great docility, yet in our interviews with him be regardful of his time and sparing in our words. In this important matter, we ought simply to consider whether a Priest possesses the necessary virtue, learning, and experience. If the Ordinary Confessor should not appear to have these requisites, fervent Religious will at least try to avail themselves of the Extraordinary. Novices, however, especially in such untoward circumstances, might find it more helpful to open their heart to their Master; and even Professed Religious would often be benefited by asking counsel of their Superior or of one of their Seniors. We should deal with Superiors just as good children with affectionate parents. Many of our little doubts and difficulties could be solved in this easy fashion to our own great advantage. We should not be bashful nor reticent. We should learn to manifest our interior to those who are qualified to assist us, and thus we shall get clearer ideas about the actual condition of our soul, and sooner become, to some extent, capable of guiding ourselves under ordinary circumstances. Besides, this laying open of our inmost conscience is the only sure means not to stray from the road to Holiness, not to be deceived by the Flesh, the World, or the Devil.

Many wise regulations have been made by the Church to facilitate the practice of Sacramental Confession. Pope Pius X, in his recent decree " Cum de sacramentalibus," has prescribed that all members of Religious Congregations of Women should be kept acquainted with the ample faculties granted to insure their liberty of conscience. At the same time, all such Religious are to be reminded that, in availing themselves of their leave to apply for a special Confessor, they should not be swayed by human considerations but only have in view their spiritual good and their progress in virtue. By a subsequent decree in favor of Religious Orders or Congregations of Men, our Holy Father the Pope has granted to all Confessors, approved by the local Ordinaries, faculty to absolve any member even from sins reserved under censure in his Institute.

Holy Communion.

Provided we are in the state of grace, have a supernatural motive, and are in earnest about making a diligent preparation and a suitable thanksgiving, we should strive to communicate every day. This, as we know on the authority of the Holy See, is the ardent desire of Jesus Christ and His Church with regard to all the faithful that have come to the use of reason. Doubtfully grievous sins, strictly speaking, do not take away our liberty to approach the Holy Table. As to admixture of other motives, the question is which one determines our choice, the natural or the supernatural. Communicating chiefly from a natural motive, such as human respect, routine, sensible sweetness, or temporal favor, even though one does not commit a sacrilege, is certain to produce very little good. Frequent Communion, especially Daily Communion, should make us gradually advance, by rendering us more vigilant and prayerful, more obedient and charitable, more patient, humble, and mortified. On the other hand, it should gradually diminish our venial faults, at least those which are fully deliberate, and intensify our detestation of sin. If on the contrary we grow more careless and more irreverential, if our preparation becomes less devout and our thanksgiving less fervent than when we communicated only a few times a week, if we continue to commit the same faults as before with equal or even greater facility and make no serious effort to improve our conduct or to check our evil habits, then there is certainly grave reason for entering into ourselves and for consulting a prudent confessor. The principles that should guide his decision are thus stated by Fr. Noldin, S. J. (III, n. 160) : "Those whose regard for the supernatural life is limited to preserving their souls free from mortal sin, and who, while neglecting their spiritual improvement, derive from Frequent Communion no other fruit than an increase of grace and charity, fail in the reverence due to this Sacrament."—"Those who do not rid themselves of their venial sins and make no effort whatever to correct such faults, who, in other words, are living in the state of tepidity and take no means at all to rise from that condition, are to be debarred from Frequent Communion." What, then, would be the result if a tepid Religious persisted in communicating frequently and even daily, contrary to the advice of his Confessor? He would eventually approach the Holy Table in the state of mortal sin and thus " eat and drink judgment to himself, not discerning the body of the Lord."

We should all make a great deal of the prescriptions of the ritual for the administration of Holy Communion and understand the meaning of the Latin formulas and prayers used by the Priest. It is also advisable during time of Retreat to examine whether we still follow the proper manner of receiving the Sacred Host. To put it briefly: we should spread and hold the cloth horizontally, raise our head somewhat according to circumstances, close our eyes, open our mouth sufficiently to allow the tongue to rest on the lower lip, and avoid moving our head suddenly forward towards the Priest's hand or drawing our tongue back with a jerk.

THE FOUNDATION, SECOND PART

Subject of this Meditation.—Three important Conclusions that follow from the fundamental truths considered in the First Part.

Composition of Place.— To see heaven opened above me — a magnificent throne — and hell yawning under my feet — a narrow cell of fire — also myself placed on this earth halfway between heaven and hell, saying to myself: "For all eternity I shall either be in heaven enjoying the glory of the Blessed, or else in hell suffering the torments of the Reprobate, and it depends on me alone, which of these two conditions will be my lot within a few years, perhaps even within a few hours; it depends on me alone whether I am to gain so great a good or to incur so great an evil."—How true! How certain! How appalling!

Petition.— Light to realize more and more intimately the supreme importance of my sanctification and salvation, to understand more and more clearly what means will most surely bring it to a successful issue; also strength to resolve firmly on using these means and then to use them perseveringly until death.

First Point. First Conclusion: "Whence it follows that man must make use of creatures in so far as they help him to reach his End, and must abstain from them in so far as they hinder him from reaching his End "; namely, the praise, reverence, and service of God here below and the possession of God hereafter.

This is an evident consequence of what reason and faith tell us about the origin and purpose of man and again about the origin and purpose of the rest of creation. It might be put also thus: "I must use creatures only in as far as God commands, counsels, or desires me to use them "; for clearly the only service we can render to God consists in the accomplishment of His Adorable Will. Hence, whether things please me or displease me, this should never influence my action and not even enter into my consideration. I should eagerly embrace and diligently use whatever is in accordance with my Rules, with the orders and directions of my Superiors, with the advice of my Confessor, with the dispositions of Divine Providence, with the promptings of the Holy Spirit. I should unhesitatingly give up and carefully shun whatever is contrary, or merely foreign to the Adorable Will of God. But when uncertain I should pray for light, and in more important matters I should, besides, take counsel with some prudent and fervent person. This is to act and to live like a rational being; this is what forms or strengthens in the soul that most wise, most noble, and most practical habit which is technically called "Indifference." To be Indifferent, therefore, means to be unbiased, impartial, disinterested, unselfish; but it has nothing in common with listlessness or apathy, with the lazy mood of "I don't care," "It's all the same to me." Indifference denotes the absence in the will of any inclination towards, or any aversion from any creature for its own sake or on our own account. Hence, Indifference does not exclude any inclination however strong towards things prescribed by God nor any aversion however intense for things forbidden by God. In fact, this holy Indifference cannot even be conceived to exist apart from an entire Devotion to the service of God, and these two combined, Devotion and Indifference, import a perfect liberty of the spirit, untrammeled by any downward tendency of nature, an undivided energy of the will centered on God and embracing everything else in God.

If I use any created thing not in accordance with this conclusion, I cease to be Indifferent, I become selfish, and my use is surely inordinate, perhaps even sinful. How wrong this is we can perhaps appreciate better by means of an illustration. If a chalice consecrated by certain ceremonies to the Divine service, should be used for any but a sacred purpose, it is profaned; and if that use should be distinctly improper, we would call it a Sacrilege. In a similar manner, creatures are profaned when we use them for any other end than the service of God, since they have been created essentially for this one purpose, and as man is a being immeasurably inferior to the Most High, by abusing creatures for our private gratification we commit something akin to Sacrilege. At the same time, every such abuse is clearly an act of base Ingratitude towards our Sovereign Benefactor. These considerations may well fill us with shame and regret for our past inordinations and sins. Evidently, we must be Indifferent, if we wish to praise, revere, and serve God our Lord, and thus to save our immortal souls. The object of the General Examen is to discover in how far our thoughts, words, and actions, have been lacking in Indifference. Have we made it diligently at the appointed times twice a day?

To act constantly according to this evident conclusion, this fundamental rule of right reason, to practise Indifference at all times and under all circumstances, on the one hand constitutes the solid foundation of the loftiest sanctity, while on the other hand
it is the most difficult task we have got to do in this
world. For the thoughts of the human heart are
prone to evil from an early age. We are reminded
of this scriptural dictum by our constant experience.
Owing primarily to the fall of Adam and secondarily
to our own sins and faults, we are not Indifferent,
we are not impartial, but on the contrary are inclined to use creatures for the sake of the satisfaction they afford to our senses, to our passions. Hence
that quasi-instinctive horror we have of poverty and
suffering. In consequence of original sin we are infected with a threefold concupiscence; sensuality,
covetousness, and pride; the threefold attachment
to health, wealth, and honor. These cravings and
repugnances of our lower appetites — our likes and
dislikes — are bad, not in themselves, but in their
having broken away from the firm control of reason
and of faith. They are bad on account of the disorder with which they make us go after some creatures and flee from others, without the slightest regard, or even in direct opposition to the Service of
God, the accomplishment of His Holy Will, the observance of Rules, the Obedience due to Superiors,
the claims of Fraternal Charity. Thus we invert the
essential order of things; we appropriate to our own
service the creatures made by God exclusively and
necessarily for His. Besides, as experience also
teaches us, everybody has some predominant inclination, some particular form of self-love or self-esteem,
which is at the root of most of his failings and short-

comings, and practically results in a decided lack of Indifference towards certain creatures. Against such a predominant passion we have to be constantly on our guard, and hence it should be thoroughly known. Here it may be well to examine ourselves once more on those common habits of thoughtlessness, inconsiderateness, precipitation; of fiction and emotionalism, sway of the imagination and of the heart; of self-indulgence, self-complacency, self-sufficiency. What could be more obvious than that we should never judge nor fancy, except in strict accordance with the truth, never pretend to possess certainty when we have only probability, never confound our subjective impressions with the objective realities. Yet how often we forget these simple principles, how often we go deliberately counter to them. The fact is, we need an unlimited amount of Self-Discipline.

Second Point. Second Conclusion: " Hence we have to Make ourselves Indifferent."
This obligation of making myself Indifferent follows directly from the two obvious truths considered just now, that I ought to be Indifferent and that I am not Indifferent. However, St. Ignatius wisely adds a restriction, " in as far it is left to my free will to do so." The reason of this is that my Indifference should be wholly regulated by my duty of serving God. Now as to many things I can no longer be Indifferent, because in their regard I know already the Divine Will. On the contrary, I must be determined to use these creatures for promoting the glory of my Creator and the sanctification of my soul. No man, for instance, can be Indifferent as to the matter of the Ten Commandments, no Catholic can be

Indifferent as to what falls under the Precepts of the Church. As a Religious I must be eager for whatever is prescribed by my holy Institute, or demanded by my sublime Vocation, or imposed by my lawful Superiors. But as to all the rest, I have got to Make myself Indifferent. How does this follow? Because otherwise, owing to my unruly passions, owing to my strong leaning towards perishable goods and vain distinctions, I shall not be Indifferent; and if I am not Indifferent, I cannot make a right use of creatures; consequently, I shall fall into inordination and sin, I shall soon become a useless and wicked servant, and in the end I shall not be saved. Besides, since my fallen nature however much remedied can never be completely cured, since my wayward likes and dislikes however much corrected can never be definitively mastered, this Making myself Indifferent will Always be necessary. A very difficult task indeed, for it means the uprooting of inclinations and aversions that have been growing up in my heart for many, many years. Imagine a tree that has its tough roots firmly fixed in the stony soil. Consider the labor required first to cut it down, and next to loosen the earth all around, in order finally to uproot the stump. My inordinate likes and dislikes are so many trees and stumps that have their roots in my own sensitive heart. To Make myself Indifferent means, then, a continual struggle against a most powerful and ever-active enemy, namely, my corrupt nature; it means a painful struggle in which I myself shall feel every wound inflicted on my opponent; it means an inward struggle and as such entirely removed from the notice and the praise of my fellow men. But, however difficult this lifelong task may be, it is necessary and hence feasible; for on those

who are willing God is sure to bestow abundant
grace.

How am I to Make myself Indifferent?   There are
three means to be used conjointly: I must resolve,
I must pray, and I must practise.   Resolution: since
it is necessary, I have got to do it; and that without
delay, for every moment my vicious propensities are
growing stronger; without intermission, for to pluck
them up by the root is not the work of one day; without restriction, for what would it profit to resist one
tendency while fostering another?   Consequently, I
must do it methodically, by means of the Particular
Examen.   Prayer: I must frequently implore the
grace of holy Indifference; more than this, I must
humbly beseech God, if conducive to His better service, to send me those very things from which I un-
reasonably recoil and to deprive me of those others
to which I am unduly attached; I must ardently beg
for the strength to embrace the former and to shun
the latter, whenever there arises an opportunity.
Practice: I must daily strive to carry out my resolution and to live up to my prayer, by resisting my
natural inclinations, by curbing my natural aversions, by checking my inordinate likes and dislikes,
so as to think, speak, or act, not from mere whim or
impulse, but only from the motive and the desire of
pleasing and serving God, my Creator and Lord.   In
fact, the whole Retreat is intended to instruct us, and
to persuade us, and to train us, in this matter of Indifference.   These Spiritual Exercises will show us
practically how to conquer ourselves, that is, how to
acquire that habitual Indifference, impartiality, and
unselfishness, which is not indolent apathy, but all
energy and exertion, self-control and self-mastery,
true nobility and intimate union with God.

Third Point. Third Conclusion: We should aim in all things at "Desiring and Choosing only what is most Conducive to the End for which we were created."

This is the mature fruit of holy Indifference, the perfect rule of conduct deduced by St. Ignatius from the Principle and Foundation. This, indeed, is to lead a well regulated life: always seeking and selecting the means best calculated to advance our sanctification, to secure our salvation, to increase the glory of the Most High. No wonder that we find this ultimate conclusion embodied in the preparatory prayer we make at the beginning of every meditation: "That all my thoughts, desires, and actions, may be purely directed to the praise and glory of Thy Infinite Majesty."—"Desiring" expresses an enlightened and fervent disposition to know and to do the Holy Will of God, not darkened by fancy, not extinguished by passion, not thwarted and vanquished by blind impulses. "Choosing" denotes an actual and perfect correspondence to this efficacious desire, embracing joyfully whatever is most advantageous to the salvation of souls or to the Service of God, and generously discarding whatever is less helpful. Hence the Saints continually prayed that they might know and do God's Adorable Will. Following in their footsteps, our constant aim and strenuous endeavor should be A. M. D. G., "For the Greater Glory of God." This is to be the fruit of our Retreat.

Colloquy, with the Blessed Virgin, free from all inordination and exempt from all concupiscence; also with our Divine Lord, Whose food it was to do the Will of His Heavenly Father. I will acknowledge my great lack of Indifference and Generosity, my poor use of the General and Particular Examens, my frequent neglect of humble and fervent Prayer. I will regret that I have been so unfaithful in the Service of my Lord and Creator, so slothful in the work of my sanctification and salvation, so cowardly in the mortification of my senses, so remiss in the subjugation of my passions. I will implore pardon for my numberless sins, inordinations, and negligences. Lastly, I will promise amendment and beg grace to take up my task with fresh vigor, to live only for the perfect accomplishment of the Divine Will.—Hail Mary. Our Father.

A. M. D. G.

"MY CHILD, GIVE ME THY HEART."

SECOND DAY

SPECIAL PATRON: St. Aloysius.

MOTTO: "Create in me a clean heart, O God."—
Ps. 50:12.

SPIRIT: Humility on account of my Sinfulness.

READING: Imitation; Bk. I, C. 21, 22.
Bk. III, C. 4, 8, 14, 52.
Bk. IV, C. 7.
Penitential Psalms; 6, 31, 37, 50, 101,
129, 142.

Prepare for a more than usually fervent Confession, including, if you wish, the time elapsed since your last Retreat, or any other portion of your past life, in so far as this may help you to deeper humility and greater contrition but will not disturb you by scrupulous doubts or groundless apprehensions.

THE TRIPLE SIN

Introductory Remarks.— We now enter upon the First Week, or first period, of the Spiritual Exercises, which is devoted to the consideration of sin and its consequences. The subject of our Particular Examen during the entire Retreat should be, how we have observed silence and recollection, how we have applied ourselves to the meditations, examens, and other prayers, and how we have kept the "additions." These additions, as stated before, are specific recommendations given by St. Ignatius, his expert advice for making a successful Retreat. In the First Week, he tells us to refrain from thinking on pleasant and joyful subjects, to darken our apartment by not admitting more light than necessary for our various occupations, and to perform some exterior penance or bodily mortification, in accordance with the prescription of our Rule, the permission of our Confessor, or the direction of our Superior.

We should all take up the Exercises of this First Week with an intense desire of realizing more intimately the heinousness of our sins, in order that we may detest them more thoroughly and humble ourselves more deeply. All should do so, whether at some time or other of their past lives they have fallen into mortal sin, or whether, in spite of their many infidelities and venial sins, they have been preserved by a special favor of God from grievously violating His holy Law. Unless we do penance we shall all

likewise perish. Unless we strive to humble ourselves with the utmost sincerity, unless we labor to
grieve over our sins from the bottom of our heart, we
are wasting this opportunity of grace, we are missing
this Divine call to complete conversion, and besides,
what is far more serious, by neglecting this indispensable preparation for future trials and temptations, we may jeopardize not only our Religious Vocation but even our eternal bliss. We must bear in
mind that the fruit of this Retreat will be exactly
proportional, not to the intensity of sensible consolation we may experience, nor to the abundance of
ascetical doctrine we may gather, but to the confusion, contrition, and detestation we conceive for our
past inordinations and sins. Hence we should apply
ourselves to these meditations of the First Week with
all the energy of our soul.

Meanwhile every one should diligently prepare to
go to Confession. In this Confession we should include an accurate and contrite Review of the last
year and also unburden our heart of anything that
may cause us doubt or anxiety.

Subject of this Meditation.— The sin of the Angels,
the sin of our First Parents, and the sin of a Soul
lost in Hell.

Composition of Place.— The actual abode of sin
and of the sinner; namely, " to see with the eyes of
my imagination and to consider, that my soul is imprisoned in this corruptible body, and my whole self
in this vale of misery, as it were, in exile among
brute beasts: my whole self, body and soul."

" To consider my soul imprisoned in this corruptible body." My soul, spiritual and immortal,

created to the image and likeness of the Ever-Blessed
Trinity, redeemed by the blood of our Adorable
Savior, a temple of the Holy Ghost by sanctifying
grace, adorned with the theological and moral virtues
as well as with the seven gifts of the Divine Spirit,
destined to enjoy the vision of God for all eternity
in heaven, after praising, revering, and serving her
Creator and Lord a short time here on earth; — this
soul of mine, instead of availing herself of the body
which she informs and animates to promote the glory
of the Most High, by holding it subject to reason and
directing all its energies towards the attainment of
her End, has surrendered to it, has allowed herself to
be ruled by its brutal instincts, and has yielded to
them even so far as to fail in her duty of serving the
Almighty, in order not to give any displeasure to
this corruptible flesh, taken from dead matter and
soon to be consigned to the grave, a mass of putre-
faction. And the body, by this continual subjection
of the soul, has acquired such a mastery over her,
that now she finds in it, instead of a useful instrument to serve God, a tangle of almost insurmountable obstacles that fetter her liberty as a prisoner is
prevented by the walls of his narrow cell not only
from going out but even from freely moving within.

"To consider my whole being as in exile on this
earth." What a shame and confusion for a person
of good parentage and lofty sentiments, to see himself shut up in a squalid and darksome prison! But
how much greater would be his shame and confusion
if, in addition to this, he should find himself exiled
to a cold and dreary region, far from the society of
his acquaintances, among a rude and savage people?
The true country of the soul that serves God faithfully is the Heavenly Jerusalem. But when a soul

has become enslaved to the body, she drags along her wretched existence as it were in exile on this inhospitable earth, so utterly unlike her Glorious Home.

"To consider myself as exiled among brute beasts." If it is a terrible disgrace for a man of noble extraction to be compelled to keep company with criminals and outlaws, what would it be to have to live among filthy animals? Yet such is the self-chosen lot of any one that gives free rein to his lower appetites and has no other rule for his conduct than pain and pleasure. For he lives, in very truth, as if he were devoid of reason and judgment, like an irrational beast.

Petition.—" Shame and confusion at my own condition, seeing how many have been lost for one single mortal sin, and how many times I have merited to be lost eternally for my numerous sins."

This is the necessary prerequisite for true and ardent contrition. We can never be sincerely sorry for our sins unless first of all we are thoroughly ashamed of them. Suppose a Religious through his own fault were sentenced to the penitentiary for life, or farmed out as a convict for hard labor, as men and women were till recently in some of the Southern States, to be treated worse than a brute; what awful humiliation, what intolerable confusion! But how immeasurably more intense would be my confusion if I could realize where I have deserved to be, perhaps already for many years: — in Hell?

First Point. The Sin of the Angels.

We may represent to ourselves the Angels as placed at their creation in an ethereal paradise, the vestibule of eternal bliss. Their number was countless. Being by nature pure Spirits, they were independent of matter for their maintenance, motion, cognition, and volition. Their knowledge was wonderfully sublime, keen, and comprehensive; the energy of their will was proportioned to the loftiness of their intelligence; and their power surpassed that of the whole physical world. Besides, from the first moment of their creation they had been endowed with Sanctifying Grace and adorned with various virtues, preeminently with Charity. And what was their purpose, their destiny? The same as ours, to show reverence and obedience to their Lord and Creator. Hence they were unceasingly singing the praises of the Most High, rapt in loving adoration before the throne of His Majesty.

How did so many come to fall? They knew what gifts God had bestowed on them, their marvelous natural and supernatural endowments. They were free to direct their intelligence either to these gifts or to the Giver; and both operations were to be done, for how can we worthily honor and thank God for His benefits unless we take care to know and value them? But in the contemplation of these gifts there lies a great danger. It should be done only to praise, revere, and love God; only in as far as it is agreeable to His Holy Will. Hence, when we are prompted by an actual grace to turn our attention from ourselves to God, we are to do so without delay. Many of the Angels, we may suppose, neglected such a grace. In itself this neglect was only an inordination, but the consequence was that they persisted in their self-contemplation beyond the proper bounds, and that their will became unduly taken up with their own beauty. Perhaps yet another and stronger grace was offered and likewise rejected. Then the final test was proposed, which probably consisted in the adoration of the God-Man, Jesus Christ, the Second Person of the Ever-Blessed Trinity, hypostatically united to a creature that was specifically far inferior to the Angels; or, what comes to the same, in the veneration of the Immaculate Virgin Mary, Mother of God, and Queen of the Universe. The greater part of the Angelic Hosts, following the lead of St. Michael, joyfully complied with the Eternal Decree, and in return were forthwith admitted to the Beatific Vision, to the bliss and glory of Heaven. But Lucifer when called upon to obey despised the Sovereign Behest, exclaiming, " I will not serve "; and in this rebellion he was at once joined by numerous other Spirits. They refused to glorify their Creator, because they had become enamored of themselves and inflated with pride.

Who can fathom the malice of this refusal of obedience, proceeding from creatures wholly destined for the Divine Service and lavishly enriched with the noblest attributes, in the very presence of the Adorable Majesty of God? But that same instant they hear the awful sentence: " Depart from Me, ye cursed, into everlasting fire." No longer adopted Sons but degraded Rebels, they are stripped of Sanctifying Grace and Supernatural Virtue. Their beauty is changed into hideousness, their wisdom has become madness, their love is turned into hatred, and from lofty Angels they are transformed into abject Demons. Driven from before the throne of God they are hurled into the abyss of Hell. How different from their former abode and from their destined home! A prison instead of a palace, a torture chamber instead of a delightful paradise, a place of utter infamy instead of a seat of ineffable glory! There

they are confined by that pitiless fire and consumed
with incessant remorse. They wanted to have their
own way, they wanted to be their own masters; and
now they are hurled back forever on their own nothingness, malice, and pride.

Consider that this punishment was visited on the
Angels, the first and most perfect creatures of an infinitely Loving God; that it was pronounced on account of one single mortal sin by Him Who is
infinitely Just, Who can, therefore, never be influ-
enced by anger or hatred; by Him Who is infinitely
Merciful and Who, consequently, always punishes
less than deserved. Yet the sentence of damnation
smote them immediately and irrevocably, because
they knowingly and wilfully committed one mortal
sin; an act of rebellion against the Sovereign Majesty,
a turning away from the Supreme Goodness, a provo-
cation of the Absolute Holiness; and on the last day
all angels and all men, both the saved and the lost,
will acknowledge the justice of this sentence.

As often as I deliberately transgressed any Commandment of God, in a grievous manner, I committed
a formal act of rebellion similar to that of the Angels,
I became guilty of a crime the heinousness of which
in the sight of God and of the Saints is so great as
to deserve no less a punishment than Hell. If, in
the very act of sinning, death had cut short my
earthly existence, I should most certainly have received the same sentence of eternal damnation, while
heaven and earth would have exclaimed, " Just
thou art, O Lord, and righteous in Thy judgments!"
And if the Angels were cast into Hell for one single
sin, what have I not deserved for so many; especially
after obtaining pardon, not only once, but over and
over again, through the Blood of Jesus Christ, in the

Sacrament of Penance? Where should I be most justly, at this very moment, except for the Infinite Mercy of God? Instead of being allowed to live amongst men, a member of Holy Church, in a Religious Community, among souls consecrated to God, I have deserved, perhaps many times over, to be at the bottom of Hell, an object of scorn to the very Demons and the other Reprobate.

But what if, with the grace of God, I never committed a mortal sin? Did I not deliberately neglect prayer which is so necessary for overcoming temptation? Did I not freely indulge in some kind or other of venial sin? Did I not thus expose myself to the imminent danger of mortal sin? It is owing, then, not to my own deserts, but to the Inexhaustible Goodness of God, that I did not go down to that depth of iniquity from which in one moment I might have fallen into the pit of Hell among the rebel Angels. Hence I too, indeed, have abundant cause for shame and confusion.

Second Point. The Sin of our First Parents.

Let us call to mind how. God had made the body of Adam most beautiful and perfect, and how He had created the soul after His own image and likeness, giving it the full use of all its faculties and endowing it, besides, with Supernatural Wisdom and Sanctifying Grace. Dwelling in the garden of Eden as lord of the whole earth, Adam had received for a lifelong friend and companion Eve, fashioned by the Almighty in every kind of perfection similar to her husband. We may contemplate the beauty and pleasantness of their early abode, the limpidity and coolness of its springs, the sweetness and variety of its fruits, the submission and gentleness of the animals, and the wondrous virtue of the tree of life which insured their freedom from suffering and death. Yet this material happiness was only a reflection of their inward peace of soul, resulting from their close union with God and the perfect harmony of all their faculties. Now, all these benefits were intended for one sole object, namely, that both Adam and Eve together with their entire offspring, by praising, revering, and serving God, might bring human nature to its highest perfection and complete in themselves the Divine likeness. Thus also this earthly paradise was a true vestibule to the Heavenly Jerusalem.

To test the obedience of our First Parents, God had forbidden them to eat of the fruit of the tree of knowledge. We see at once how just this prohibition was, how easy, and how weighty. By respecting this Divine injunction, Adam would have secured, both for himself and for his posterity, the gift of Sanctifying Grace together with many other extraordinary favors. He was offered a choice between the fulness of life, natural and supernatural, and a miserable death of body and soul; a choice between perfect felicity and utter affliction.

However, they did eat of the forbidden fruit and sinned. Lucifer, the leader of the fallen angels, appeared to them under the form of a serpent, which probably was then, not the insidious and repulsive reptile that most men now instinctively avoid, but an attractive and even sociable animal. With perfidious cunning he began by tempting Eve, in order through her also to seduce Adam. First he suggested to her fancy that the restriction put upon them was in no wise intended for their happiness; next he instilled into her heart a desire of becoming

completely independent of God; and then he drove
her from this inward disloyalty into open disobedience. Eve in turn, by her bad example and insinu-
ating manner, prevailed upon Adam to set aside the
Divine Prohibition.

Their eating of the forbidden fruit, though in itself
a very small thing, was nevertheless a deliberate and
wilful act of rebellion against Almighty God. Nor
was the threatened penalty long in being inflicted.
That same moment our First Parents were deprived
of all their Heavenly Graces and special endowments;
they were driven out of the terrestrial paradise into
the wide world which thenceforth was to yield only
thistles and thorns; and filled with shame at the lust-
fulness of their bodies, they were obliged to cover
them with the skins of animals. They too had
wanted to have their own way and to be their own
masters, but they found that their flesh had revolted
against their spirit and that the whole earth had
shaken off their former supremacy. Their remaining life was spent in constant and manifold misery,
which finally culminated in the terrible ordeal of
death. Yet all these sufferings would have availed
them naught to escape eternal perdition, had it not
been for the Infinite Merits of the Redeemer promised them by their most Merciful Creator. But even
so, what lamentable consequences this one sin entailed for all their descendants: loss of Sanctifying
Grace and other precious gifts; darkness of the mind
and weakness of the will; subjection of the soul to
a threefold concupiscence; numberless hardships and
ailments of the body rapidly preparing the way for
death.

We should consider well that this punishment was
inflicted not on angelic spirits but on human beings,

who in so many respects are dependent on the lowliness and limitation of matter, and who had been led into sin by the deceits of Satan, the implacable enemy of God; that it was inflicted for one single sin of disobedience, which had lasted but an instant and had soon after been most sincerely detested; that it was inflicted by Him Who is infinitely Holy as well as infinitely Loving, but Whose Justice was acknowledged from the first by the Angels and the Demons as well as by our guilty Parents, and will be recognized by the whole human race, on the day of judgment, for all eternity.

Consequently, even this awful chastisement, visited on Adam and Eve and their entire posterity, does not fully correspond to the wickedness of even one mortal sin. If I had been placed in the same position as Adam, the poison contained in each of the offenses committed by me, would have been sufficient to infect all mankind. What punishment, then, can be commensurate with my numerous sins? What shame and confusion should I not be made to suffer before the whole world on account of so many iniquities? What place could I ever claim to occupy among my fellow men except the very last and lowest?

But if, through the Mercy of God, I should till now have been preserved from mortal sin, I yet have every reason to be filled with shame and confusion on account of my numberless inordinations in the past; and more especially in view of my frequent indulgence of idleness, vanity, self-complacency, anger, impatience, curiosity, sensuality, disobedience, and pride. How often, indeed, have I been prevented from committing mortal sin, only, as it were, by a miraculous intervention of Providence?

Third Point. The Sin of a Lost Soul.

There yet remains to be considered a still more striking instance of Divine Retribution; the case of "some person who for one mortal sin has gone to Hell, and many others without number that have been condemned for fewer sins than I committed." No one can entertain a reasonable doubt about what St. Ignatius here proposes to us as a certain truth; namely, that many a Soul is actually in Hell in consequence of one single mortal sin. Hence the instant doom pronounced on hosts of Angels, for one act of rebellion, cannot be accounted for by the fact that they had been gifted with a more exalted nature than ours; nor can the severe treatment meted out to our First Parents, for their one sin of disobedience, be explained on the ground that they had been created in original justice.

But how did such a Soul get to that place of never-ending punishment? Let me consider one whose natural difficulties, supernatural endowments, and various other circumstances were pretty similar to those in which I grew up, who was exposed to temptations very like those to which I yielded, and who fell into exactly the same sin that I also committed. Then death overtook that Soul before it returned to God, and now it is forever tormented in the unquenchable flames of Hell. If I could ask that Soul, "Do you consider your punishment just?" there is no doubt as to what it would reply.

"Yes," I should hear it say, "my punishment is eminently just, for I received precisely what I had before clearly understood would be the consequence of my sin. I knew that God had threatened the sinner with everlasting damnation. I knew that in creating me out of Pure Goodness He had destined me for

Heaven, and that He had even gone so far as to die for
me on the Cross in order to bring me to eternal bliss
and glory.   I knew that in His All-Wise and All-Loving Providence He had disposed every detail of my life
for the best.   I could easily have abstained from that
sin, but nevertheless I committed the crime with full
deliberation and consent.   The fact is I wanted to
be my own master, I insisted on having my own way,
and I justly went down to Hell.   Besides, my punishment considered in itself is most appropriate.
For surely the penalty ought to bear some proportion to the offense.   Therefore, inasmuch as I turned
away from the Sovereign Good, it should comprise the
pain of loss; in so far as I abused God's creature, it
must include also the pain of sense; and since I dared
to insult His Infinite Majesty, it could not be other
than eternal.

"Moreover, this punishment being certainly
merited was also rightfully inflicted immediately
after my first mortal sin.   For, evidently, the Almighty was not obliged to suspend in my behalf the
operation of the natural causes that were about to
effect my death at the very time when I was burdened with the guilt of grievous sin.   He very seldom interferes with these created agencies even in
behalf of those who are innocent.   On the contrary,
the wickedness of mortal sin would rather seem to
demand that the physical laws be suspended the very
instant a man attempts to violate the moral laws, so
that he may forthwith be thrown into Hell as a warning to all.   Any one who in his frenzy and villainy
rebels against the Adorable Creator and outrages
the Absolute Holiness, should expect to be cut off at
once, like a horrid monster, from human society, and
to be cast headlong into that moral cesspool of the

universe which is called Hell. Hence what has happened to me has likewise happened to many others, who passed into eternity defiled with the guilt of one or more mortal sins, and are consequently ever since suffering these same inconceivable torments. And their number is still increasing every day." Such would be the answer of that Soul, if I could question it.

In the light of this fact that so many are lost for one single sin, how silly appears the presumption that it is easy to avoid Hell after committing a grievous offense, and what utter folly it was for me to remain so long on the brink of perdition or even within the reach of temptation. Where should I be now, if God had wished to deal with me as He most justly dealt with countless other sinners perhaps far less guilty than myself? Is there any humiliation however profound that I should not look upon as a signal distinction in comparison with what I have deserved? Is there any practice of penance that I should not be eager to adopt with the sanction of my Confessor? Should I not gladly prostrate myself on the ground, if commanded, and lower myself in the dust before every creature? Should I, henceforth, not deem it a real honor to be allowed to assist my fellow Religious or to serve my neighbor in any office however menial, for the sake of God? And shall I still presume to find fault with my Companions, their words, ways, or actions? Shall I ever again forget myself so far as to criticise the management or command of my Superior? or to show lack of respect and submission towards this legitimate vicegerent of Almighty God? By my sins,— by my ingratitude, perfidy, degradation, and malice,— I have rendered myself unworthy and unfit not only to be a member of this Religious Community but even to have any intercourse with the rest of mankind. If God had treated me as was only right and just, I should long since have been an outcast of creation, a prisoner in Hell, abandoned to perpetual torment and infamy. And even now, the vices fostered by my sins in my soul, if they could be seen by my fellow men in all their hideousness, would fill them with a most profound loathing for my person and make them shun at any cost my presence and my very neighborhood. But what, then, ought to be my shame and confusion when appearing in prayer before Almighty God, when acknowledging my sins to the Minister of Christ, and especially when preparing to receive my Adorable Savior in Holy Communion?

Colloquy. "Imagining Christ our Lord before me and placed on the Cross," says St. Ignatius, "I will ask Him how, being my Creator, He has deigned to make Himself Man, and from eternal life to come to temporal death, thus to die for my sins. Again, looking at myself, I will inquire what I have done for Christ, what I am doing for Christ, what I ought to do for Christ. And then seeing Him, the Eternal Son of God, thus fastened to the Cross, I will give expression to what shall present itself to my mind."

Kneeling down in spirit on Mount Calvary, my face buried in my hands for shame, near those pierced feet which I dare not touch with my sinful lips, but allowing my tears to mingle with that sacred Blood, I will consider that He who is nailed to this awful Cross, is the Son of God, coequal with the Eternal Father, the Almighty Creator of angels and of men, and that now He is racked with bodily suffering, consumed with thirst, crushed with anguish, overwhelmed with insults, and dying in unutterable torments and ignominy, not only on account of the sin of Adam and the sins of other men, but in particular on account of my personal sins. Yes, my sins made Him come down from heaven to earth; my sins fastened Him to this horrible Cross; my sins inflicted this awful punishment on the Son of God. But that is also why, in spite of my numberless and shameful sins, I was called to repentance, why I was even favored with a Religious Vocation; whilst so many others, millions of men and angels, who committed far fewer sins than I, are already buried in the flames of Hell. What merciful preference, what singular predilection, of Christ the Lord, for me, most wretched and ungrateful, sinner! He loved all His creatures and He died for all mankind, but me He loved and for me He died with special efficacy. O wonder of Divine Goodness, beyond all human power to express!

And in return for so much love, what have I done for Christ in the past? Surely this is not the first time I hear of the Son of God dying for me on the Cross. No, I learned this already in early childhood. But what return did I make to Him? I offended Him by numberless and grievous sins. Can there be any ingratitude worse than mine? What am I doing for Christ now? I am meditating on my sins. Am I now at least filled with shame and confusion on account of these heinous crimes? Alas, how cold and proud I still am! What ought I to do for Christ in the future? I must completely break with sin; I must carefully shun all dangerous occasions; I must use the means of grace, Confession, Penance, Prayer, and Holy Communion; I must strive to do the Will of God perfectly, in the observance of my Rules, in

the practice of Obedience, in the fulfilment of my
Duties, in the exercise of Charity, in the patient and
joyful bearing of whatever Hardships and Humiliations He may deign to send me in expiation of my
sins.   In this way, I must remove whatever obstacles
I have placed so long to the love of His Sacred Heart.
For though He has no need of us, no need of our labor, our teaching, or our ministry, yet He longs for
our love.   And love Him I will, at any cost.   Sweet
Heart of Jesus, by my love! — Our Father.

MY PERSONAL SINS

Introductory Remarks.— If I have obtained the fruit of the preceding meditation, I shall be fully convinced that I am unworthy to be numbered among the Chosen Companions of Jesus our Lord; that if God had allowed me to run my course and had not prevented me, by most unmerited favors, from falling into worse sins, I should deserve to be actually in the company of hideous Demons and miserable Reprobates. This realization will fill me with a most salutary and holy confusion, since there is nothing so vile, so loathsome, so abominable, as the society of the Devils and the Damned. Even to be forced here on earth to associate with a gang of convicted criminals, with the most vulgar and most degraded wretches, would be nothing compared to being cast for all eternity into that vast sink of moral impurity and infamy, which we call Hell. Once we have succeeded in thus realizing where we should deserve to be but for the Incomprehensible Love of God, oh! how we feel urged to lower our eyes and cover our face for very shame, to cast ourselves on the earth in profound self-abasement, to humble ourselves before all those who represent to us God's Infinite Majesty, our Superiors and our Companions, all Men in fact, and to render them the most menial and most laborious services with the disposition and the bearing of a devoted slave. This, indeed, is the only correct attitude of mind for every one of us, from which we should never depart.

But, besides this deep conviction that I am unworthy to be among the Cherished Companions of our Lord, I should have gathered from the preceding meditation also a generous resolve to Remove the Obstacles which I have placed so long to the Love of the Sacred Heart of Jesus, and to render myself less unfit to receive those treasures of Grace which He has yearned to bestow upon me all along during so many years. This is certainly what He looks for on my part.

Meanwhile we should long for the hour when we can lay open our inmost soul to the Minister of Christ, in the Sacrament of Penance, being determined to use this opportunity in order to humble ourselves as sincerely and as deeply as possible. As to our annual Review, we should bear in mind that the object is not so much to have the guilt of our sins forgiven — for this, we may trust, was done long ago — but to obtain if possible the full remission of the penalty and the complete removal of the effects of these sins. Oh! might we bring to this Confession a contrition like that of St. Aloysius, fainting through shame and grief on account of some semi-deliberate venial sins, or like that of St. Ignatius, doing such terrible penance in the lonely cave near Manresa.

Whatever advice or command anyone may have received, on former occasions, about never mentioning again certain faults of the past, for this one Confession every one should consider himself entirely free to go over any part or any sins of his whole life; not, however, from idle scrupulosity or groundless fears, but from the desire of obtaining deeper humility and greater sorrow. Lastly, whatever doubts or difficulties one may have, he should propose them

in this Confession with childlike openness and
docility, in order that he may secure perfect peace
of mind.

Subject of this Meditation.—My own personal Sins.

Composition of Place.— The same as in The Triple
Sin; namely, my soul imprisoned in this corruptible
body and my whole self in this vale of misery, as it
were, in exile among brute beasts.   That this is not
an exaggerated figure but a sober truth, must be evident to any one who considers how man, though by
God created king of the universe, is now in consequence of sin compelled to conceal the nobility and
beauty of his form under dead vegetable fibers and
animal skins.

Petition.— Great and intense grief together with
abundant and burning tears.

**First Point. The Process or Indictment of My
Sins.**

This Indictment is to be drawn up by calling to
mind all the Sins of my past life.   Several things
will help me in this work; the places where I have
stayed and the houses in which I have dwelled, the
persons with whom I have lived and the companions
with whom I . have associated, the occupations in
which I have been engaged and the amusements in
which I have spent my time.   But since I am a Religious striving after Perfection, this Indictment or
Process against myself may include, besides my
many more or less grievous Offenses, also my countless Inordinations.

As to the Sins and Faults that have marred our
Life in the World, we should exert ourselves — either

by a diligent survey, if we have made this meditation already several times before, or else by a careful examination, if we have never yet entered thoroughly into ourselves,— to recall their immense number and their various kinds. Without letting our imagination dwell on any circumstances that might prove a source of disturbance and temptation, we should transfer ourselves back to the moment when each sin was committed and its guilt was realized, when we found ourselves inwardly defiled under the very eyes of the All-Holy God, our most Loving Creator and Father. It will also be very useful on this occasion to arrange those sins under a few heads, so that we can always keep their recollection vividly before our mind. But as to the Sins and Faults of our Religious Life, we should search them out with great earnestness and sincerity, especially those committed since our last Retreat. For we are extremely prone to hide from ourselves our real defects, and to trouble ourselves less about our true failings than about the consequences of our failings. We must, therefore, endeavor to go to the root of the evil, to discover the cause or motive of our faults; for instance, why we break silence, why usually at such a time, why frequently with such a person, and so forth.

Again we should strive to examine our conscience and to estimate our sins in the light of the Divine Holiness and Justice, to judge of our guilt as we shall be judged when standing before the tribunal of our Lord Jesus Christ, utterly discarding all the vain excuses and paltry extenuations with which we are accustomed to hide from ourselves our own iniquities, and even presume to make them a matter of self-commiseration and self-complacency. We must resolutely tear off the false mask we are habitually wearing, in order to see ourselves as we really are in the sight of God, the infinitely Pure Spirit, and as we are seen by our Guardian Angels and Patron Saints. How could we afterwards, as we intend to do, lay bare in confession our inmost soul, if we remain satisfied, as usual, with an indolent, superficial, self-blinded, self-approving review of the past? Hence, to draw up this Indictment against ourselves truthfully and sincerely, we need a very special Grace, and for this we should pray most earnestly. Even after having made this meditation dozens of times in successive annual Retreats, there is still ample room for forming a more correct estimate of our sinfulness and for conceiving a correspondingly more intense Shame and Confusion.

Second Point. " **To Weigh My Sins, considering the foulness and malice that every mortal sin contains in itself, even supposing it were not forbidden.**" In fact, sin is not bad because it is forbidden, but sin is forbidden because it is bad, because it clashes with the harmony of creation, because it is destructive of all order, well-being, progress, and happiness. But without indulging in any philosophical speculations, let us strive to realize first the Folly or Frenzy of sin, secondly the Malice or Fiendishness of sin, and thirdly the Foulness or Villainy of sin.

The Folly or Frenzy of Sin and, consequently, also of the Sinner.— Here we may note; first, the Blindness of Sin, because God forbids only what is contrary to our real Welfare and our true Happiness; then, the Madness of Sin, inasmuch as by sinning man cuts himself loose, forever, from God, the Source of all Blessing, on Whom he is actually dependent for his very life; and lastly, the Insolence of Sin, considering a mere, puny creature disobeys God's Immaculate Law, violates God's Inalienable Right, offends God's Infinite Majesty, and commits these outrages in God's Immediate Presence, that Presence which fills with awe the loftiest Seraphim.

The Malice or Fiendishness of Sin and, consequently, of the Sinner.— Here we may observe first, the Cruelty of Sin, how it upsets our organic Functions, poisons our Blood, impairs our nervous System, soils our Memory, obscures our Intellect, enfeebles our Will; in a word, how it undermines our bodily, mental, and moral Energy. Secondly, we can view the Malignity of Sin, how it infects our neighbor worse than the most Contagious and Virulent Plague, not only by positive seduction or complicity, but also by the inevitable scandal of bad example and the downward influence of evil dispositions; in short, how Sin tends to inflict on our fellow men the same Harm as it does on ourselves. Thirdly, we should dwell on the Atrocity of Sin, how it destroys our Heavenly Merits, kills our Supernatural Life, and thus brings on us an Everlasting Punishment.

The Foulness or Villainy of Sin and, consequently, of the Sinner.— Here we may consider; first, the monstrous Ingratitude of Sin, inasmuch as we not only abuse God's own Gifts but actually turn against Him the very Proofs of His Love; then, the utter Degradation of Sin, for by sinning man lowers himself to the very Level of the Beast, preferring to be ruled by his Sensual Passions and to be enslaved by his Animal Instincts, instead of being guided by Reason and by Faith; lastly, the Horrible Treason of the Sinner against God, presuming, as he does, to refuse the Service that is absolutely Due to his Almighty Creator and attempting to cast off the

Dominion of his Sovereign Lord, intending, in fact, as far as lies in him, to annihilate the Infinite Goodness.

Now, what practical conclusion am I to draw from this very imperfect analysis of the Foulness and Malice of Sin? Though even the smallest sin is so great an evil as to defy all human power of expression, yet evidently the answer to this question must depend somewhat on whether my transgressions of the Ten Commandments have been mortal or venial. In the first case, I ought to realize with shame and sorrow, that in view of my sins I have no right to expect anything but to be designated and treated by everybody as a downright maniac, a dangerous fiend, and a despicable villain. In the other case, knowing that, except for the special protection of Heaven, I certainly should have forfeited Sanctifying Grace in consequence of my innumerable faults, and that even though none of them constituted in itself a grievous offense, yet they were all deliberate and wilful violations of the Divine Law, I ought to realize with humility and contrition, that I deserve to be looked upon and dealt with by my fellow men as one guilty of countless acts of indescribable folly, cruelty, and baseness. But in either case, the fruit of this Second Point should consist in a genuine horror and an intense hatred of my wicked self.

Third Point. Who am I that Committed so many Acts of inconceivable Frenzy, Fiendishness, and Villainy?

What am I in comparison with the other members of this Community, with the other subjects of my Order or Congregation? How easy it is to fill the place of any Religious, even though he be an efficient teacher, or an eloquent speaker, or an able administrator; and how soon is the loss forgotten! Not seldom, in fact, far from being a regrettable loss, his death is felt to be a distinct relief. Some Religious, either through their own fault or through bodily infirmity, become a real burden, though borne with patience and charity. What, then, am I in comparison with all those actually living on this earth in the state of Sanctifying Grace? What, in comparison with all the Saints and Angels in heaven, myriads of blissful and glorious spirits, together with their most exalted Queen, the Immaculate Virgin Mary? What, then, can I be in comparison with Almighty God, whom I have dared to insult so often by my Sins? Less than a grain of sand on the seashore, less than a tiny drop in the ocean, less than a mere atom in the universe.

Again, what am I as to my material component, my body? How great and manifold is even its present misery, the consequence of original and actual sin! In how many ways it is exposed to injury, to how many diseases it may fall a victim! And what will it be a few hours after death but a disgusting mass of corruption? Yet the misery of my body is only a faint image of the wretchedness of my spiritual component, my soul. To what else can I liken my soul, from which have issued so many sins, so many iniquities, but to a hideous sore or a loathsome abscess? In fact, what thoughts usually occupy my understanding even in Religion? — vanity, self-complacency, pride,— what desires are cherished by my will? — self-exaltation, envy, resentment,— what recollections haunt my memory? what images fill my fancy? what cravings engross my heart? — sensuality, self-indulgence, worldliness.

Fourth Point. Who is God against Whom I have Sinned?

Just as my own nothingness, so His Essential Greatness is altogether beyond my power of conception. How immeasurably high, for instance, His Sovereign Wisdom soars above my extreme ignorance! God knows all things without any obscurity or confusion; and each thing individually, down to its minutest details and most intimate composition, with the same perfection and clearness as all. Truly, everything is naked and open to His eyes; yes, even the deepest recesses of the human heart. He knows me at this moment with absolute completeness and certainty, even my future is seen by Him as distinctly as my present and my past. What is more, He knows with equal precision how I would act under any possible circumstances which will never become real. Besides, He knows thus not only every single being that He ever created, but also the innumerable other beings which He might, but never will create. And all this Immense Knowledge He exercises unceasingly by one absolutely Single Act which is identical with His own Divine Substance. Contrasted with this Infinite Intelligence, what is all the boasted science of mankind but dense stupidity? Yet how infinitesimal is my personal share in the hazy, crude, and superficial notions men have so laboriously acquired in the course of so many centuries?

Again, what incalculable distance there is between His Unlimited Power and my utter weakness! What stand, for instance, could I make against the crash of a thunderbolt, or against the rush of a cyclone, or against the descent of an avalanche? What resistance could I offer to the shock of an earthquake, or to the motion of the tide, or to the impact of a planet? But how inconceivably helpless, then, I would be in face of all the forces of the universe combined! Yet God moves them with His finger, yea, by a Mere Act of His Will. "He spoke and they were made, He commanded and they were created."

Once more, what point of contact can there be between His Supreme Goodness and my abject iniquity? I, so injurious to myself, so offensive to my fellow men, and so unjust towards God; He, infinitely Perfect in Himself, most Liberal towards all His creatures, and towards me in particular so Loving and so Merciful. This last consideration, especially, should overwhelm me with shame and confusion, fill me with burning contrition, and make me shed bitter tears of grief. Here I may call to mind how many extraordinary proofs I have received all along of God's Tender Love and Admirable Solicitude, not only before I began to lead a life of sin but even during my most heinous excesses. At my first Holy Communion, what sweet attractions, what powerful impulses I felt in His Adorable Presence! Already then He desired to possess my soul as His spouse. Yet what subsequent forgetfulness, unfaithfulness, ingratitude, and rebellion; what abuse of all His gifts and favors; what wanton destruction of every trace of His Divine Likeness! Who could even with tears of blood wash away so many hateful offenses committed by so vile a wretch against a God so Gracious and so Good?

Fifth Point. Consequent Feelings of Wonder.
After this, surely, I ought to be lost in astonishment, wondering how God's faithful creatures could

suffer me to live at all, and even assist me in prolonging my sinful existence; how the Angels that ever stand ready to avenge any insult offered to the Divine Majesty have guarded me in all my ways; how the very Saints and the Immaculate Virgin herself have constantly prayed and interceded for me; how the sun and the earth, fire and water, plants and animals, and thousands of my fellow men, have kept ministering to my wants and even to my pleasures, at the very time when by my crimes I deserved that the ground should open under my feet and cause me to drop, body and soul, to the very bottom of Hell.

Colloquy, as in the preceding meditation, at the feet of Christ our Lord, Who for love of me came down from the inaccessible throne of His Majesty, and now, in my behalf and on my account, is dying in the most atrocious torments and the most profound ignominy, nailed naked to this frightful Cross. I will beg again with all the energy of my soul, for intense and perfect contrition, for bitter and abundant tears; a contrition that may cause me also to faint for shame and grief; a contrition like that of St. Peter, St. Mary Magdalen, St. Mary of Egypt, St. Margaret of Cortona, St. Rose of Lima, or Bl. Margaret Mary Alacoque. I will also render most sincere and heartfelt thanks to God, my Savior, for preserving my sinful existence till now, for opening my eyes to see the frenzy, the fiendishness, and the villainy of my numberless iniquities: and I will renew my determination, with the help of His grace, to labor at my thorough amendment for the future; to begin a new life free not only from sin but also from inordination; and, as far as possible, to do daily penance for the past. Yes, henceforth I will do all the

penance I can, in accordance with the Holy Will of
God, in keeping with my Religious Duties, in compliance with the inspirations of Grace, and in conformity with the advice of my Confessor.— Our
Father.

EMENDATION OF LIFE

We are all more or less suffering from tepidity and routinism; we know it, we regret it, but we seldom go to the root of this evil, which is our lack of self-knowledge, our neglect of self-examination. Our mind may be daily crossed by multitudes of frivolous, self-complacent, uncharitable thoughts, of which we take no more notice than persons addicted to profanity do of the number and character of their curse-words; while our heart may be so completely taken up with the attractions of sensible objects, that we are continually led astray by the inordinate tendencies of our Nature and almost blindly follow the suggestions of the Devil, often without realizing our danger till it is too late. These habitual dispositions of mind and heart are so closely interwoven with our daily lives that they may for some time escape the attention even of the vigilant and fervent, thus paralyzing their efforts towards Perfection. Without the grace of God it would be well-nigh impossible to detect them. Still, while putting our trust in the Divine Mercy, we ought also to do our own share by making a searching Examination of Conscience. The faults set forth in this Conference, being largely the record of an individual soul, are intended only to give an idea how one ought to scrutinize his past conduct at this stage of the Retreat. But this indirect self-accusation, of course, does not pretend to furnish anything like an ex-

haustive list of the defects to which Religious may
be subject, and hence it may profitably be supple-
mented from other sources according to each one's
personal needs.

I will, then, examine myself seriously,— not my
Companions, much less my Superiors, but my own
inmost heart,— before God, my Heavenly Father, my
Sovereign Lord, and my Unerring Judge, after first
humbly imploring the Light and Grace of His Holy
Spirit.

I will examine whether I am in the habit of offending against both **the Vow and the Virtue of
Poverty** by disposing of things independently, that
is, without the sanction of Superiors. Or while
keeping my Vow, do I perhaps sin against the
Virtue of Poverty by being unduly attached to
the goods of this world or to the articles given
me for my use; by desiring greater conveniences
or something above and beyond what is necessary; by retaining clothes, furniture, books, or
other objects of which I have no longer any need;
or by allowing what has not been put under my special care, to be spoiled, wasted, or lost? When outsiders make me a present, do I insist on leaving it
with the Superior, that he may dispose of it as he
may think best in the Lord? Do I sometimes elicit
such presents by hinting to outsiders at my needs or
tastes? Do I keep such presents for my own use,
without asking leave? Or again, have I violated
Poverty, by giving to relatives, friends, or pupils,
expensive rosaries, valuable pictures, and such like
objects; acting, perhaps, under the spell of some spiritual illusion?

I will examine whether I am habitually neglectful

of the safeguards of both **the Vow and the Virtue of Chastity;** namely, the custody of my senses, especially my eyes and my touch, the custody of my imagination from all dangerous representations or recollections, the custody of my mind from all curiosity about things the knowledge of which we should leave to the disposition of Providence; and the custody of my heart from all particular friendship or sensual affection. Again, do I resist temptations with sufficient promptitude and with exclusive trust in God?

With regard to **the Vow and the Virtue of Obedience,** I will examine whether I am in the habit of recognizing, revering, and loving in my Superior, only the Adorable Person of Jesus Christ, of Whom he is the true representative, approved by our Holy Father the Pope, the Successor of St. Peter, and, hence, referred to by our Divine Lord when He said, "Whoever heareth you heareth Me, and whoever despiseth you despiseth Me." Or have I perhaps accustomed myself to see in my Superior only a man, endowed with various natural qualities, good or bad, and to obey him from temporal, worldly, or selfish motives? If so, I should consider that I have entirely failed in the most essential obligation of my Sacred Profession, and that I have been a Religious only in name, but not in deed; and that I must bend all my efforts to live henceforth a life of Supernatural Obedience animated by Faith. Have I spoken or acted disrespectfully towards my Superiors, and if so have I done all I could to make up for such an insult to the Divine Majesty? Do I obey promptly and exactly in execution, lovingly and cheerfully in will, blindly and intelligently in judgment? Am I in the habit of obeying the sign of the bell, both for community exercises and for personal duties, just as if it were the voice of our Blessed Lord? Do I ever criticise the arrangements or orders of my Superior, merely in thought, or also in words, either privately by breaking perhaps the Rule of silence, or publicly and thus destroying the peace of the Community? Do I ever go so far as to judge and condemn his intentions? Have I, perhaps, committed such serious faults even more or less habitually? It may be well for me to remember, what some Religious seem to ignore, that irreverence and disobedience towards Superiors are violations of the Fourth Commandment, just as breaches of poverty are of the Seventh, and offenses against chastity of the Sixth. Similarly, one may sin against the Fourth Commandment by disrespect for those who are much older in Religion or for those who have been raised to the Priesthood. Lastly, I will examine whether I practise towards my Superiors that childlike openness even with regard to matters of conscience — my desire of perfection, my success in prayer, my use of the Sacraments, my conduct in temptation,— which is so strongly recommended by the Saints and so conducive to progress and perseverance.

I will examine whether I observe **Enclosure**, that is, Separation from the World, both physical and spiritual. Am I in the habit of looking for current news or for intercourse with outsiders? Have I ever presumed to communicate with relatives, friends, or pupils, by word or by letter, without the approval of my Superior? Do I strive to keep my heart constantly united to God, and occupied not with the fleeting shadows of earth but with the lasting realities of heaven, not with the temporal concerns of those whom I have left in the world, but with the spiritual interests of my Divine Lord and His Holy Church, the salvation and sanctification of men? Is it only through obedience and from a supernatural motive, that I assist at games, entertainments, picnics, excursions, and similar gatherings?

I will examine myself, as to my Meditation, Office, and other **Spiritual Duties**; whether I perform them through mere routine or put into them fresh fervor and love day after day; whether I am exact in keeping the "Additions"; whether I give the full time to my Examinations of Conscience, spending it in earnest prayer and not in distractions; whether I attend faithfully and energetically to my Particular Examen; and whether, as far as my health permits, I preserve at all Devotional Exercises, both public and private, a reverential and manly attitude.

I will examine myself with regard to Practices of **Mortification and Humiliation**, fasting, abstinence, discipline, girdle, waiting at table, public self-accusation, and similar means of self-abasement. Do I embrace every one of these precious opportunities, as far as I am permitted, with an ardent desire of atoning for my past sins and of becoming like to my Crucified Lord, or am I, perhaps, also in this vital matter, a slave to routinism and a sample of tepidity?

I will examine myself as to my **Daily Occupations**. Do I apply myself to my appointed task from a spirit of cheerful obedience, sincere humility, and ardent charity? In other words, do I labor from supernatural motives; or from natural reasons; for instance, because I have to in order to get on at all, or because

I wish to stand well with the Superior or the Community, or because I like to indulge my inborn activity and love of distraction, or because I look on my work as a means of maintenance, a source of support for the House? Do I prefer the humbler charges and the harder duties, at least as far as my strength will allow? And while I am engaged in these occupations, do I strive to keep my heart on God, or do I allow myself to be wholly engrossed with my task, giving way to impatience, precipitation, dissipation, uncharitableness, suspicion, faultfinding?

I will examine myself on **Silence**, whether I have failed in its observance under ordinary circumstances or have presumed to talk even during times and in places of Great Silence; and whether I break it through childish levity, or through particular friendship, or to vent my uncharitable thoughts and feelings, or perhaps to get others to support me in my criticism of Superiors. Especially in this last case, I ought to humble myself deeply before God, considering that unless I diligently correct and duly expiate such faults, I run a great risk of eventually forfeiting my Religious Vocation. Again, have I kept strict Silence during these holy Exercises? Without Silence, I need not expect to reap from the Retreat any other fruit than an increased responsibility for neglecting the grace of God.

I will examine myself as to my **Speech**, whether I have always been truthful, or whether I have told falsehoods, through vanity, fear, or flattery. Have I misrepresented matters to Superiors in order to gain my point? Have I made unwarrantable mental reservations? Am I in the habit of exaggerating things; am I fond of using superlatives? Do I strive to be truthful also in my Thoughts, by checking all self-complacency in my work, my talents, or my success, and by not substituting fancies for facts, assumptions for proofs, prejudices and prepossessions for unbiased opinions?

I will examine with regard to **Fraternal Charity**, whether I have offended against this sovereign virtue, in thought, in word, in deed, or by omission. Have I indulged in rash judgments, have I yielded to envy, have I harbored, even for a moment, feelings of resentment? Have I brought unfounded or false accusations against any of my fellow Religious, or reported every detail of their conduct and every word from their lips, as if I were a salaried spy, or as if they were perfidious enemies and sworn traitors? Have I in any other way injured their reputation with Superiors, companions, or outsiders. When I come from another House, do I take care not to talk of its affairs or inmates, except in such wise as will edify my hearers? Have I been cold and unsympathetic towards my Religious Brethren: showing no concern for their troubles and sufferings; attributing their ailments to their imagination; taking offense at their peculiarities because different from my own; making no allowances for nationality, temperament, education, age, and so forth; holding them up as cranks because they do not share my views or my ways of speaking and acting, or even because they are more strict in the observance of the Rules, more fervent in the practice of self-denial and penance; meddling and finding fault with their discharge of official duties or with their personal habits;

ignoring, slighting, ridiculing, or exasperating them through either thoughtlessness or malice? Do I strive to be present at the common recreation, not only in body, but also in mind and heart? Do I take the necessary precaution not to be hindered from this very important duty; or, on the contrary, do I perhaps avail myself of every excuse to absent myself? If I gave any scandal, have I taken care to repair it fully? Even for Religious it is well to bear in mind the words of St. John (1:4:20): "If any man say, I love God, and hateth his brother, he is a liar. For he that loveth not his brother, whom he seeth, how can he love God, whom he seeth not?"

Lastly, I will examine whether I have been constant and earnest in striving after the **Perfection of Divine Love**, after intimate Union with God. Have I been careful and eager to avail myself of all the means put at my disposal by my holy Institute to fulfil this chief obligation of the Religious State, to reach this one object for which I was honored with a Special Vocation? Have I at least striven to keep alive and nourish in my heart the desire of Evangelical Perfection, the resolution of treading in the footsteps of my holy Founder and his saintly Children? Or, have I perhaps been satisfied with the life of an ordinary Christian, avoiding grievous sins but neglecting the promptings of the Holy Spirit? Again, instead of working for the approbation of the Most High, have I perhaps degraded myself to labor for the praise of my fellow men, or to curry favor with my Superiors, in a spirit of servility or ambition; endeavoring to ingratiate myself by the simulation of sentiments and opinions I did not entertain, or by the dissimulation of my real thoughts and feelings;

by rendering them acts of service that belonged to another's office; by signifying exaggerated or indiscreet approval of their views, their plans, their words, their actions; or by practising any other unworthy tricks and false devices? If so, I have surely good reason to fear that I too shall be counted amongst those who have received their reward here below, and who for the sake of some passing gratification or some trifling preferment have jeopardized their eternal crown of bliss and glory in Heaven. Besides, who can estimate the immense harm which the introduction of this political spirit into a Religious Community will cause not only to the actual members but even to many future generations? Oh! if in my past conduct I detect any indications of my having been a time-server, a sycophant, a politician, I must use every effort to break completely and forever with such a detestable, subversive, and irreligious procedure.

In conclusion, these are serious consideration, and each one should make a similar examination of his own actual condition, humbly and sincerely, in the Presence of God, our All-Knowing and All-Holy Judge, setting aside the deceitful excuses of self-love and despising all the perfidious pretexts of Satan. But we must not rest satisfied with a clear knowledge of our failings; we should exert ourselves still more earnestly to conceive a true sorrow, an intense contrition for our faults. For this end, we should help ourselves also by a wholesome fear, remembering that God is not mocked, that we must beware of exhausting His Patience and Mercy by our folly and ingratitude, that by our infidelities and our sins we are in danger of losing the priceless pearl of our holy Vocation, which the Saints sought and kept at the cost of the greatest privations and sufferings. But on the other hand, we must also bear in mind that God will not despise a contrite and humble heart, and that like St. Paul, we can do all things in Him Who strengthens us.

SIN, INORDINATION, AND WORLDLINESS

Subject of this Meditation.— A repetition of the two preceding exercises, followed by a triple colloquy.

Composition of Place.—" To see with the eyes of the imagination and to consider that my soul is imprisoned in this corruptible body, and my whole self in this vale of misery, as it were, in exile among brute beasts: my whole self, body and soul."

Petition.— Intense shame and deep confusion joined to great grief and burning tears, for all my iniquities.

First Part. A Repetition of the two Preceding Meditations.

This repetition will prove very beneficial, if, in going over the successive points of The Triple Sin and My Personal Sins, we take care to impress on our minds and to treasure up in our hearts particularly those considerations in which we have experienced either a stronger disgust or a greater relish. The points of The Triple Sin were: the sin of the Angels, the sin of Adam and Eve, and the sin of many a Soul lost in consequence of one mortal sin or of fewer sins than I committed. The points of My Personal Sins were: an indictment of all my sins; their frenzy, fiendishness, and villainy; my

insignificance, my bodily corruption, and my
spiritual misery; my ignorance, weakness, and
malice in contrast with the Wisdom, Power, and
Goodness of God; lastly, the Admirable Mercy of
my Lord and Creator in bearing with me so long, so
patiently, and so lovingly.

In this repetition, then, I should especially strive
to bring home to myself that, if ever I committed
even one grievous sin, I acted like a maniac, a fiend,
a villain, and deserved to be buried for all eternity
in the flames of Hell with the demons and the
damned; that if ever I committed even one venial
sin, deliberately offending God, my Absolute Master and Supreme Benefactor, I did something very
foolish, cruel, and base, while besides I put myself
on the highroad to mortal sin and to everlasting perdition. I should note particularly that all this holds
good of sin committed by man, as he is by Unregen-
erate Nature, an intelligent and free being. How inconceivably more heinous, therefore, sin must be in a
person raised by Sanctifying Grace to the dignity of
an adopted Child of God, in a Soul daily nourished
with the Adorable Body of Christ our Lord, in a Religious entirely consecrated to the Special Service of
the Most High!

It cannot be emphasized sufficiently that all without exception stand very much in need of the graces
asked for in these meditations on sin; namely, deep
shame, intense contrition, abundant tears. For
either we have as yet kept our baptismal innocence or
else we have contracted grievous guilt. Now, on the
one hand, those favored souls who, owing to a most
unmerited mercy of God and in spite of their numerous inordinations and venial faults, were preserved from falling into mortal sin, should labor

with the utmost earnestness to conceive a burning
and lasting contrition for all their past infidelities,
because otherwise, not sufficiently realizing that
their freedom from grievous guilt is a pure gift of
God, they will remain very deficient in humility and
watchfulness, and consequently may find themselves
sooner or later exposed to strong temptations and
terrible dangers. This is why some Religious that
left the world before they knew its corruption, after
spending many years within the holy walls of the
convent, sometimes even lose their Vocation and die
like reprobates. Others, without going quite so far,
habitually indulge in a multiplicity of venial faults,
and consequently lead very imperfect and unhappy
lives, precisely because they never humbled themselves completely in their own inmost hearts, in the
sight of Almighty God, at the feet of the Minister
of Christ. But, on the other hand, those who have
had the misfortune of committing mortal sin, just
as they far surpassed the more highly favored in
wickedness so they should also strive to surpass them
in penance. Now it does happen that the contrary
is found, either because such persons never yet ex-
erted themselves to obtain that overwhelming confusion and ardent contrition with which even a
single mortal sin should fill every upright soul, or
else because they neglected to intensify these dispositions of shame and sorrow in proportion to their
growing knowledge of God and their increasing years
in Religion. Also Religious of this description have
good reason to fear that their lukewarmness and
routinism will eventually drag them down to spiritual death and eternal perdition. Therefore, to
whichever class we belong, we must strive to produce
genuine fruits of penance, and for this purpose apply

ourselves to these meditations on sin with the utmost energy and fervor. The deeper our confusion, the greater our shame, the more bitter our grief, and the more copious our tears, the more certain and thorough also will be our amendment, the more constant and rapid likewise our progress in Perfection. For the future, our customary acts of contrition ought to be very different from what they have been but too often in the past.

Second Part. The Triple Colloquy.

This Triple Colloquy prescribed by St. Ignatius, is intended to complete the cleansing of our soul from sin, of our heart from inordinate desires, and of our mind from worldly views. The First Colloquy is directed to our Lady, that she may implore for me from her Son and Lord these Three Graces: first, an intimate Knowledge and real Hatred of all my Sins, so that I may never commit them again; secondly, a keen Perception and profound Abhorrence of my manifold Inordinations, so that I may amend my whole conduct; thirdly, a clear Recognition and utter Detestation of the World, so that I may rid myself of everything worldly or vain. The Second Colloquy is addressed to our Divine Redeemer that He may obtain for me the same Three Graces from the Eternal Father. The Third Colloquy is made to God the Father that He, in His Infinite Mercy, may grant me these same Three Graces.

First Grace; an intimate Knowledge and real Hatred of all my Sins, that I may never commit them again. My hatred of Sin will always be exactly proportional to my knowledge. It is because I do not sufficiently realize the true character of Sin, its frenzy, its fiendishness, and its villainy, that I am so negligent about the avoidance of temptation and so remiss in the practice of penance. Hence natural reason alone is not enough; I need supernatural illumination, to give me that intimate knowledge of Sin which will make me flee with horror from any future consent and will cause me to embrace eagerly every means of expiating my past indulgence. The more fully I shall become convinced of this evident truth, that Sin is the greatest of all evils and, in fact, the only evil I have to fear, the more spontaneous will be my flight from any temptation to Sin, however alluring its aspect or painful its rejection, and the more insatiable will grow my longing for every form of mortification and humiliation to purify my heart from the effects of Sin.

Second Grace; a keen Perception and profound Abhorrence of my manifold Inordinations, that I may amend my whole conduct. Since Inordination is the root of Sin, I am not likely to keep from Sin, unless I labor to destroy Inordination. My past life has been full of Inordination, of spiritual Disorder, inasmuch as I have habitually thought, spoken, and acted, without first considering the Adorable Will of God, my Creator and Lord. If I am really in earnest about my amendment, I must cease to have my own way, to do as I please, to follow slavishly the promptings of my Fallen Nature. It is this widespread leaven of Inordination that till now has vitiated by far the greater part of my conscious existence, and prevented me from devoting all my energy to the service of the Most High. For every Inordination is an exhibition of injustice and ingratitude towards God, a piece of self-stultification and self-injury, an abuse and profanation of the creature. With what ardor, therefore, I should implore this grace of keenly

discerning and deeply abhorring all the Disorder
of my past life, and of henceforth regulating the
activity of my senses and faculties only by the Divine Will in whatever way manifested.

Third Grace; a clear Recognition and utter Detestation of the World, that I may completely rid
my mind of all its deceit and vanity. Just as Sin is
the consequence of Inordination, so Inordination is
the result of Worldliness. The World comprises all
those who lead a merely natural existence and labor
exclusively for earthly interests, while entirely neglectful of the supernatural life and of the endless
hereafter. Their chief concern is " to have a good
time." Hence, the World embodies the spirit of nat-
uralism, materialism, and unbelief. It stands for
the unrestrained and unremitting pursuit of health,
comfort, enjoyment, wealth, distinction, and independence. Its views and doctrines are diametrically
opposed to the principles and teachings of Christ and
His Saints, to the Evangelical Counsels and the
Eight Beatitudes. I was infected with this worldly
spirit already before my birth, I lived many years
in the midst of this pestilential atmosphere, and even
in Religion I cannot altogether escape its poisonous
breath. No wonder, therefore, if I should detect in
myself a more or less considerable residue of Worldliness. " We offend people by our poor clothes."—
" A person cannot live without some fun."—" Without money we can do nothing."—" Why should I still
be treated like a little novice? "—" I am not going
to let everybody walk over me."—" Don't try to be
better than the rest." Surely, these and other such
sentiments are neither based on sound reason nor inspired by the Holy Ghost. I should pray, then, for
abundant grace, not only to recognize clearly the

blatant sophistry and worthless tinsel of the World, but also to detest it so thoroughly as to break forever with its deceitful maxims and pernicious tendencies.

In conclusion, let us strive to make this Triple Colloquy with all possible humility, confidence, and fervor. If we should derive from our whole Retreat no other fruit than these Three Graces, it would still be the best we ever made. It is because we have till now been wanting in this real Hatred of Sin, this profound Abhorrence of Inordination, this utter Detestation of Worldliness, it is because there has been as yet no entire conversion of our mind and heart to God, the Absolute Holiness, the Sovereign Truth, the Infinite Goodness, that our desires to advance in perfection have proved so ineffectual and ephemeral.

In making this Triple Colloquy, says St. Ignatius, " I should in spirit prostrate myself before the throne of the Eternal Father, at whose right is seated Christ our Lord, and next to Him the Most Holy Virgin Mary, all three looking down on me with eyes full of the tenderest pity and love." Then addressing first our Heavenly Mother, I should plead my cause with her, in childlike simplicity and candor, insisting on my extreme misery, on my pressing need, on her marvelous exemption from every stain of Sin and Inordination, on her all-powerful influence over the Sacred Heart of Jesus, supplicating and conjuring her by all she suffered here on earth but especially under the Cross of Calvary to obtain for me these Three Graces, and then recite the Angelical Salutation. In the same manner I should afterwards, with her assistance, have recourse to our Adorable Savior, and add the Anima Christi. Lastly, through the intercession of our Blessed Lady, and the mediation of her Divine Son, I should present my petitions to the Eternal Father, and finish with the Lord's Prayer.

"MY CHILD, GIVE ME THY HEART."

THIRD DAY

SPECIAL PATRON: St. Francis Borgia.

MOTTO: "Pierce Thou my flesh with Thy fear."—
Ps. 118:120.

SPIRIT: Hatred and Horror of Sin, of Inordination,
and of the World.

READING: Imitation; Bk. I, C. 6, 13, 14, 23, 24.
                Bk. II, C. 2, 10.
                Bk. III, C. 24, 41, 53.

Strive to intensify more and more your sorrow for
sin and your desire of penance. Bear in mind that
the fruit of this Retreat will be proportioned to the
humility, sincerity, and docility, with which you
seek to manifest your past faults and your actual
dispositions to the Minister of God.

HELL

Introductory Remarks.— While the consideration
of Hell tends directly to inspire fear, it indirectly
also helps to enkindle love. Yet even fear is something we cannot afford to discard as long as we are
living in this world. If we could realize the deadly
hatred that Satan bears us and the violent temptations to which we may be suddenly exposed, we
would not let a single day pass without seriously
reflecting on Hell. Even after St. Francis Borgia
had attained a high degree of holiness he very frequently meditated on Hell, declaring that he derived
great benefit from this exercise every time he made
it. But for this it is necessary to make Hell an actual reality to ourselves, not looking upon it as a
plausible opinion or a philosophical theory but as a
certain and awful truth, revealed and vouched for
by God Himself. In the Gospels alone there are at
least fifteen distinct references to this place of everlasting punishment, of unquenchable fire, recorded
from the lips of our Divine Lord. For Catholics,
however, and all the more for Religious, it ought to
be enough to know on this point the explicit teaching
of His Holy, Infallible Church.

Subject of this Meditation.— The endless affliction
of the unrepentant sinner in Hell.

Composition of Place.—The length, breadth, and
depth of Hell; or else, the narrow space destined

there for me if I should continue in my tepidity, such as was shown in a vision to St. Theresa to rouse her to greater fervor.

Petition.—"An interior sense [or intimate realization] of the pains which the Lost suffer; in order that if ever through my faults [my inordinations and venial sins] I should forget the love of the Eternal Lord, at least the fear of punishment may prevent me from falling into [mortal] sin."

First Point. The Pains of Hell.

The Pain of Loss: "Depart from Me."— This peremptory command means separation from God as He is our Supernatural End and Recompense; in other words, it means our being once for all excluded by the Most High from that Intuitive Vision which would make us share in His own Infinite Happiness. Here on earth the loss of fortune, health, or companionship, tends to fill us with sadness; what, then, must be the effect of losing God, of this immeasurable and irreparable Loss? To understand fully what this Pain of Loss implies, we ought to have experienced already the bliss and glory of the Saints in Heaven. But as such is not the case, we can only say that the Reprobate are forever deprived of that Divine Vision which unceasingly keeps the Angels and the Blessed immersed in an ocean of ecstatic delight, a delight ever new and ever full, without any shadow of alteration or any fear of diminution; a delight such as, in the words of St. Paul, no eye has seen, no ear has heard, and no human heart has ever been able to conceive. The Reprobate, however, suffer not only the absence of this unspeakable happiness, but also an indescribable anguish arising from

the fact that they were positively created for the
enjoyment of the Infinite Truth and Goodness. The
Loss of God, consequently, leaves in the souls of the
Damned a frightful void which nothing can ever
fill.

Again, as the Lost are fully aware that God is su-
premely Happy, their impotent hatred fills them with
extreme bitterness, while the glory of the Saints and
Angels, from whose society they are forever excluded,
consumes them with fiendish envy. Moreover, they
are now forced to acknowledge the Sovereign Beauty
and Loveliness of God, and though irrevocably ban-
ished from His Presence, though forever deprived of
His Love, yet, by the very law of their being, they
vehemently long for Him and are irresistibly drawn
towards Him, inasmuch as they clearly perceive in
Him the sum total of all happiness. For there exists
in every soul a natural craving for happiness, which it
now recognizes can be found only in God; while at
the same time, through its own perverse choice, it is
swayed by a fierce hatred, a wilful aversion from
God, as the unsurmountable obstacle to its selfishness
and pride. Thus the Lost are being continually at-
tracted and repelled by one and the same object. And
these two conflicting tendencies, namely, this powerful inclination to God and this strong aversion
from God, will tear asunder, so to speak, the Reprobate Spirit for all eternity, causing it to undergo an
everlasting death or rather a never-abating agony,
incomparably more excruciating than that inflicted
by any torments on earth. Still, since we can never
form directly an adequate idea of this Pain of Loss,
let us strive to realize it indirectly by considering
for a few moments the far less terrible Pain of Sense.

This Pain of Sense we may take to be the effect of

the Divine Malediction expressed in the words, " Ye
cursed." The Lost are separated, cut off from God,
not only as He is in Himself, but also as the Source
of every physical and moral good, of every natural
blessing. Hence they suffer utter destitution, that
is, the most complete privation of whatever is necessary to supply their manifold and ever pressing needs.
What hardship it is to be without food or drink for
an entire day, or even for a few hours; what misery
it is to be deprived of one's eyes, feet, or fingers!
What, then, must it be to be absolutely and forever
deprived of everything? Dives imploring the boon
of a drop of water in vain, such is the object-lesson
furnished us by the Son of God, the Infallible Truth.
In brief, each of the Lost will be filled with every
kind of affliction to the full of his capacity.

In Hell, consequently, there is no action but all is
passion; there is no pleasurable exertion of any kind,
nothing except conscious suffering; a punishment of
spiritual sloth, of moral stagnation. In Hell there
is complete and universal disorder, in the faculties
of the soul as well as in the senses and organs of the
body; a punishment of spiritual negligence and
moral crookedness. In Hell there is no light, except perhaps to reveal to the Lost the terrors of their
prison, but all else is shrouded in impenetrable
gloom; a punishment of unguarded looks, of dangerous readings. In Hell there is no sound, except such
as can afflict the hearing, but otherwise all is absolute silence, the horrid stillness of the tomb; a
punishment of the abuse of speech, of the craving
for voluptuous music. Worse than all this, however,
in Hell there reigns a universal and deadly hatred; a
punishment of the irregular love of self and creatures. The Damned animated with a most vehement

detestation, a most profound loathing for everything created, are continually cursing the hour of their birth, the authors of their existence, the friends that seduced them, the persons on whose account they sinned, and especially their own selves. In Hell, then, there is no affection, no love.

While the Reprobate are thus completely abandoned and isolated in their unutterable wretchedness, only their vices remain with them to exercise a despotic sway over their entire being and to inflict on them a ceaseless persecution. This inevitable result of not practising penance and self-denial begins already here on earth and is a matter of daily experience. In fact, our greatest misery and keenest suffering is brought on us by our own vices in proportion as we get enslaved to them. What must it be when their tyranny has become absolute and all gratification is rendered impossible? Thus gluttony, avarice, lust, pride, will each torment its helpless victim forever in Hell.

The Pain of Fire: "into everlasting fire."— We know from Revelation that the Lost in Hell will be punished, both in soul and body, by this "Everlasting Fire prepared for the Devil and his Angels," that is, called first into existence for the punishment of the Demons the moment they were cast into Hell. It will afflict each Reprobate in exact proportion to the number and gravity of his sins, and each member of his body in the measure in which it has been the instrument of evil. "They shall be salted with fire." (Mark 9:48.) It is certainly real and physical, but whether the suffering caused by it is altogether distinct from the Pain of Sense just considered, is not certain. At all events, even if not distinct, it furnishes us with a different aspect of the Pain of

Sense, and so renders our knowledge and appreciation more complete.

The proud rebellious spirit, then, is imprisoned by a physical Fire, it is held at the mercy of matter. What awful pain, what frightful torture may be inflicted by our earthly fire, we all know by experience; yet, in comparison to the sufferings caused by the Fire of Hell, according to St. Augustine, it is only as it were a painted fire, or like the picture of a fire. Now, unless we have a very strong imagination, a mere pictorial reproduction of a fire would surely cause us little inconvenience. Well, such is the fire of earth contrasted with that of Hell. But even if it were no worse than our earthly fire, who would not shudder with horror at the prospect of being chained down on a burning pile of wood or shut up in a roaring blast-furnace or submerged in a caldron of molten metal, and that not for a second, not for a minute, not for an entire day, or a week, or a month, or a year, but forever and ever? Yet no such crude imagery as this can at all approach the tremendous reality.

And in the midst of these awful afflictions the Damned are devoured with the most intense Remorse. It is a matter of daily observation how painfully men are affected by the loss of a valuable object, the missing of a splendid opportunity, or the failure of a promising enterprise, when the blame is entirely their own. So each Reprobate Soul keeps repeating to itself incessantly: "It is all my own doing, my own choice, my own fault. I insisted on having my own way, and I got it. Now I am forever buried in Hell; in spite of the sufferings of Christ, in spite of the intercession of Mary, in spite of the prayers of the Saints and Angels, in spite of the example of parents, the help of friends, the advice of priests, in spite of all the numberless favors and special graces lavished on me by God, I am lost."

Hence, in conclusion, the worst calamities of this world, all the multitudinous horrors of cyclones, floods, earthquakes, conflagrations, collisions, and shipwrecks, of plagues, famines, revolutions, and wars, are but the distant foreshadowings of what will come upon the unrepentant sinner. This, then, is what I have deserved, perhaps over and over again, by my sins; this, then, is what I should be suffering already now, and even since many years, if God in His Admirable Mercy had not so patiently prepared and awaited my conversion, if Christ, my Adorable Lord, had not died on the Cross amid unspeakable anguish and ignominy, for Love of me and on account of my Sins. This, then, is the final result of wanting to have my own way, of wishing to be my own master, of not submitting to those appointed to rule and direct me, of following slavishly my likes and dislikes, my blind propensities and repugnances. And this is where my Sins, yea, even my Inordinations will yet lead me inevitably, unless like St. Theresa, I exert all my energy to cooperate with Divine Grace for a thorough and lasting Reformation of Life.

Second Point. The Eternity of Hell.

The Fact.— Though Eternity cannot be expressed in terms applicable to time, yet probably the simplest way in which we can form some imperfect notion of Eternity is by means of an endless succession of years. Hence we may say, for instance, that after a hundred thousand years Hell will still be only beginning, and that after a hundred thousand million years it will not have advanced any further than when the Lost Soul first received her sentence of damnation. But we must bear in mind that the Eternity of Hell is in reality far worse than all this, inasmuch as it presses on the Reprobate at each instant with its entire weight. Almost any hardship here on earth becomes bearable, provided the end be not too far distant and be certain to come within a limited number of hours, days, weeks, or even months. But if our sufferings are prolonged indefinitely for many, many years, how the dark prospect seems to crush our spirit and fill our soul with such sadness and melancholy as actually to bring about death. What then, must be the anguish caused by the certainty that they will never, never come to an end; and sufferings not of earth, but of Hell?

The Reason of this Eternity is the Divine Decree that death should fix man's destiny forever after, either in Heaven or in Hell; in other words, the irrevocable sentence of the Sovereign Judge. But a deeper reason lies in the very nature of mortal sin, which of itself is irremediable. Just as the Blessed are confirmed in grace, and love, and holiness, so the Lost are confirmed, or rather abandoned, in guilt, and hate, and wickedness. While yet on earth, they abused their liberty; while it was yet in their power to listen to grace and to return to God, they refused to avail themselves of His Mercy; now no more grace is offered them since the period of probation is past, and accordingly their evil will remains forever turned away from God, full of sin, full of hatred, full of wickedness.

The Consequence is that Hell is not only Everlasting but also Invariable. There will be not one moment of respite, not the least token of sympathy, not the faintest glimmer of relief. No companions ex-

cept the Reprobate and the Demons. No hope, forever; and hence the most absolute, the most frantic
Despair. Therefore, in opposition to the Eternity
of Heaven, which is the actual, total, and simultaneous possession of a life of bliss and glory, whose
duration shall have no end; the Eternity of Hell may
well be called the actual, total, and simultaneous in-
fliction of an agony, both spiritual and physical,
whose duration shall have no end; in other words, an
Everlasting Death, or rather an Everlasting Dying,
to be suffered with unmitigated intensity, at every
single instant, both soul and body being made to undergo unceasingly all the torments of which they are
capable, in exact proportion to all the natural gifts
and supernatural graces which they did or could receive during this earthly existence, but which they
deliberately, obstinately, and scornfully squandered
and rejected. Is this, then, Hell? No, this is only
a very imperfect description of it. Just as Heaven
is entirely beyond our intellectual grasp, so is Hell.

Third Point. The Way to Hell for Religious.—
How did they get there, these wretched souls who
once, perhaps, were members of this same Order or
Congregation, had made the Noviceship, had taken
the Vows, and had filled several Offices? This Fire
was " prepared for the Devil and his Angels," not
for Men, not for Religious. If we could ask some of
them how they got into this place of torment, what
would they answer? Being completely isolated from
one another, they could only reply in the singular.

" First; there was lack of earnest correspondence
to the grace of God; no desire, no effort to practise
penance, self-denial, and self-abasement; relaxation
of fraternal charity; frequent inordinations; gradual

substitution of the natural for the supernatural; I became satisfied with avoiding deliberate Venial Sin.

"Next; there was routinism in spiritual things; partial omission of prayer; negligent performance of duty; liberty of the senses, no guard over eyes and touch; giving the body every little gratification and comfort that could be had; taking in all the distractions and amusements that offered themselves; wilful transgression of the rules; I did not stop at anything except deliberate Mortal Sin.

"Lastly; there were numerous and habitual venial sins; confessions without true sorrow or sincere purpose; communions without preparation or thanksgiving; indulgence of unlawful curiosity; seeking proximate occasions of sin, places, books, persons; total neglect of prayer; then deliberate mortal sins; grievous violations of the vows; complete abandonment of vocation; and thus I fell into Consummate Pride." Such in outline would be the reply of almost every Lost Religious.

How, then, can I afford to make light of matters of such inconceivable importance as those which concern my Eternal Salvation? Must I not rather be most eager to give up everything and anything that may prove an Obstacle or constitute a Danger? And how highly I should esteem my Vocation, how sincerely devoted I should be to my Community, for the manifold and powerful Helps afforded me to get farther and farther away from Hell! What, if I had been left in the World? Besides, should I not embrace every kind of Penance, except when prevented by age or infirmity, or rather by Holy Obedience? No Religious is safe that does not practise in addition to Interior Mortification also Exterior Penance; such as self-denial in food, in comfort, in rest; custody of the eyes and the tongue; affliction of the sense of touch by praying on one's knees with arms extended, by wearing small chains, by taking the discipline. This chastisement of the body is one of the most efficacious means for checking our Sensuality and humbling our Pride, for obtaining Recollection and regaining Fervor, and thus for increasing our inward Peace, our true Happiness.

Colloquy.— Once more kneeling at the foot of the Cross, I shall give expression to my contrition, my gratitude, and my determination of using henceforth all the means afforded me by my holy Institute to persevere at any cost, until death.

Here I should also represent to myself the immense multitude of souls that are already in Hell, either because they would not believe in Christ, or because they refused to keep the Commandments; that is, either for lack of supernatural Faith or for lack of Good Works. How many were lost before the Coming of our Lord, how many even during His Stay on earth, and how many again after His Ascension! Alas! what frightful ruin caused by Sensuality and Pride! How thankful I ought to be that God did not call me into existence during those dark ages when the whole world was groaning under the dominion of Satan, or that He did not give me my being during these modern times in the midst of some idolatrous nation or in the bosom of an irreligious family! If with all my advantages of birth and education I committed so many sins, what should I not have done under less favorable circumstances? O wonderful preference of Divine Love towards me, chosen out of such countless numbers of souls, many of whom, if they had received the same graces as I, would have corresponded to them so much better! But while they were justly condemned to Hell, God has till now only shown me the most tender Pity and Mercy.

Nevertheless, all those who are now lost forever were once truly destined like myself for Everlasting Bliss. How, then, did they happen to perish eternally? Many went astray for want of apostolic men to teach them the truths of Revealed Faith, to set them the example of Meritorious Works; many lived and died in Sin, because there was none to pray, labor, and suffer for their Conversion. And the same holds good of all those millions and millions in every part of the globe who are actually in imminent danger of Damnation. Whose heart would not melt with pity at this thought? Whose breast would not be inflamed with zeal? It is also for their Salvation, that I should henceforth apply myself in real earnest to my own Sanctification, by the exercise of Prayer and Penance, by the practice of Poverty, Chastity, Obedience, and Charity.— Our Father.

THE KINGDOM OF CHRIST

Introductory Remarks.— Let us suppose a certain man has been appointed directly by God Himself to rule all Christians. This king issues a proclamation to his subjects informing them that, in virtue of his Divine commission, he intends to subjugate the whole country of the infidels, and that those who wish to follow him in this glorious campaign will have to share with him in its various hardships in order that afterwards they may likewise share in his certain victory. Surely, every loyal subject would eagerly accept such a benevolent and liberal offer, and any one who did not, would incur the just blame and contempt of all his fellows. St. Ignatius uses this reference to a temporal ruler in order to fix our attention on Christ, our Heavenly King, and on His Paramount Claims to our Devoted Service.

Subject of this Meditation.—The Call of Christ our Lord.

Composition of Place.—" The synagogues, towns, and villages, through which Christ our Lord used to preach," on the sunny hills of Judea, the fertile plains of Galilee, and the lovely shores of Gennesareth. This includes every locality where the call of Christ our King actually went forth; to remind us that there is question, not of a fictitious call, but of a real and historic call.

Petition.—"That I may not be deaf to His Call, but prompt and diligent to accomplish His most Holy Will."

First Point. How Christ Calls All Men.—"If we consider," says St. Ignatius, "the summons of the temporal king to his subjects, how much more worthy of our consideration it is to see Christ our Lord, the Eternal King, and before Him the whole human race, all of whom and each in particular He calls, saying: 'My will is to conquer the entire world and all My enemies, and thus to enter into the glory of My Father. Whoever, therefore, desires to come with Me must Labor with Me, in order that following Me in hardship he may likewise follow Me in glory.'"

The Person of Christ our Lord.— This is the same Divine-Human Person Whom, already in the meditation on The Triple Sin, I beheld nailed to a Cross, wondering how He, the Almighty Creator, could have condescended to become Man, and from everlasting life could have come down to temporal death, thus to die for my Sins, that I might not be cast into Hell, like the rebel angels and so many millions of men, condemned for fewer sins than I committed, or even for one single mortal sin. This is the same Adorable Lord, Whose admirable Mercy and singular Predilection — as I considered in the meditation on Hell — are the only cause why I am not already burning in that unquenchable fire, with so many others far less guilty than I. This is the same Eternal King, to Whose Love and Preference I have till now corresponded with so much ingratitude, but Whom in future I desire to love with all my heart, in return for so many signal favors, by applying myself in real earnest to the practice of every Virtue, to the observance of every Rule, and to the performance of every Duty.

His Actions.— He stands "before the whole human race," as their True and only Sovereign King, by nature as God and by grace as Man. Oh! might He be soon acknowledged as such by all. "Thy Kingdom Come!"—"He calls all and each in particular." All are called absolutely to follow Him by the profession of the Faith and the observance of the Commandments; and, besides, all are called, at least conditionally, to the practice of the Evangelical Counsels. I too have been called, but I was favored with a Special Vocation, that is, I was invited in an absolute manner to the embracing of the Counsels, to the Perfection of Charity, to Sanctity. Christ also said to me, "if thou wilt be perfect," while at the same time He inspired me with the desire to become perfect. And I am still being called day after day, by the prompting of His Holy Spirit, by the disposal of my Superiors, by the exhortation of my Rules, to an ever closer following of my Divine King. In other words, my Vocation did now cease at my taking of the Vows, but is continuous and ever more urgent. Oh! may I never be deaf to that Sacred Call, may I not rest satisfied with merely keeping up the fervor of my noviceship,—"to have never lost the fervor of one's noviceship" is at best a very doubtful praise — but especially during this Retreat may I be attentive and obedient to that Heavenly Call as to the Voice of my only Beloved. May I welcome His Call, may I embrace this Vocation to ever greater Holiness, with the utmost alacrity and generosity!

His Words.— His Royal Proclamation is brief: "My will is to conquer the entire world and all My

enemies, and thus to enter into the glory of My
Father." For this purpose He came down upon the
earth. His Sacred Heart cannot bear to see humanity, like a wild torrent, rushing into the infernal
abyss, into the everlasting torments of Hell. O Admirable Love and Mercy of my God and my King!
" To conquer the whole world," to subject all men, all
hearts, to the Sweet Yoke of poverty and humility, to
the Heavenly Law of purity and charity, by the acceptance of Divine Faith and the exercise of Good Works,
and even by the practice of the Counsels of Perfection,
that is, by the pursuit of the highest possible Sanctity:
thus to deliver them from the tyranny of their passions, from the slavery of Satan, from the imminent
danger of perdition; and to render them truly happy
here below, eternally blissful hereafter. What Tender Compassion of the Lord God for my miseries!
and this, in spite of my former sinfulness, my black
ingratitude, my foul rebellion. Adorable King, conquer also my heart, though so utterly unworthy of
Thy Divine Solicitude, subdue it, enslave it forever.
" And all My enemies." What enemies are these except my own irregular inclinations, my own evil
passions, which ever tend to drag me down into sin,
to render me miserable? These are His enemies precisely because they are mine; they are hateful to Him
because they are injurious to me: Sensuality, Covetousness, and Pride; that is, my inordinate leanings towards comforts, possessions, and distinctions; or, in
one word, the Flesh ever in league with the World
and the Devil. "And thus to enter into the glory
of My Father." In triumph, leading innumerable
bands of souls, enchained by His Love, united by mutual Charity; He being the Head, and they forming
His Mystic Body, acquired by His Passion and Death;

that they may share with Him unending Bliss and inconceivable Glory.

But besides, He wants our cooperation in this Spiritual Warfare, in this Supernatural Conquest. Here is His appeal: " Whosoever, therefore, desires to come with Me." All are invited, but none is compelled. Our King looks for voluntary service. His kingdom is one of devotion, sacrifice, and love. But what condescension on His part to invite us to a share in this Divine Enterprise. Instead of reserving all the glory to Himself, He desires every man to have a share in it, those very men, so ungrateful and sinful, for whose Redemption He has conceived and undertaken this wonderful conquest of Infinite Mercy. Who then could refuse to listen to His Call? " Must labor with Me." Of course; but what happiness to labor and toil and suffer with Him, our King, our God, laboring, toiling, suffering with us and for us; what a privilege to have part in His Afflictions, in His Cross, for the sake of our Brethren, each of whom He longs to bring under the empire of His Love! What selfishness, what meanness it would be not to be contented with His food, His rest, His drink, His raiment, and His shelter! " In order that following Me in hardship, he may likewise follow Me in glory." What liberality! Our recompense, our share in His triumph will be exactly proportionate to our share in His labors and watches. Though by nature we are only His servants, and by sin His debtors, yet He desires to treat us as His intimate friends. It is true, there is the cowardly fear of our natural Self to alarm us, there are the deceitful suggestions of the Devil to discourage us; yet we know that we can do all things with the help of Grace, and that there is no higher happiness than that of the Saint.

Second Point. How Men Listen and Correspond to the Call of Christ, their King.

Many do not listen at all but, on the contrary, reject the Call of Christ and positively refuse to do anything for our Lord. They have either no Faith or no Works. Not a few of them are Nominal Catholics. These are men that follow instead the vanities of the world, the promptings of their passions, and the deceits of Satan, men whose main object is to make money, to seek amusements, to gain distinctions. They have no sense, no honor, no gratitude, and no love. Many amongst them remain knowingly and wilfully outside the True Church, many others have deserted Her and turned traitors. They all oppose the Kingdom of Christ by contributing to the spread of error and immorality, some even persecute His faithful followers by acts of violence and iniquitous laws. Perhaps I too have been at one time amongst these blind ingrates: — for how long, for how many years? O shame and confusion, for such folly and perversity!

Many listen to the Call of Christ, but only in so far as to keep themselves ready to carry out any particular command or obligation laid upon them by their Divine King. They make no spontaneous offer of Service. These are ordinary, or rather Lukewarm Catholics, who habitually strive to keep from Mortal Sin and to do what is enjoined under pain of damnation, but do not exert themselves to avoid Venial Sin. Surely, they show no generosity, manifest scarcely any zeal, and give proof of very little sense, in not availing themselves better of such an advantageous and glorious opportunity to which they are invited by Christ our Lord. Yet even these, in spite of their poor service, provided only they persevere in Sancti-

fying Grace, will receive an eternal reward. Such is
the Magnanimity, the Prodigality of our King. But
how completely a Religious would miss the spirit of
his Sublime Calling, if he were contented to belong
to this class.

Not a few, indeed, go further and offer their possessions and their talents for the Service of Christ.
These are earnest, Practical Catholics, that lead the
life of the Precepts but devote their goods, their time,
and their energy, to the cause of the Church, to the
relief of the poor, to the instruction of the ignorant,
to the comfort of the sick and afflicted. Not satisfied
with what is of obligation, they attend special exercises of Worship and frequently receive the Sacraments. They thus show their good sense, since for
everything they now sacrifice they will receive a most
ample compensation both here in this world and in
the next; here, preservation from mortal sin and even
from venial sin, with peace of soul; hereafter, endless
bliss and glory in Heaven. To this class, then, all
those belong who, " having the use of judgment and
reason, offer their whole selves for labor." Even
this, however, is by no means enough for a Religious.

**Third Point. How a Religious should Listen and
Correspond to the Call of Christ.**

" But there are some," St. Ignatius says, " who wish
to show greater affection and to distinguish themselves in every kind of service of their Eternal King
and Universal Lord." These are persons that, besides
reason and judgment, possess a generous disposition
and a loving heart, and who, in order to make the
greatest possible progress in Perfection, have surrendered themselves unreservedly to the Adorable
Will of God. Is not this exactly what we had in view

when we conceived the idea of entering the Religious State? To show greater affection towards Him, our Creator, Who for love of us, His sinful creatures, embraced all the torments and ignominy of the Cross; to signalize ourselves in His Service, to do for Him something special and arduous in return for such Wonderful Love; namely, to strive after real Holiness, to become entirely His. This is surely the spirit of our Vocation. Oh! let us resolve not only to persevere in these same desires, but daily to fan them into a more ardent flame, to be wholly consumed by the vehemence of this celestial fire. But from these generous aspirations we must proceed to energetic action.

For these, in the words of St. Ignatius, " not only offer their whole persons to labor,"— even to perform the lowest drudgery, in which there is no opportunity of vainglory,— but also begin to " act against their own sensuality, their carnal and worldly love." Sensuality; the inclination to things agreeable to the senses, namely, earthly goods and pastimes, and the aversion for things painful, such as poverty and suffering: Carnal Love; the sympathy we feel for persons that please us by their appearance, kindness, or accomplishments, and the antipathy we experience for such as displease us by their defects, rudeness, or drawbacks: Worldly Love; the craving for esteem and honor, and the shunning of contempt and insult. Comparatively few Christians understand this point, that, since Christ our King came to conquer His enemies, our inordinate passions, they themselves should start at once, with the help of His grace, to wage war against these domestic, most dangerous, and most persistent foes, whose existence they realize constitutes an immense obstacle to the carrying out of their generous desires and lofty aims. This means more than to offer one's goods and talents, this is the Actual Following of Christ our King.

However, let us not forget that to belong to this class we must " act against " our rebellious inclinations, not simply restrain them, check them, or stand on the defensive, but take the offensive, exert ourselves in the contrary direction, do the very opposite of that towards which they tend, determined daily to make the greatest possible progress.   These, then, are Fervent Catholics, such as lead, in so far as circumstances will allow, the Life of the Counsels, of Evangelical Perfection, and who sincerely devote themselves to the work of their sanctification.   They realize that, before helping to extend the Kingdom of Christ over other hearts, they must first establish it firmly in their own, by complete self-conquest, by continual self-denial.   Am I too thoroughly convinced that this is my most pressing need, my most important task; self-denial, self-conquest? that, without this, my activity, learning, reputation, or talent is useless and worse than useless; that all these things, far from being conducive to the Kingdom of Christ, will only prove detrimental and destructive?   Not that I should ever cease begging to be wholly spent with zeal for souls; for the Son of God has come for this purpose, to conquer the whole world, to extend the empire of His Love over all men, over all hearts.   But in order to assist Him in this Divine Enterprise and to follow Him in this Holy Campaign, I must begin with completely subduing His enemies in my own inmost soul, namely, my inordinate self-love and self-esteem. Hence, whenever I pray " Thy Kingdom Come! " I should add, if not in words, at least in spirit: " Yes, Dearest Lord, Thy Kingdom Come, but first of all in my own heart!   Oh! help me by Thy Grace to make it wholly Thine; Thine by poverty, by mortification, by humiliation; Thine by spotless purity, by unalterable meekness, by ardent charity, by perfect obedience."

Yet not a few go still further and enter the Religious State, that is by the Sacred Vows they embrace the State of Perfection. Just as some people strive to become merchants, lawyers, or doctors, and others are bent on becoming artists, statesmen, or millionaires; so these have irrevocably bound themselves to live exclusively for this one object, to become Saints. Hence the permanent "status" of every Religious is his own sanctification. These, then, to follow Christ their King even into the fiercest conflict and to display on all occasions His glorious Livery, long with deep earnestness and great confidence to bear every kind of insult, contempt, and ignominy, every kind of toil, poverty, hardship, and suffering; provided only it be for the better Service of their Lord, that is, in so far as He will deign to give them these opportunities of distinction, through the direction of Holy Obedience or the disposal of Divine Providence. He does so to some extent every day. But shame on us, if we should allow ourselves to be surpassed in zeal and generosity by persons in the world on whom this priceless favor of a Religious Vocation was not conferred.

In conclusion, Only One Person deserves our unlimited and undivided veneration and affection; namely, the God-Man, Jesus Christ: Only One Work claims our unreserved and unceasing attention and devotion; namely, His Work, the salvation and sanctification of souls: and Only One Means will enable us to love that Person and to embrace that Work with energy and perseverance; namely, Self-Denial, the

restraining of our rebellious passions, the mastering
of our unruly senses, the renouncing of our perverse
will; a continual and painful struggle, it is true, but
nevertheless sweet and easy through the all-powerful
grace of God.   In other words, the Only One Way
to Perfect Charity as well as to Genuine Happiness
is the Way of the Cross.

Colloquy with my Patron Saints, my Glorious
Models; with the Blessed Virgin, my Heavenly Queen;
and with Christ, my Eternal King.   Full of shame
and sorrow, I will ask pardon for my past cowardice
and infidelity, and acknowledge myself utterly unworthy to be numbered among the members of my
Institute.   Then I will fervently renew my Vows and
Resolutions, and again dedicate myself, body and
soul, to the Divine Service.   Realizing more clearly
than ever that in my own weakness I can do nothing,
but that I can do all things in Him Who is my
strength, I will offer myself to be disposed of in whatever way Providence may intimate through my Superiors; I will beg to be employed in any position, however
low, hard, or isolated, for any length of time, even
until death; and I will implore the favor of bearing
actual want, unmerited reproaches, and manifold affliction, in union with Jesus, my Adorable Lord.   At
the end I will recite the Our Father.

THE RELIGIOUS STATE

The State of Perfection, also called the Religious State or the Religious Life, is constituted by a public and permanent obligation to aim at Perfection, which obligation is assumed with the taking of the Three Perpetual Vows. By taking the Vows of Poverty, Chastity, and Obedience, we publicly profess that we have irrevocably bound ourselves to the pursuit of the Perfection of Divine Charity.

The Perfection of Charity after which a Religious has engaged to strive perseveringly, is not the common degree necessary to all that wish to be saved and consisting principally in the exclusion of whatever is contrary to the Habit of Charity; but it is a higher degree which consists in loving God as much as we are capable and, consequently, comprises, besides the Habit of Charity, the Removal of all Obstacles and the frequent Making of Acts.

Now, a Religious is bound to strive after this Higher Degree of Perfection by a serious obligation, which arises from the virtue of Religion and is distinct from the obligation of the three Vows. For, in consequence of his engagement contracted with the Order or Institute, he cannot licitly abandon the Religious State. But he who is bound to a state, is likewise bound to what is demanded by the essence of that state. In other words, by embracing an Institute whose only reason of existence is the pursuit of the Higher Perfection of Charity, we bind our-

selves at least implicitly to strive earnestly after the
attainment of that object.

The Religious State, then, is a stable manner of
life led by persons who profess, by means of the Vows
of Poverty, Chastity, and Obedience, to tend in the
Church towards the Perfection of Charity. Voluntary Poverty uproots the concupiscence of the eyes
and removes the solicitude about temporal goods.
Perfect Chastity uproots the concupiscence of the
flesh and removes the solicitude about wife and
children. Holy Obedience uproots the pride of life
— that craving for independence and superiority
which may also be called the concupiscence of the
mind — and removes the solicitude about the use of
our freedom.

Poverty, in general, consists in the absence of
worldly possessions. Considering it from the Religious standpoint, we usually distinguish the Vow, the
Virtue, and the Spirit of Poverty.

The Vow of Poverty is an outward renunciation
of earthly goods, made in accordance with the general
laws of the Church and the particular constitutions
of a Religious Order. The Laws of the Church have
determined that the Vow of Poverty, whether simple
or solemn, prevents the person who takes it from disposing freely, that is, without permission, of any
material goods. The Constitutions of each Religious
Order, with the previous approbation of the Pope,
settle the details of this self-spoliation. Hence it is
contrary to the Vow of Poverty to take things
without permission, to use things longer than
allowed, to hide things that the Superior may
not deprive us of them, to eat or drink without leave, through carelessness to cause what is

committed to our charge or given us for our use to be damaged or lost, to spend money received to defray traveling expenses for other purposes, to be either too liberal or too economical in the administration of temporal goods. Briefly, a Religious sins against his Vow of Poverty, when he gives, accepts, buys, sells, exchanges, lends, borrows, uses, or destroys anything, beyond the regulations approved for his Order and without the permission of his Superior. We should note here also that a Religious breaks his Vow of Poverty whenever he transgresses the Seventh Commandment, it being immaterial whether or not his action redounds to his own personal advantage. This would happen, for instance, if as a subordinate official he were to engage laborers to do necessary and useful work for less than a living wage; or if he were to secure funds, favors, or exemptions, under false pretenses or to the detriment of third parties; or, in general, if in his business transactions he were to follow the pernicious principle that whatever is not punishable by the law of the land is permissible by the law of God.

The Virtue of Poverty consists in the detachment from earthly possessions, in the absence of all inordinate affection to temporal goods. Hence, while the Vow is the means, the Virtue is the immediate end; while the Vow directly regards only the outward act, the Virtue perfects our inward disposition. Consequently, a Religious may offend against the Virtue of Poverty without violating the Vow, but one can never violate the Vow without at the same time offending against the Virtue. The Virtue, therefore, has a far wider scope than the Vow. It is against the Virtue of Poverty to entertain any inordinate leaning toward temporal goods; to foster the desire for a more abundant use of them than allowed by the Rule; to nourish a love of conveniences, valuables, curios, or superfluities; to look for the best in things placed at the disposal of the whole Community; to give no account of money spent unless positively asked; to elicit presents from outsiders with a view to one's own satisfaction; to show displeasure if a permission is refused, or if things are not so nice, comfortable, and plentiful as one expected.

The Spirit of Poverty goes still further. It enters more deeply into the intention of our Blessed Lord, when He gave us this Evangelical Counsel: "Go, sell all thou hast, and give to the poor, and come follow Me." This Spirit of Poverty will enable us not only to bear patiently but even to accept eagerly whatever privations we may have to undergo in the observance of our Vow or in the practice of the Virtue, and will cause us to feel more happy the nearer we can approach our Divine Model. A Religious who has acquired the Spirit of Poverty, will on every occasion choose for himself only the least and the worst; will cheerfully welcome the withdrawal of human favor or the loss of temporal means; will be glad to experience the sting of actual want in hunger, thirst, cold, heat, fatigue, sickness, and similar trials; will be delighted when obliged to beg from door to door for the support of the Community or for the maintenance of its work; and, in short, will continually aspire after the most complete destitution and the most painful abandonment in order that he may place his entire trust in the Providence of his Heavenly Father. This is that genuine Poverty which seems so repugnant to worldlings, this is that thorough Detachment from all earthly goods of which our Divine Master has set us the Example.

Surely, on the one hand we have abundant reason to humble ourselves, seeing how little progress we have as yet made towards Perfect Poverty. But on the other hand we ought to realize with joy and gratitude, that we truly possess nothing as our own; that the things we use with leave — our clothes, books, bed, desk, chair, and so forth,— are only lent to us and may be taken away or exchanged at any moment; that we can dispose of nothing according to our own independent choice; that every time we receive food, drink, or other necessaries, we are like beggars who have to ask for alms and live on charity; in one word, that to some extent at least we have fellowship with the Son of God, Who had not even a stone on which to rest His weary head. Besides, "Blessed are the Poor in Spirit, for they shall possess the Kingdom of Heaven."

Chastity, with reference to unmarried persons, consists in the abstinence from all carnal pleasures. For the better understanding of this important matter, we should consider successively the Vow, the Virtue, and the Spirit of Chastity.

The Vow of Chastity.— Every violation of the Sixth Commandment is an offense against both the Vow and the Virtue of Chastity. But, in consequence of the Vow, the guilt of a sin against the Sixth Commandment would be augmented by the malice of a sacrilege. On the other hand, the Vow not only imparts to our Chastity the character of a Divine Consecration, but also, in the case of those who have never fallen, confers upon it the special glory of Virginity. How thankful we ought to be to our Adorable King for having called us, in spite of our past failings, to a state of life so similar to that of His Immaculate

Mother Mary. And again, how determined we should be, by every means in our power, to preserve our soul from any thought, desire, or affection that might sully this sublime gift of Angelic Purity. Even in these modern times an occasion may still arise for displaying the same heroism as animated those Saints of the age of persecution who steadfastly suffered a Cruel Martyrdom rather than forfeit their Virginal Chastity.

The Virtue of Chastity.— As already stated, the Virtue of Chastity coincides with the observance of the Sixth Commandment; and, with regard to this matter, nothing need be added except that a merely sensitive delight, such as may be experienced at the sight of a beautiful flower, or even a sensual pleasure, such as one might feel about the heart on meeting a dear friend, is by no means a carnal gratification. At the same time we should not forget that sensitive delight is apt to become inordinate, and that sensual pleasure may easily lead to something sinful. Hence it will be very useful to consider here the precautions we have to take, in order that we may never mar or lose this Angelic Virtue; for, unfortunately, we are liable to go wrong even in the cloister and at any period of our Religious profession, yea, as St. Jerome assures us, even on the very threshold of death. However, this misfortune can happen only to such as wilfully neglect the powerful safeguards designed to protect this Heavenly Prerogative.

The first of these is Humility. Some Religious imagine that they are firmly established in Chastity because they do not feel the sting of the flesh. No delusion could be more dangerous. The absence of temptation may be due to various causes, and may be nothing else than a stratagem of the devil. The

sure test of Chastity is sincere Humility.   Do I keep
constantly before my mind, that is, do I practically
realize in my thoughts, words, and actions, my own
absolute nothingness, my profound sinfulness, and my
unlimited capacity for evil?   Or would I find on
close examination, that I am still full of vanity, of
self-complacency, of self-assertion, of pride?   In other
words, am I unremitting in the exercise of self-humiliation and self-abnegation?   If so, I need not fear
any temptations against the Angelic Virtue; though
I must, of course, avoid them with the utmost vigilance and banish them with the greatest promptitude.

The next safeguard is Prudence, which is to guide
us in all exterior occupations, readings, visits, tokens
of friendship.   It will make us resist all personal attractions, and shun all tender disclosures, and abstain
from all undue familiarity.   It is Prudence that dictated the laws of Papal Enclosure or equivalent prescriptions of Rule and Custom.   But vain would be
the observance of Enclosure as to the letter, if we
should neglect to cultivate the spirit, by unnecessarily
looking through secular newspapers or periodicals, or
by freely conversing about worldly amusements,
sports, plays, concerts, balls, weddings, and such like
events.

The third safeguard is Modesty, which constitutes
the outward ornament of a virginal soul.   Modesty
makes us keep a habitual guard over ourselves, over
our body, our senses, our imagination, our thoughts,
our words, our actions, so that as far as we are concerned they may never become a source of temptation
against Chastity.   It regulates every motion so as to
show that, whether alone or not, we are conscious of
the presence of God.

The fourth safeguard is Mortification. Without Mortification it is evidently impossible to observe modesty or to avoid temptation. We have to practise Exterior Mortification of the senses, not only in bearing cold and heat, hunger and thirst, fatigue and suffering, but also, as far as circumstances will permit, by inflicting bodily pain with discipline, girdle, and other instruments of penance. Though indispensable, this is not enough. We have, besides, to practise Interior Mortification of the mind and heart, especially by repressing all undue curiosity, carnal affection, and particular friendship.

The Spirit of Chastity.— Chastity, as well as Poverty and Obedience, is only a means to unite the soul to her Heavenly Spouse, Jesus Christ, by a union of love so holy, so close, so tender, that even the noblest affection known on this earth is nothing but its feeble shadow and dim reflection. The Spirit of Chastity, then, aims at perfecting this union, on the one hand, by the complete detachment from creatures, not only from all material objects but also from every sensible attraction; and, on the other hand, by the diligent practice of those virtues especially which stand out more prominently in the life of our Divine Lord, such as humility, obedience, meekness, patience, charity, and zeal. These virtues are, as it were, the perfume exhaled by the lily of purity. In proportion as we advance in this Spirit of Chastity, we shall experience even while yet on earth the truth of the Sixth Beatitude: " Blessed are the Clean of Heart, for they shall see God."

Obedience, in general, consists in the subjection of our own will to that of another. Religious Obedience denotes the loving and intelligent submission of our will to the Will of God, manifested to us by the will of our lawful Superior. Also in the matter of Obedience, we may distinguish the Vow, the Virtue, and the Spirit.

The Vow of Obedience.— This Vow is of all the most excellent, because by it a Religious consecrates to God those goods which men value most highly; namely, his liberty of action, of will, and of judgment. While human weakness is, consequently, very apt to fall into various faults and imperfections contrary to the Virtue of Obedience; yet sins, especially grievous ones, are not so easily committed against the Vow of Obedience as against the other two Vows of Poverty and Chastity. The obligation of the Vow of Obedience consists in this, that a Religious is bound under pain of sin to carry out the lawful orders of his Superiors. He commits a grievous sin against his Vow when he refuses to obey in an important matter enjoined upon him by his Superior — who should but very seldom adopt this course —" in the name of Jesus Christ," or "in virtue of Holy Obedience," or in some equivalent phrase; also when he answers his Superior, who gives him an order, " I will not obey," " I won't do it," or similar words that express formal contempt of authority, even though the thing commanded be unimportant; and, lastly, when his disobedience gives great scandal or causes serious inconvenience, either to the Community or to outsiders. The most grievous sin that can be committed against the Vow of Obedience, is apostasy from the Order.

The Virtue of Obedience has for its intrinsic motive the moral beauty of our complete subjection to the Divine Will interpreted by the will of our Superior; while its extrinsic motive lies in our desire to

please God, to love God, and to be united with God.
Religious Obedience occupies the first place among
the moral virtues inasmuch as it serves to implant
and foster in our soul all the others. However, the
perfect acquisition of this Virtue is conditioned by
the diligent and constant exercise of Faith, Humility,
and Confidence. Faith makes us see the government
of God in the exercise of authority by our Superiors
and fills us with deep reverence and sincere affection
for their persons as the duly accredited Representatives of the Most High. Owing to lack of Faith, the
very foundations of human society are nowadays
being shaken. Those who are swayed by the spirit
of the age are inclined to see in authority only the
preponderance of power, wealth, ability, or votes.
Religious too are liable to become infected by this
pestilential atmosphere, through newspapers, periodicals, books, and intercourse with seculars. Let us
be on our guard. Humility causes us to recognize
our own utter baseness and absolute nothingness, and
consequently enables us to love our obligation of submitting to the Divine Will as manifested to us by
Superiors. Confidence assures us that, since God is
infinitely Powerful, Wise, and Loving, and can never
be outdone in liberality, our Superiors will rule us in
everything for our own greater good as well as for that
of our neighbor.

The Three Degrees of Obedience form the successive steps that lead up to its perfection. The First
Degree, Obedience of Execution, consists in doing
what has been enjoined promptly, without excuses
or delays; exactly, not resting till the order is entirely
accomplished, whether agreeable or not; and perseveringly, especially in those charges which extend
over some period of time or are to be performed either

at stated intervals or whenever the occasion arises.
The Second Degree, Obedience of Will, consists in
submitting neither from self-interest nor through
compulsion but with our whole heart, and hence enables us to obey universally, any Superior or
Official in everything that falls under his juris-
diction, not waiting for his express command but at
a mere sign of his deliberate wish; joyfully, ready to
continue in the same duty as long as it shall please
the Superior; and lovingly, desirous to carry out the
Superior's directions exactly according to his mind.
The Third Degree, Obedience of Judgment, is by far
the most difficult and constitutes the crowning perfection of this Virtue. It consists in obeying supernaturally, firmly convinced that what has been
ordered is, here and now, under these actual circumstances, the best for us and the most conducive
to the Divine Glory; blindly, shutting our eyes, so to
say, to all considerations about the mental or moral
qualifications of our Superior, and likewise to whatever objections may present themselves, as, for instance, that the command bears no relation to the
object intended, that we have not got the requisite
strength, time, or ability; and intelligently, striving
to penetrate the intention of our Superior, especially
in the case that unforeseen difficulties or opportunities should arise.

A very apt illustration of the necessity of Perfect
Obedience is furnished by train orders. Being ·hu-
man, they may be imperfect and thus cause disagreeable delays. But if not obeyed, there will be disaster
and destruction. Our train dispatcher is He who
governs the whole universe and each individual soul
with Sovereign Wisdom and Unspeakable Love,
through the automatic workings of natural forces

and the free will of intelligent men, especially our
Superiors. It may appear to us like an unnecessary
delay, a mistaken purpose, a senseless waste. But,
provided we obey, He will guide us infallibly to happiness and holiness, to temporal peace and eternal
bliss.

The Spirit of Obedience consists in being entirely
possessed and energized by the Adorable Will of God,
so that in all our thoughts, words, and actions, we
remain intimately united to Him by an almost ecstatic love. Such was the life of our Divine Lord, a
life of Obedience. His very food was to do the Will
of His Heavenly Father. And day after day, He
still continues this life of Perfect Obedience, after a
mystic manner, in the Adorable Eucharist. But how
can we acquire this sublime Spirit of Obedience? By
practising simple and childlike openness, not only
towards our Confessors, but also towards our Superiors, so that we become wholly dependent on them,
in the internal affairs of our own conscience no less
than in the external matters under their charge.
Desirous of having our whole soul intimately known
to them, we should manifest, of our own accord, not
only our faults and temptations, but also our virtues,
devotions, mortifications, and penances. Some Superiors, from scrupulosity or overwork, are unwilling
to receive such spontaneous communications. For
this they will one day have to render a rigid account
to Almighty God. A Religious Institute is surely not
to be governed as if it were simply a close corpora-
tion, whose shareholders by means of strict economy,
voluntary celibacy, and domestic discipline, manage
to run schools, asylums, or hospitals, at the lowest
possible figure. As was explained before in this
Conference, the first and foremost object of every

Order or Congregation is to procure the salvation
and perfection of its own members. This is the end,
the rest is only a means. And, consequently, just as
subjects should avail themselves of every help afforded them by their Vocation to attain Sanctity, so
Superiors are bound to use all their influence to second the Call of Christ our Lord, and to lead the souls
entrusted to their care, by exhortation, guidance, and
example, to the acquisition of even the most Heroic
Virtue.

THE INCARNATION

Introductory Remarks.— We now enter upon the Second Week of the Exercises. Having clearly recognized in our Religious Vocation the Personal Call of Christ our Heavenly King, inviting us to follow Him in the conquest of souls, we are going to study for several days His Divine Example. Hence during this period of the Retreat we should keep our mind steadily occupied with the Life of our Lord down to the event which we are about to contemplate. Meanwhile we should make such use of light or darkness, of comfort or penance, as we think will be most helpful to obtain the graces we are looking for.

Subject of this Meditation.—" The three Divine Persons, beholding the entire surface of the earth covered with men, and seeing how all were falling into hell, decreed in their eternity that, to save the human race, the Second Person should become Man. Thus when the fulness of time had come, they sent the Angel Gabriel to the Virgin Mary to announce to her the accomplishment of the Divine Promises."

Composition of Place.—" To survey the whole surface of the globe inhabited by so many and such diverse nations; in particular, to see the humble dwelling and the little room of our Lady in the town of Nazareth."

Petition.—" An interior knowledge of our Lord,

Who for me has become Man, that I may love Him
more ardently and follow Him more closely." What
St. Ignatius, in these words, directs me to pray for is
evidently a very comprehensive grace. An interior
knowledge is one which penetrates deep down into
my soul and remains indelibly engraven on my mind;
it is a knowledge which, moreover, enters into the
very Heart of Christ our Lord, and realizes the Desire
that burns there for the salvation of the whole world
and every single human being, but in particular for
my salvation, since it was for me that with special
efficacy He became Man, preferring me in His Singular Love to all the rebel angels and to so many
men who, for one single sin, or for fewer sins than I
committed, were lost forever in Hell. This knowledge, then, both subjectively and objectively intimate,
keen, and vivid, is to move my will not only to love
Him, but to love Him more; more than I have loved
Him till now, while as yet I did not know Him so
well, and more than others who have not such powerful
reasons for loving Him, inasmuch as they have not
experienced so much Tenderness and such marked
Preference. But this greater love, born of my better
knowledge, must not be limited only to words however
sincere, nor stop short at mere affections however
ardent. It has to pass on to Deeds, as did the Love
of Christ towards me; and these Deeds are to be noble
and arduous in order to correspond somewhat to so
Singular a Predilection on His part; and the precise
manner in which I have thus to prove the reality of
my greater love, nourished by that more intimate
knowledge of the Lord God Who for me has become
Man, consists in following Him, my King, to the conquest of all those who dwell on the surface of the
earth and are rushing into Hell, by the mortification

of my Sensuality and the humiliation of my Pride,
by the acceptance of Poverty and Pain, by the bearing
of Contempt and Insult, to whatever extent He may
deign to mark me out for such distinctions.

" Observe," says St. Ignatius, " that whenever we
meditate on the Life of Christ our Lord, substantially
the same three preludes are to be made, their form
only changing in accordance with the subject-matter."

**First Point. What Men are without Christ,
without Redemption, without Sanctifying Grace:
Sinners, Atheists, Idolaters.**

Their Persons: " so varied in dress and manners,
some white and others black, some in peace and others
in war, some weeping and others laughing, some in
health and others sick, some being born and others
dying."— Though so different in many respects, they
all agree in this, that they are on the highroad to perdition, either because they do not believe the Teachings of Christ or because they do not observe His
Commandments. Who would not be moved to compassion at so pitiful a spectacle as the Eternal Ruin
of so many millions and millions of men? For us
living in the twentieth century of the Christian era,
it is difficult to figure to ourselves the condition of
human society as it was before the coming of Christ
our Savior; the horrors of warfare, the tortures of
imprisonment, the cruelties of slavery, the tyranny of
power, the worship of vice, the shocking degradation
of woman, the brutal perversity of man. Even now
how frightful a state of things we witness in China,
India, Africa! Yet mankind was at no time entirely
without the Grace of Redemption. How immense,
then, would have been our misery, if the Redeemer
had never even been promised?

Their Words: "what people are saying, how they converse, how they swear and blaspheme."— The ordinary conversation of worldlings is likely to give us a better idea of their inward dispositions than their studied appearance and outward manners. For it is usually out of the abundance of the heart that the mouth speaketh. Their favorite topics are, the best opportunities of making money, the chances of the political game, the latest fashions in clothing, the newest types of auto, the glories of their family, the shortcomings of their neighbor, the indulgence of their passions, the defense of their rights, the avenging of their wrongs. Their daily speech is largely a tissue of flatteries and insults, of lies and slanders, of boastings and indecencies, of complaints and curses. Not one word that bespeaks pure affection or genuine happiness.

Their Actions: they eat and drink, they buy and sell, they toil and travel, they quarrel and fight, they steal and squander, they marry and divorce, they seduce and murder, they die and go down to Hell.— The actions of men are but the natural outcome of the blindness of their understanding, the malice of their will, and the fury of their passions. They are exclusively occupied with earthly goods, sensual pleasures, and empty honors, while totally forgetful of their True End and their Eternal Destiny. Hence they go on breaking every Commandment and running from bad to worse, not to stop till they meet their final doom in Hell.

All this should fill my soul with Grief, Gratitude, and Humility. Grief: for these men not only are very unhappy but also greatly offend the Divine Majesty. Gratitude: for I too might have been born under sundry disadvantages, in vicious surroundings, of infidel parents, or among idolatrous savages. Humility: for in spite of so many and such precious advantages, I lived perhaps even for several years, no better than the rest, sharing in their folly and in their wretchedness. And even now, how sensitive I am still to the joys and ills of this world, how sloth-ful in the sanctification of my soul, how negligent about the salvation of my neighbor, how indifferent towards the imperishable and inconceivable treasures of Heaven. Yet, of one bound by such solemn and so oft repeated protestations of devotion to Christ the Lord, what else could be expected than that he should be wholly engrossed with the interests of his Adorable King. Thus the bad example of others should only serve to reanimate my desire and confirm my determination, henceforth to take as large a share as possible in the conquest of souls, by the generous and continual practice of Self-Denial.

Second Point. The Blessed Virgin and the Angel Gabriel.

Their Persons.— How utterly different Mary had been from the rest of mankind since the first moment of her existence, through that unique privilege, her Immaculate Conception. Truly, she was the glory of womanhood and the pride of our race. What humil-ity, what purity, what charity! What union with God! How lively her Faith, how holy all her Works! How poor her narrow cell, but also how peaceful! I must remember that she received these wonderful gifts and graces also for the great benefit of men and in particular of myself, that I might learn to imitate her, as my Heavenly Queen, and might be prompted to implore her all-powerful intercession. In the same manner, whatever favors I have already received or may yet obtain, are intended by God not only for my own advancement but also for the good of my neighbor. As to the Angel, he was unceasingly engaged in praising, revering, and serving the Most High. How sublime his praise, how profound his reverence, how loving his service! Oh! that I may soon become similar to this lofty Spirit. With what joy, in obedience to the Divine Behest, he descended as a messenger from Heaven to announce the coming of our Redeemer. Is this not also to be my favorite occupation: to prepare the way of the Lord?

Their Words: " what the Angel and our Lady are saying."—" Hail, full of grace, the Lord is with thee, blessed art thou among women! "—" Behold the handmaid of the Lord, be it done unto me according to thy word."— I must strive to imitate the Holy Angel in repeating his salutation, by doing so with greater attention, veneration, and devotion, than heretofore. I must strive to imitate also the Blessed Virgin by generously embracing whatever my Superiors, as the messengers of Almighty God, may propose, request, or command me, for my own sanctification or for the salvation of my neighbor.

Their Actions: " what the Angel and our Lady are doing; namely, the Angel fulfilling the functions of a heavenly legate, and our Lady humbling herself and giving thanks to the Divine Majesty."— Both apply themselves with the utmost humility and fervor to their respective tasks assigned by Almighty God and thus procure Him great satisfaction and glory. How much trouble we could avoid and how much merit we could gain, if we would strictly mind our own business and give our undivided attention and energy to the performance of our own duties. Let us beg leave to join the Blessed Virgin and the

Holy Angel in adoring and thanking God made Man, in that lowly dwelling at Nazareth, for the salvation of the world, for the love of every single child of Adam.   May we too by prayer, penance, and charity, become fit instruments for causing Christ our Lord to be born in the hearts of sinners and unbelievers, and for bringing them thus to the unspeakable bliss of Heaven!

Third Point. The Adorable Trinity.

Their Persons. " Consider the three Divine Persons as on the royal throne of their majesty, how they view the whole surface of the world and all nations in such blindness, and see them dying and descending into Hell."— Yes, such wilful blindness; obstinately refusing to acknowledge God their Creator or to obey His Holy Law, and dying consequently devoid of Supernatural Faith and destitute of Good Works, they go down to Hell. Alas! I too, for a considerable time, shared in the delusion and wickedness of sinners, but while the three Divine Persons are filled with the most tender Compassion and Mercy towards all men, I have experienced in my own preservation, conversion, and vocation, the wonderful effects of their singular Providence and Predilection. " Glory be to the Father, and to the Son, and to the Holy Ghost."   To Each I owe an everlasting debt of boundless praise.

Their Words. " Consider what the three Divine Persons are saying; namely, ' Let us bring about the redemption of the human race, and so forth.' "— What inconceivable Mercy!   While they were actually being offended so grievously by this miserable and perverse race of Adam, the Ever-Blessed Trinity decided in their eternity to accomplish its Redemption by the

Incarnation of the Second Person, the Son of God and the Son of Mary. In this Adorable Decree each one of us was present to the Divine Mind, and it was out of Personal Love for every single man that the Eternal Word undertook to be born in this world, to labor, to suffer, and to die on the Cross. What return could I ever make for so much Love? Even if I were to spend every moment of my earthly existence in lowly toil, in complete destitution, in acute torment, it would be as nothing in comparison with what Christ has deigned to do for me, His faithless servant.

Their Actions. "Consider what the three Divine Persons are doing; namely, working out the most Holy Incarnation:" the Father creating the soul by His Almighty Power, the Holy Ghost forming the body in the most pure womb of the Blessed Virgin, and the Son taking to Himself this human nature in the unity of Person.—"And the Word was made Flesh." God had become Man. O truly Infinite Condescension! He came into the world, and the world, blinded by greed and lust and pride, refused to acknowledge Him. But we, believing, adore and love.

The Sacred Humanity, then, on coming into existence, was hypostatically united to the Person of the Word. Christ, even as Man, clearly saw the Divine Essence and enjoyed, consequently, the bliss of Heaven. He was fully conscious of being constituted the Head of angels and of men, adorned with every Supernatural Virtue and Godlike Gift in the very highest degree in which they can be bestowed on a human soul or a created spirit, and in such fulness that from Him Grace is derived to all mankind. He further recognized that all these priceless favors, all this incomparable greatness, had been lavished on

Him without any antecedent merit of His own, but through the pure liberality of the Adorable Trinity. On seeing Himself thus adorned, preferred, and elevated, above every other creature, and possessing a Soul preeminently noble and grateful, He could not but conceive a most ardent desire to acknowledge so many Blessings and to correspond to so much Love, by wholly immolating Himself to the Eternal Will.

But as He witnessed at the same time the sad condition of the human race and of each individual on the face of the earth, and beheld the far sadder fate of the numberless victims of sin in Hell, He understood that this immense wealth of Heavenly Favors had been conferred on Him also for the relief of His brethren exposed to such imminent danger of everlasting perdition. And this realization enkindled in His most Generous Heart that tender sympathy for all mankind and that ardent zeal for the glory of His Eternal Father, which made Him embrace a Life full of toil and hardship, and a Death most cruel and shameful, for the sanctification and salvation of every single human being. He would start the Divine Conquest, but he would also invite other men to continue and complete it, and these His companions were to learn from Him the tactics of this Spiritual Warfare, this Warfare of Humility and Love, in order that they might likewise share in His endless Glory.

However, what I must bear in mind especially, is that the Love burning in the Sacred Heart of Jesus was from the beginning a Personal Love for each one of us, and hence that it was truly for the sanctification and salvation of every child of Adam, that He entered upon this Life of poverty, obscurity, labor, and suffering, which He knew would terminate in the unutterable torments and ignominy of the Cross.

In return for so much Love, surely, the least I can do is to follow Him in actual poverty, in humble labor, in constant self-denial, in sincere charity, in perfect obedience. But day after day I must strive to follow Him more faithfully and more closely. By thus beginning to share in His Self-Immolation, how many souls I can help to save for time and eternity! Already now I must long for my death, in whatever manner it may come and by whatever sufferings it may be preceded, as my supreme sacrifice in union with Jesus Crucified. For not until the seed fall on the earth and pass through corruption, will it produce fruit. Meanwhile, to realize more thoroughly my paramount obligation of imitating Christ my Savior, I cannot do better than to study and invoke the Immaculate Heart of Mary ever most intimately united to the Adorable Heart of Jesus, from the first moment of the Incarnation.

Colloquy.—" At the end," says St. Ignatius, " a colloquy is to be made, thinking what I ought to say to the three Divine Persons, or to the Eternal Word made Flesh, or to His Mother and our Lady; making petition according to what I feel in myself in order better to follow our Lord just now become Man." I will give humble and heartfelt thanks for the immense Benefit of Redemption, the grace of baptism, the advantage of a good education, but especially for the signal favor of having been called out of the world to share in the labors of Jesus Christ, the Son of God. I will beg for supernatural light and energy to follow Him as closely as possible in the conquest of souls, by my own sanctification, by the practice of prayer, humility, penance, charity, and obedience. For only thus can I become a fit instrument for the salvation

of my neighbor. In conclusion, I will pray that my
proud and selfish heart may become animated and
inflamed with the most holy and generous dispositions of Jesus and Mary. "Then I will say an Our
Father."

A. M. D. G.

"MY CHILD, GIVE ME THY HEART."

FOURTH DAY

SPECIAL PATRON: St. Ignatius of Loyola.

MOTTO: "Lord, what wilt Thou have me to do?"—Acts 9:6.

SPIRIT: Self-Devotion in following our Lord.

READING: Imitation; Bk. I, C. 7, 17, 19.
Bk. II, C. 1, 7, 8.
Bk. III, C. 18, 27, 37, 39.
Rules and Customs.

Strive to embrace your Vocation with intense gratitude as a wholly unmerited favor of Christ our Lord, and study how you may henceforth correspond to it more faithfully and more generously. Go over the work of the three preceding days and gather up your Lights and Resolutions.

THE HIDDEN LIFE AT NAZARETH

Introductory Remarks.— Let us continue the Retreat with great earnestness, confidence, and generosity. To slacken is dangerous. Life is a warfare. We entered the Religious State, not to escape from the troubles and burdens of a life in the world, but to follow Christ our Lord, to embrace His Cross, with all its labors, sufferings, and humiliations. We entered in order to save our souls at any cost, by first sanctifying ourselves with all the means at our disposal, and then also becoming instrumental in the salvation of others. This Retreat will show us how to attain our purpose.

Unless we ourselves possess the solid principles that are to shape our efforts towards perfection and unremittingly apply ourselves to the difficult task of our own sanctification, how can we dream of ever doing any good to those entrusted to our care or guidance? Instead, we shall both delude ourselves and delude others; far from leading our neighbor to God, we shall lead him into worldliness, vanity, sensuality, sin, and perdition. The only way to benefit a single soul is the one marked out by our Divine Savior.

How is it that so many of our colleges and academies turn out so few earnest, whole-souled, and zealous Catholics? How is it that, generally, they yield so few Vocations? There must be a reason for this. Let us not put the blame where it is not. No doubt, in many cases the early home training of those chil-

dren has been very deficient. Yet we ourselves also
may be largely the cause of these poor results, through
our lack of prayer, of humility, of mortification, of
obedience, of apostolic charity. If, instead of aiming
at substantial results, we are satisfied with making
a show by the number of our pupils, by their elegant
and smart appearance at commencement exercises and
theatrical displays, by the sumptuousness of our
houses and parlors, by our extensive learning and
polite manners and distinguished looks; we are simply thwarting the loving designs of Christ, and the
upshot will be a multitude of worldly young men and
women, without firm faith, without solid morality,
without self-sacrificing devotion, people that look
chiefly for wealth, amusements, and distinctions.

Let us, then, during this holy Retreat, strive to get
a clear idea of our numerous failings, but especially
of the daily imperfections and venial faults of last
year. Let us strive to get a clear idea of the means
we have to adopt in order to expiate fully our past
sins, whether committed in the World or in Religion.
Let us strive to get a clear idea how we can improve
our vocal and mental prayer, how we can derive more
profit from our examens and confessions, how we can
live more closely and lovingly united to God our
Lord. This Retreat should not be suffered to pass
before all these matters are thoroughly settled.
Everything should be set right both with Almighty
God and with ourselves; with Almighty God, by confessing our faults with sincere contrition and earnest
resolution to amend; with ourselves, by removing all
our doubts, difficulties, and perplexities. We must
not hesitate to ask advice. It will never harm us to
be too open, too candid; but it may harm us very much
to be too close, too reserved. The only guarantee to be

guided safely is readiness to manifest our whole heart.

Subject of this Meditation.—" He went down with them, and came to Nazareth; and He was subject to them. And Jesus advanced in wisdom and age, and grace with God and men."— Luke 2:51-52.

Composition of Place.— The home of the Holy Family at Nazareth, built against the side of a hill and comprising a small grotto formed in the rock.

Petition.— An intimate knowledge of our Lord, Who for me led a life of Poverty, Labor, and Obedience, that I may love Him more sincerely and follow Him more generously.

First Point. The Poverty of Nazareth.

The earnings of a common artisan in a small village like Nazareth must surely have afforded but a very stinted maintenance. We may be pretty sure that Joseph could barely procure the necessaries of life, and that sometimes, both he and those dependent on his care, were in actual want. Thus Jesus, for love of me and to atone for my seeking after material comforts and sensible gratifications, wished to suffer the sting and the reproach of Poverty. For, of course, the son of a poor carpenter was looked down on and despised by other people that were better off. Yet what serenity, what peace, what happiness, in this heavenly home! How gladly and generously Mary and Joseph shared in the voluntary Poverty of Jesus. Every one that wants to live on intimate terms with Jesus must strive to become truly poor. Thus the Apostles were sometimes content to pluck a few ears of wheat to still their hunger. What is my regard, my love for Poverty? Do I esteem and cherish the poor

more than the rich, inasmuch as Jesus forsook riches
to embrace Poverty? Do I at least receive and treat
poor people with the same regard as I would wealthy
persons? Do I love the accompaniments of Poverty,
mean clothes, old shoes, a hard bed, a bare room,
simple or even somewhat scanty food? Do I rejoice
in being made to experience at times some of its effects: hunger and thirst, cold and heat, inconvenience
and privation? that thus I may become more like to
my Lord and Savior, Who suffered all these things for
my sake and on my account, a sinner, " propter me
et pro me, peccatore." Am I ready to solicit alms, to
beg from door to door, after the example of the Saints,
— Francis of Assisi, Ignatius Loyola, Benedict Labre?
Do I at least avail myself gladly of every opportunity
to appear poor, by humbly asking my Superior for the
necessary apparel, stationery, carfare, and so forth?
Am I delighted to get a taste of real want, in finding
myself deprived of human aid or involved in serious
difficulty, that thus I may practise sweet and firm reliance on the Providence of our Heavenly Father,
Who feeds even the birds of the air and clothes the
flowers of the field?

But to return to the Holy Family at Nazareth, what
order, what cleanliness in this humble dwelling, in
spite of their limited resources! So every Religious
House, in spite of its Poverty, should be conspicuous for its neatness. Each inmate should do his
share. No disorder, no dirt, either in the main build-
ing, or in the annexes or grounds. A slovenly Religious is a burden to a poor Community, a disgrace to
his holy Profession, and a scandal both to his companions and to seculars. Apart from exceptional
circumstances, how can a Religious pretend to keep
his soul free from sin, if he cannot even keep his room

free from dust and disorder? Where there is no
spirit of regularity and cleanliness, there is no Spirit
of Poverty either.

Again the home of the Holy Family was not devoid
of some simple ornaments, but how unworldly they
were, how apt to raise the mind to Heaven. Sometimes, through misplaced amateurism or through sheer
thoughtlessness, there may be found in Religious
Houses paintings or pictures that one would hardly
expect to see in the home of an ordinary Catholic.
If they are really valuable works of art, they had
better be sold; if not, they should be burned.

Poor people usually lead a very obscure existence,
and so it was with our Divine Lord. Jesus remained
hidden in that lowly home at Nazareth from His return out of Egypt till the opening of His ministry.
He who had come to convert mankind by the Preach-
ing of the Gospel, thus spent by far the greater portion of His life in Obscurity. How foolish, then,
must it be to make so much of whatever brings us
before the public. Do I love to remain hidden, do I
really seek to be ignored, do I aspire to be employed
in the lowliest office and the commonest work? Do I
rejoice at being set aside to make room for others,
and at getting to be considered as of little use or of
no account? These trials will come sooner or later
for most of us, until, with increasing years, we are
definitely laid on the shelf. Oh! what a shame for me
to be still dreaming of some high office, some place of
authority, some position of influence. How unlike to
my Savior and my God! But while I yet feel full
of health and energy, let me not go about my occupations, be they loftly or lowly, in such a manner as to
remind everybody of my presence. Precipitation,
hurry, and noise, characterize the promptings of Na-

ture, whereas the workings of Grace are marked by reflection, self-control, and quiet.   I should apply this test to my thoughts, my words, my actions, my correspondence, and even to my resolutions.   What is done hastily, is in most cases badly done.   And since our Lord, the Incarnate Wisdom, seeks Obscurity and Oblivion, why should I strain to make a little show in this world?

Yet, notwithstanding His love of remaining hidden, Jesus caused His light to shine in the narrow circle assigned to Him, for the time, by the Providence of His Eternal Father.   He advanced in age, in wisdom, and in grace, before God and men.   Poor in earthly goods, He abounded in heavenly favors.   My immediate surroundings, the Religious Community of which I am an unworthy member, this should be, before everything else, the object of my fervent Prayers and apostolic Zeal.   Does my light — my good example, my regular observance, my charity, my obedience,— shine before my companions?   Have I too, with advancing years, grown in True Wisdom and Heavenly Grace before my brethren, my pupils, my acquaintances?   Or, as to wisdom, have I, on the contrary, not become somewhat inflated with my wider business-experience or greater book-learning?   And as to grace, have I, perhaps, not grown remiss in my earlier fervor of spirit, in my former eagerness for Mortification and Humiliation, in the generous Imitation of Christ my King?   But the means of Holiness are still within my reach.   The only thing needed is the will to use them with energy and perseverance.   By doing so, I yet can render my few remaining years fruitful of supernatural blessings to innumerable souls. Trusting, therefore, in the Divine Power, I now renew my determination to strive after Sanctity; and I will

begin this very instant by retrenching ever superflu-
ity in clothing, furniture, food, drink, rest, and recreation, as well as by renouncing the object of every undue attachment and the indulgence of every faulty
habit.

Second Point. The Labor of Nazareth.

Jesus was truly in Labor from the days of His childhood, according to the scriptural prophecies. First
He helped His Holy Mother, then He assisted also His
beloved Foster-Father, and later on He Himself exercised the trade of a carpenter. Why? To teach us
the dignity, the necessity, and the value of Labor.
Labor, indeed, in as far as it means activity, is honorable and ennobling; since God Himself is perfect and
substantial Activity. But in as far as it means
fatigue, it is a penalty, a penance, imposed on Adam
and on all his children. " In the sweat of thy brow,
thou shalt eat thy bread." Jesus, by His toil, set us
the example of submission to this Divine Sentence,
pronounced, not against Him, but against our First
Parents for their disobedience, and merited no less
by ourselves on account of our own transgressions.
It was to atone for my sins, in particular, that He
suffered, during so many years, the inconvenience,
hardship, and weariness attached to earthly Labor.

Besides, our Lord wished to animate us to constant
toil, because it is the great means to subdue the animal body and its unruly passions. Just as the
pleasurable cultivation of the garden of Eden would
have hindered Adam from falling into that disgrace
which covered him with confusion at the voice of God,
so the penitential exertion to which he was henceforth
subjected, was intended by God to enable him to rise
from his degradation. Since man had refused alle-

giance to his Maker, the earth had rebelled against its
master, and since the soul had aspired to be like the
Lord of Glory, the body had striven to enslave her
spiritual faculties to its brutal instincts.   But the
penalty for all this disorder would also prove its remedy.   By Labor, the earth was again to be made sub-
servient to man, the body to be subjected to the mind,
and the soul to be rendered obedient to God.   Thus
Labor,— and consequently also fatigue, weariness,
exhaustion,— if borne generously, besides being a
powerful help to Humility and an excellent instrument of Penance, is the great safeguard of Holy
Purity.   Let us bear this also in mind when we have
to do with lazy children or indolent students.   They
are necessarily proud and sensual and bad, because
they discard the God-given means to correct themselves.   Labor, however, is not any frivolous pastime
or self-chosen occupation, lounging, talking, reading,
playing, sightseeing, or visiting; but exertion of mind
or body, imposed or sanctioned by Holy Obedience.
All else, for us Religious, is idleness.

But it was not enough for Jesus to devote Himself to Labor, no; He chose, besides, manual and
humble Labor, such as is required in the care of a
household and the trade of an artisan.   Sometimes
we are inclined to think little of our occupations, because they are commonplace and lowly.   Let us give
up these unreasonable, unchristian, irreligious views,
by considering the example set us by our Divine Lord,
and let us strive, for His love and reverence, to shun
what would make us prominent, and be eager to renounce pleasant pastimes for useful drudgery.   Particularly as a poor village carpenter, the lot of Jesus
must, indeed, have been very humble.   We can easily
fancy how He would be received rudely by those coun-

try folk, commanded imperiously, criticised unjustly, and sent away scornfully, without the payment needed to buy bread for the Holy Family. But oh! how joyfully He anticipated such humiliations, how His Sacred Heart relished the consequent confusion! With what Meekness He would answer or even apologize, with what Patience He would endeavor to satisfy the whims of His employers! All this to confound my self-conceit, to rebuke my self-will, to uproot my pride, to convert my heart.

How does Jesus Labor? With what Purity of Intention, with what Recollection of Demeanor, and yet with what Thorough Application to even the smallest details! And while His hands are thus busily engaged, where are His Thoughts, where is His Heart? My thoughts are usually wandering on almost any subject, or else my heart is wholly engrossed with some pet creature, some trifling hobby, some worldly news, some fanciful project. But His Thoughts are constantly dwelling on the things of Heaven, the glory of His Father, the salvation of His brethren; while His Sacred Heart is completely absorbed in Prayer and in Love. I must strive to behold and watch my Savior at His Daily Toil; I must learn from Him how to sanctify myself in my various occupations.

Third Point. The Obedience of Jesus at Nazareth.
Who Obeyed? The Incarnate Word, the Wisdom of the Father, the Almighty Creator, the Eternal Lord. If, then, He deemed it expedient and necessary to obey, how futile must be my pretexts, how senseless my repugnances that hinder me from yielding Perfect Obedience? Of all things this is the one I must realize most thoroughly, namely, the value of Obedience as the practical expression of Humility, and hence

the necessity of steadily advancing in this virtue, so as to reproduce in all my actions the Wonderful Example of Jesus Christ.

For how did He Obey? Our Savior was subject in all things, even in the most menial duties, even in matters He understood incomparably better than those who commanded. Let me, then, often contemplate this Divine Obedience, so prompt and exact in Execution, so joyful and loving in Will, so blind and intelligent in Judgment, reflecting on my own Obedience in things temporal and spiritual, and recognizing, full of shame and sorrow, how far I am still from closely imitating my Adorable Master.

Lastly, whom did Jesus Obey? His Parents, His own creatures. What an immense distance between the superior and the subject! the superior a mere man, the subject Almighty God. Yet Mary and Joseph, as well as the religious and civil magistrates, were for Jesus the Official Representatives of His Eternal Father. That was enough to show them profound Reverence, loving Submission, and unhesitating Obedience. Who are in my regard the Special Representatives of the Most High? Am I impressed chiefly by the good or bad qualities I see in them, inasmuch as they are weak and fallible men; or am I guided solely by Supernatural Faith, acknowledging in them the Interpreters of the Divine Will and the Vicegerents of the Supreme Majesty?

Colloquy.— Since it was for me, in particular, that Jesus led this life of Poverty, Labor, and Obedience, with what confidence ought I not to beseech Him, through the intercession of the Blessed Virgin and His holy Foster-Father, for a deep and ardent love of actual privation, humble toil, and complete subjec-

tion? How earnestly I should beg of Mary and
Joseph, that, as they daily derived such immense
profit from the Divine Example which they had constantly before their eyes, so they may obtain for me
the grace of ever keeping before my mind and earnestly pondering in my heart, the Perfect Virtues of
Jesus, my Savior and my God, toiling for me at Nazareth. Lastly, I will pray that I too, by the steady
and loving Imitation of my Heavenly King, may
daily grow in grace and wisdom before God and
men, before the other members of this Community,
which is to be a copy of the Holy Family, before all
seculars and outsiders with whom I have to come in
contact, but especially in the sight of Jesus, my Adorable Master.— Our Father.

THE STAY IN THE TEMPLE

Subject of this Meditation.— Jesus being twelve years old, the Holy Family went up to Jerusalem according to the custom of the feast. When the days were completed, Mary and Joseph set out on their home journey, while the child Jesus remained in Jerusalem without their knowledge. They missed Him at nightfall, looked for Him in vain among their kinsfolk and acquaintance, but found Him on the third day in the Temple amidst a group of doctors.— Luke 2:42-49.

Composition of Place.— The road from Nazareth to Jerusalem, the narrow streets of the Holy City, the Temple.

Petition.— An intimate knowledge of my Lord, Who for me made the sacrifice of His tenderest affections,— for my instruction by His example, for my comfort by His affliction, for my pardon by His merit, — when He remained in the Temple without informing His parents, that thus I may love Him more sincerely, and follow Him more courageously.

First Point. The Journey of the Holy Family to Jerusalem.

They went, says St. Luke, according to custom, but they certainly did not go merely through custom. To do things according to custom, means for us Religious, to do them according to the letter of our Rule and the spirit of our Institute, and hence to seek in them always fresh occasions for practising humility, mortification, and charity. But to do things merely through custom, means to do them mechanically because one has got into the habit of doing them from a kind of inevitable necessity, or to do them passionately because one has become strongly attached to them in consequence of some selfish motive, some natural aptitude. How do I perform my Spiritual Duties, according to custom or merely through custom? How do I fulfil my other duties, thoughtfully and religiously, or now mechanically, now passionately?

Let us also consider that it was quite a journey in those days to go from Nazareth to Jerusalem; particularly for poor people it meant a great deal of fatigue, hardship, and even danger. Yet Jesus, Mary, and Joseph undertook it joyfully, knowing how many special graces God is wont to bestow under such circumstances. How easy, on the contrary, it is for us Religious, to go to our chapel or our church, where we find not only the Majesty of the Most High but the very Person of the Word made Flesh. Do I adore Him there as often as the accomplishment of His Holy Will allows me? Again, am I practically convinced of the paramount importance, the priceless advantages of my Spiritual Duties? When I have a pretext to defer them or to shorten them, am I not too ready to avail myself of it? and do I not sometimes sacrifice them entirely to what is far less urgent? Nothing can wait, nothing can be put off, except our examens, our beads, our visits to the Blessed Sacrament. It is true that we may at times have to forego our prayers for the sake of charity or obedience, but in a well-regulated Community this happens rarely and not without an opportunity of repairing our loss.

It was during this journey that Jesus decided on leaving His Parents by staying back in the Temple without their knowledge. It is particularly in the observance of silence and the exercise of prayer, in the secret sanctuary of our soul, that we can learn to correspond to the manifold graces of Heaven, to yield to the ceaseless promptings of the Holy Spirit, to follow the powerful attractions of Divine Love towards self-sacrifice. It is only when we are recollected that we can at all expect to hear the voice of our Adorable Master calling us to greater exertion and loftier perfection. Hence the diligent practice of the Presence of God is indispensable for our happiness and our sanctification.

I may in spirit accompany the Holy Family on this journey, following a little in the rear as their most unworthy servant. With what genuine and charming recollection they proceed on their way, except at certain intervals, when Joseph reopens the conversation with a joyous " Alleluia," " Praise ye the Lord." Hence, what Union with God, what peace of soul, what Perfection of Charity! How each one strives to profit by the beautiful example of the others, and how each is to the others an inspiring model! What gentleness, what gravity, what patience! But now they are going to make a short halt. I will approach Saint Joseph and ask him whether I may fetch some water to wash the dust off their feet, or may care for the ass which is to carry the Blessed Virgin over the mountain passes. Meanwhile I hear Joseph giving directions to Jesus about gathering some dry grass, and also to Mary who wished to know where he would like them to take their little repast. And I see how Mary and Jesus obey, so promptly, so exactly, so lovingly. Then they bring out their provisions, they are scanty and simple, the bread is pretty hard and the cheese looks stale. But how devoutly they say grace, not as a mere formula recited carelessly through routine, but as a real and earnest prayer coming from their inmost hearts. I notice how the Blessed Virgin strives to serve Saint Joseph and even Jesus with the better portion, and how the Holy Child begs His dear Mother to take it herself, since for Him the other will do just as well. And how modest they are in all their looks and movements, though evidently their little meal is thoroughly seasoned with hunger. How careful also, almost scrupulous, some one might think, not to waste anything! But they are poor people, and they realize it, and they are glad to be so. What heavenly joy is all the while mirrored in their saintly countenances! And how delightful their conversation, about the coming festivity, the sacred buildings, and so forth! How eagerly and respectfully Jesus is asking questions, and with what docility and attention He listens to their answers.

Second Point. Jesus Remains Behind in the Temple.

I may now accompany the Holy Family right up to the Temple. That is their place of rest; for they are spiritual persons, not carnal, and their souls are able to pray in spite of the weariness of their bodies. On the contrary, my soul is so truly imprisoned in this corruptible body, that the least physical indisposition interferes with mental application, especially with Prayer and Meditation. But it shall be so no more. In imitation of the Divine Child and His holy Parents, I must strive to overcome myself, I must discard the complaints of the flesh, and if necessary, I must chastise it and force it into submission. Besides, on reaching a destination or stopping in a town, my first and foremost care shall be to visit the church or chapel and adore the Blessed Sacrament.

Keeping, then, in mind their great fatigue, let me contemplate the Holy Family during the religious functions in the Temple. Saint Joseph is with the men in the court of the Israelites, the Blessed Virgin is with other women from Galilee in the outer court, while Jesus is in one of the porticos amid a group of children under the supervision of some relative. I may note particularly the deep reverence manifested in all their outward bearing and relish their inward devotion, the faith, the confidence, and the love that filled their hearts. What they implored most earnestly from God, was light to know His Adorable Will and strength to accomplish It perfectly. I will presume to join them and offer my prayers in union with theirs. Here, in their company, I must learn how to make my Meditation. Yes, I must learn to pray. For without the habit of Prayer, without constant and ardent Prayer, in Meditation and Mass and Communion and Examens and Beads and Office and throughout the day, there is no detachment from creatures, and without detachment from creatures there is no Following of Christ, no conquest of souls.

But Jesus has abandoned Himself entirely to the Holy Spirit. I will strive to realize all that passes in His Sacred Heart, for though Divine inasmuch as It belongs to the Person of the Eternal Word, It is also Human, full of sympathetic love and tender solicitude for His earthly Parents. Indeed, the affection of Jesus towards Mary and Joseph is incomparably more deep and ardent than any other child of His age can ever feel towards its father and mother; and if He has decided on leaving them for a few days, let us be convinced that it is not through any coldness or indifference. No, His Gentle Soul is racked with pain, His Loving Heart is crushed with anguish, at the prospect of the separation. But He knows how to sacrifice His Purest Affections to the Will of His Heavenly Father. And though Mary and Joseph are the Holiest Persons that ever lived, though they would never place the slightest obstacle to His work for the glory of God, yet He is resolved to abandon them as soon as the appointed hour strikes. How much more reason, then, have I to conquer my affections for persons dangerous to my spiritual welfare, such as by word or example might hinder me from doing the Divine Will, and to tear myself loose from any creature, towards which I begin to feel an undue inclination or attraction. Evidently, I ought to be no less generous and resolute in overcoming any undue repugnance or aversion that should come between my soul and the call of Grace.

Jesus, however, not only suffers intensely because He is to be deprived of the company of His beloved Mother and cherished Foster-Father, but He is still more distressed because of their own bereavement and desolation. For He knows and realizes all the pain He is going to cause them by this unexpected separation; their restless anxiety, their heartbreaking sadness, their bitter and ceaseless tears. Yet even this fact cannot alter His decision. When God deigns to manifest to us His Adorable Will or merely His Good Pleasure, we ought to obey Him without delay, in spite of the sorrow and affliction we may thus bring on those near and dear to us. Our affection for persons, however good they may be, ought always to retain its supernatural purity and nobility; it must never degenerate into merely natural sentiment. On certain occasions we may have even to set aside every human consideration and cut asunder every tie of kindred or friendship, for the sake of the Heavenly Kingdom. It may be either wicked persecution driving us into exile or Holy Obedience assigning us to a distant post. In all such cases let this be our consolation, that our sacrifice will turn to the great benefit not only of ourselves, but also of the very persons whom we forsook at the Voice of God. On the other hand, let us be convinced that by entertaining, or rather by not extirpating, an inordinate attachment, we shall not only inflict great harm on ourselves, but also bring spiritual injury on others. Many a budding Vocation to the Religious Life has thus been choked by unmanly softness and sentimental indulgence, by indiscreet praise and silly flattery. When we notice that a child has been especially favored by God, let us rather strive to awaken and foster in that soul the spirit of gratitude, of self-devotion, of humility, and of self-denial. But if instead we rouse and feed its selfishness, its sensuality, its idleness, its worldliness, and its vanity, far from seconding the work of Grace, as we intended, we run a great risk of strengthening the power of Evil. A most lamentable and baneful error, which can be avoided only by such as labor constantly at curing the corruption of their own heart.

The lesson, therefore, I have to learn from this Heroic Conduct of Jesus my Lord, and the grace I have to implore from Him in this Contemplation, is that of an entire Detachment from all objects, places, offices, and especially persons, in order to be like to Him, to Mary, and to Joseph; a Detachment so thorough and perfect as to enable me to bear at any time the complete spoliation of things created, even of spir-

itual friendships and supernatural consolations, not
only with patient resignation but with the utmost
readiness and joy.   In the light of the Divine Example set me by Jesus Christ, my most Loving Savior,
I must examine myself carefully on this complete Detachment from all creatures, I must search my heart
and discover those inordinate, unmortified tendencies
of sympathy or antipathy, of attraction or aversion,
which up to this have kept me back from God and prevented me from belonging wholly to Him, from advancing towards real Sanctity.   Unless I do this now,
unless I find them out now, unless I resolve to root
them up now, the coming year will be the same as the
outgoing and this Retreat will prove even more barren
of results than any previous one.

However, there is yet another matter that deserves
our attention.   If Jesus was so painfully affected by
the leaving of His most holy Parents, without any
fault or imperfection on their part; who can tell what
agony His Sacred Heart experienced at the thought of
so many a Soul enriched with Sanctifying Grace, so
many a Religious favored with signal privileges, wilfully separating from Him by inordination and sin!
Am I not, perhaps, of the number of these ingrates?
What, then, am I going to do in order to atone for my
past ingratitude and to console my Sorrowing Lord?

Third Point.   The Finding of Jesus in the Temple.
Mary and Joseph seek the Holy Child during three
days.— I will endeavor to realize their apprehension
and their grief.   I will follow them in their fruitless
search through the streets of Jerusalem.   Yet what
predominated in their souls was profound humility
and loving conformity to the Divine Will.   They too
offered to God the sacrifice of even their noblest affec-

tions, and it was in this way that the absence of Jesus contributed to their progress in Perfection. Who, indeed, could measure the tenderness and ardor of their love for Jesus, the All-Beautiful, or express the intensity and fulness of their happiness in His Heavenly Company! But it is precisely this immolation of our heart, from the motive of Charity or at the word of Obedience, which is sure to draw down upon those we love the most abundant graces.

Mary and Joseph find Jesus in the Temple.— They had sought Him in vain among their kinsfolk and acquaintance; but they found Him as soon as they entered the Sanctuary of Jehovah. If we make to God the offering of our feelings, if we sacrifice to Him our natural affections, we shall find them again, purified, intensified, divinized, often already in the Religious Cloister, in the House of the Lord, oftener still in the Sacred Heart of our Lord, in the Adorable Eucharist, and unfailingly in the Heavenly Jerusalem. And in proportion to the generosity of our Detachment, shall we be compensated with a tenfold, a thirtyfold, and even a hundredfold. More than this: Jesus Himself will be our Reward exceeding Great; already here on earth, our soul will enjoy the Intimate Friendship of Almighty God and be inundated with torrents of delight in the midst of suffering and humiliation.

Let me also reflect, however, that while Mary and Joseph sought the Holy Child so sorrowfully and perseveringly, I, after losing His sweet intercourse through my own fault, remained not seldom for days and weeks, perhaps even for months and years, without recognizing my misfortune and my guilt, without taking a single step to recover His former Friendship and gladsome Presence. Oh! how I ought to be over-

whelmed with shame and grief at the recollection of
so senseless, so heartless, so inhuman a conduct.

Mary humbly and affectionately remonstrates with
Jesus, and receives a most loving and satisfactory
reply.—"My son," said the Blessed Virgin, "why
hast Thou done so to us? Behold, Thy father and I
have sought Thee sorrowing." And Jesus answered
them: "Why did you seek Me? Did you not know
that I must be about my Father's business?" This
reply was dictated by His ardent Zeal for the glory
of God, His tender Affection for His Parents, and His
prudent Reserve towards the doctors of the Law. " I
acted thus in order to do the work given Me by My
Heavenly Father, and you knew that I could not be
engaged in anything else than the accomplishment
of His Adorable Will. You had not lost Me through
any fault of yours. Why, then, did you seek Me? It
was only because of your great love and burning solicitude." Am I too always about the business of my
Heavenly Father, in union with Jesus, after the example of Mary and Joseph? Or do I still use my time
independently of Obedience, just according as I feel
impelled by my own likes and dislikes, by my natural
indolence or restlessness?

Colloquy with Saint Joseph, the Blessed Virgin,
and the Holy Child Jesus; beseeching each in turn for
some share in those heroic virtues of which they set
such shining examples during their visit to Jerusalem.
I will ask in particular that, through the continual
and diligent exercise of Prayer, my heart may become
like to theirs, thoroughly detached from all earthly
bonds, completely engrossed with the things of heaven,
and solely intent on the fulfilment of the Divine Will.
I will also implore my Adorable Master that, in my

daily Meditation, He may take my cold, wretched, selfish heart, and give me instead a pure, humble, and generous heart, a heart ready to make some genuine return for His Boundless Love when He comes to me in Holy Communion.—Our Father.

THE MOTIVES OF HUMILITY

Humility is that virtue which, by the loving acknowledgment of our own utter vileness as contrasted with God's Sovereign Excellence, checks our false, disorderly self-esteem, and fosters our true, orderly self-contempt. Unfortunately, we are all blinded and hardened by pride. This is one of the worst effects of original and actual sin, a spiritual disease almost identical with our very nature. The remedy is to consider attentively and prayerfully what we are of ourselves, what we made ourselves, and what we ought to become for the love of Christ our Lord; in other words, to meditate on the Motives of Humility, our Nothingness, our Sinfulness, and our Vocation. While the first and second considerations serve chiefly to enlighten our mind, the third consideration aims principally at moving our will. For even though we should be fully convinced of our own unlimited baseness, yet as long as we do not cherish this conviction in our inmost heart nor strive to express it in every detail of our conduct, we have not reached even the lowest degree of the virtue of Humility.

First Motive of Humility. Of myself, I am a mere Nothing.

God, of Himself, is Infinite Being and Perfect Activity, Pure Intelligence and Essential Love. What am I, of myself? I did not make myself; I was made. Of what? Of nothing. Nothing is the direct and absolute negation of all being. A blade of grass is

something, a speck of dust is something; but I, of
myself, am less than either, less than the most
infinitesimal atom; I am nothing. Without God, I
am the most beggarly of all beggars, the most helpless
of all weaklings, the most wretched of all unfortu-
nates; no, I am immeasurably less; I am nothing.
Whatever good I possess, natural or supernatural, is
not mine but God's. Whatever power, wisdom, or
goodness I perceive in the various beings round about
me, comes all from God, is all God's. But, on the
other hand, whatever is defective, whether in myself or
in others, reminds me in loud and unmistakable
accents of my own utter nothingness. For what is a
defect save the absence of some requisite being or some
necessary quality, an approach to nothingness? So,
whatever is poorly planned or clumsily arranged, re-
calls to me that absolute void of intelligence which is my
own. Whatever is bad or hurtful, speaks to me of that
thorough lack of goodness which is my own. I cannot esteem what is defective, ill-managed, injurious;
hence, if I wish to be consistent and just and truthful, I am not to value myself nor to be pleased with myself, but I must make of myself no account whatever.
Am I, then, to despise myself? No, at least not inasmuch as I am only nothing. As such, I need not seek
contempt but may rest satisfied with being completely
ignored. But if I want to be esteemed and honored,
or rather if I am not willing to be treated as perfectly good-for-nothing, I do not seek the truth, I cherish falsehood, I am not walking in the light of God,
I do not love God. Being thus thrown back upon my
own nothingness, I must needs be miserable. On the
contrary, what happiness to recognize that God is
really all to us, and worthy of our most profound
adoration and most ardent love! How sweet this con-

sciousness of being utterly destitute of all goodness
and compelled, as it were, to place our entire confidence in God, to rely completely on Him, the Source
of every blessing! The humble man alone can say
from his heart: " My God and my all! I rejoice that
Thou art infinitely Mighty, Wise, Good, Just, and
Perfect; that Thou only art the most Holy, most High
Lord. Thou art my All, and I, Thy creature, am
wholly Thine, Thine by nature and Thine by love! "

This, then, I should constantly keep before my mind
and strive to realize more fully every day, namely,
that of myself I am nothing; that for me it is the most
natural thing to blunder and to fail; that, if I do any
good it is God's grace, if I understand anything it is
God's light, if I possess anything it is God's gift. As
long as I am in this mental attitude — which is the
only correct one for any man and the only possible one
for an honest person — how could I be scandalized at
the words or actions of others? They are simply
doing what is natural to them and natural to me. If
God were not to sustain me continually, at this very
moment, I should commit faults far more serious, sins
far more shameful, crimes far more detestable. Besides, what do I know about their circumstances or
their intentions? With an understanding so limited
and so darkened as mine, how can I assume and usurp
the office of judge, reserved exclusively to God? Let
us, therefore, never condemn any man, never think
harshly of any man, never look down on any man.
Whether he be a bad Catholic or a bitter Protestant or
a benighted Infidel, let us always have a kind word
for him and bear him a compassionate heart. How
many of them, with only a small fraction of the graces
heaped upon us, would have turned out good and
holy! Just as some persons have received a larger

share of temporal benefits, of wealth, learning, or energy, that they might be the open channels and willing instruments of the Divine Bounty towards those less richly endowed; so others have been blessed with a greater abundance of spiritual favors, that they might communicate them, in God's name, to their less privileged brethren.   To use one's talents any other way is nothing but ill-disguised self-idolatry.

Again, if I honestly recognize my own numberless shortcomings and sincerely desire not to be esteemed except for God's gifts, what difficulty can I have in manifesting my interior to those appointed for my guidance on the road to Perfection and in laying open my heart as it really is; my miserable correspondence to Divine Grace; by being taken up so deeply with earthly things and so slightly with the things of Heaven; the many distractions I entertain in Prayer; the scanty profit I derive from the Sacraments; my uncharitableness, my impatience, my self-complacency, my self-indulgence; my frequent violations of Rule; my careless performance of duty; my general lack of holy enthusiasm and ardent zeal?   Even if manifestation of conscience were intended only to furnish us with a spur to self-examination and a lever for self-humiliation, it ought to be diligently practised by every sincere Religious, or rather by every sensible Christian.

Second Motive of Humility. I Made Myself a Sinner.

Were I only nothing of myself, I might rest contented with being utterly ignored.   But no, I am less and worse than nothing, inasmuch as I made myself a sinner.   For this means that I repaid God's incomprehensible bounty with the blackest ingratitude and the grossest offenses. It means that I preferred a mere creature, another nothing like myself, to Him, the Infinite Goodness, Wisdom, and Power. And this shameful outrage I committed in His immediate Presence — much more immediate than is our mutual presence — in the Presence of so Holy a God, so Loving a Father. More than this, I have thus abused His own liberality, turning His own gifts against Himself; I, an utter nothing, against Him, the Sovereign Lord.

No wonder that St. Aloysius fainted away while confessing merely a few venial sins. But I who committed so many and, perhaps, such grievous sins, what contempt can be too severe for me, what humiliation too great to atone for the insults I have inflicted on the Infinite Majesty? How profoundly I ought to despise myself, and how earnestly I ought to desire to be despised by all according to my deserts! I must use every allowable means to expiate my offenses, and invite all creatures to assist in punishing me for my ingratitude. What rebuke have I not merited? What labor can be too hard for me? Am I still to follow my likes and dislikes in everything, or shall I, henceforth, seek to prefer everywhere God's Adorable Will in whatever way manifested? Indeed, I ought to look upon it as a special favor, to be burdened with the lowliest drudgery. I ought to be thankful when blamed or scolded, considering it a splendid opportunity to make some reparation for my past faults. Not only must I persuade myself that the meanest things in the house should be assigned to my use, since they could suit nobody better; but I must also, of my own accord, choose for myself always the poorest and the worst. I ought no longer to use anything as my own, for the simple reason that it is God's. Even if I had not taken a vow of poverty, I should still be careful not to waste or destroy any of His gifts. I must not only readily forgive those who have done me harm, but I must treat such as have in any way afflicted me, as my real benefactors and devoted friends. Having in the past, for the sake of creatures, become a rebel against God, I will in the future, for the love of God, become a servant to all men. But I will particularly strive to practise Perfect Obedience, prompt, exact, with thorough union of will and full conformity of judgment.

By my sins I have greatly fostered my inborn tendency to evil, for every fault disfigures and weakens the soul in proportion to its gravity. Therefore, I have a special reason to keep strict guard over my senses, over my imagination, over my heart; and not to seek my ease, my rest, or my comfort, except when really necessary, though even then never at the sacrifice of religious decorum or to the detriment of outward modesty. Not content with the various mortifications imposed by rule on all the members of the Community, I will beg permission for additional penances, and daily, if possible, inflict chastisement on my sinful flesh. For, besides having to wage a relentless war against my corrupt self, I must also make due satisfaction for all my past sins to the Divine Justice. It is true that the Blood of Christ our Savior was shed to atone for our offenses; yet, even so, there remains much to be paid for by ourselves, either in this world or in the next. So horrible and loathsome is the stain left by sin on the Soul, that if it were to be presented in this state before the throne of God, it would spontaneously plunge itself into the terrible fire of Purgatory. To stay in the Divine Presence, if such were possible under these circumstances, would be to it a torment incomparably more intense than all the sufferings inflicted by those cleansing flames. And the same holds true to some extent also in this life, of a soul that begins to love God in real earnest. It cannot bear to appear in prayer before Him, the Infinite Holiness, unless it has used every means to expiate its sins. It longs to wash away even the least stain, to pay off its debt to the last farthing; and hence it eagerly embraces every mortification and humiliation as a most valuable opportunity to attain its object.

Third Motive of Humility. I Ought to Become a Saint.

Though by nature a mere nothing, and by sin a horrid monster, yet by grace I am called to become like to Jesus, my Divine Master, Who is Meek and Humble of Heart. To this, in fact, I have already bound myself by my Vows; this is to be the exclusive aim of my remaining years, to imitate my God made Man for love of me. God made Man; what an unparalleled self-abasement, particularly as the nature He assumed was a fallen nature, the nature of degraded, sinful man. He became Man to serve man. He served His Parents as a Child; He served those who engaged His labors as a village carpenter; He served in healing, in teaching, in correcting, in commanding. For we must not think that teaching, correcting, or commanding, is less of a service than other work done for our neighbor. No; on the contrary, the higher we are placed the more it is our privilege to serve. Hence our Holy Father the Pope, in calling himself the Servant of the Servants of God, is merely stating something inseparable from his sublime office of Pastor of the Universal Church. But Jesus, our Lord, became Man to serve with such entire self-forgetfulness, with such boundless devotion, that no slave ever rendered his master more perfect service. He truly made Himself the slave of all, though it was an infinitely loving slavery. "For the Son of Man is not come to be ministered unto, but to minister, and to give His life for the redemption of many." This then is our Example, our Model. By nature we are the slaves of God, by sin we made ourselves the slaves of Satan, by grace we must become the most humble, most devoted slaves of every man with whom we come in contact. If engaged in mental occupations, we will study not for the pleasure we may get out of books, but to fit ourselves to be the slaves of our fellow men. If performing household duties, we will do so not for temporal gain or from mere necessity, but because we desire nothing better than to be the slaves of our brethren. In fact, we will make it our constant practice to look upon all as our superiors, whom it is our glorious task to serve at the call of God and for the love of Jesus.

But more than this, Christ our Lord became Man to be humbled for my sake and to suffer on my account; and I in return ought to welcome contempt and hardship for love of Him, in order to become like to Him, my God. No higher nobility, no truer happiness can be conceived in this world than that which is found in being ignored and despised with Jesus, in bearing poverty and pain with Jesus, in being bound and buffeted with Jesus, in being trodden down and spit upon with Jesus, in being falsely accused and barbarously mocked with Jesus, in being cruelly scourged and put to a most shameful death with Jesus, the Son of God. He Divinized revilings and sufferings, and those who accept them and seek them for His sake, are really pursuing the greatest good on earth as well as the loftiest glory in Heaven. Christ rejected honors, riches, and pleasures; and we too should consider them of no account. For if these things were worth having, certainly the Eternal Wisdom would have coveted them; but on the contrary He coveted contumely, destitution, and affliction.

" Learn of Me for I am Meek and Humble of Heart." This, our Lord assures us, is the only way to find rest for our souls, that rest, that peace which surpasses all understanding and in comparison with which even the noblest enjoyment in the natural order is but bitter desolation. Let us not think Humility hard to practise or difficult to acquire. " My yoke is sweet and my burden light," says the Infallible Truth. No; Pride is hard, sin is hard, inordination is hard, worldliness is hard; while Humility is the heavenly balm that sweetens and softens all the ills of this time of exile and temptation. And with the help of grace, which is ever offered us in profuse abundance, we now resolve to apply ourselves to this virtue unremittingly for the remainder of our lives.

TWO STANDARDS

Introductory Remarks.— All mankind may be said to follow either of two banners: " the one of Christ, our sovereign Leader and Lord; the other of Lucifer, the mortal enemy of our human nature."—" He that is not with Me, is against Me," says the Son of God, " and he that gathereth not with Me, scattereth." In this Exercise there is, of course, no question of choosing between these Two Standards. That we have done long ago and forever. But St. Ignatius proposes this Meditation that we may recognize more clearly the Irreconcilable Opposition between the two Leaders of this present world, that we may realize more intimately the Terrible Dangers to which men are constantly exposed in this life, that we may understand more thoroughly the Solid Principles which should ever govern the work of our personal sanctification as well as our labors for the salvation of our neighbor, and that thus we may become more intelligent, more sincere, more ardent, more steadfast Followers and Apostles of Christ our Lord. Two Standards emphasizes the momentous truth, that unless we are wholly imbued with the teachings of our Divine Savior, unless we strive to lead men, our pupils, our charges, or our penitents, in perfect accordance with the directions of our Heavenly King, we shall only be playing into the hands of Satan, our infernal enemy. Neither gold, nor might, nor learning, will convert or even in the least benefit a single soul.

Subject of this Meditation.—" Christ calls and desires all under His banner, Lucifer on the contrary under his." God most sincerely wishes the salvation of all men, their temporal happiness and their eternal bliss, by the profession of faith and the practice of good works; while Satan and his demons strive to bring about men's temporal misery and everlasting ruin.

Composition of Place.—" A vast plain in the region about Jerusalem where the Supreme Leader of all the good is Christ our Lord; and another plain in the country of Babylon, where the chief of the enemy is Lucifer.

Petition.— Knowledge of the deadly deceits of the wicked chieftain and help to guard against them; knowledge also of the life-giving truths which our Sovereign Leader points out and grace to follow Him.

First Point. Persons.
" Imagine," says St. Ignatius, " the chieftain of all the enemy as seated in that great plain of Babylon on a lofty throne of fire and smoke, in aspect horrible and fearful."—" That great plain," indicates vast resources and momentous issues,—" Babylon," the center of disorder,—" a lofty throne," pride,—" fire," perpetual unrest,—" smoke," darkness,—" horrible," means loathsome in himself, " and fearful," breathing cruel hatred to others.
On the other hand, " consider how Christ our Lord, in aspect fair and winning, takes His station, on a lowly spot, in a great plain of the country near Jerusalem."—" Our Lord," by birthright as God, by donation as Man,—" fair and winning," ineffably Beautiful and infinitely Loving,—" takes His station," not

like a selfish tyrant but like a Devoted Captain,—
"on a lowly spot," in true humility,—"in a great
plain," the immense realm of grace,—"near Jerusalem," the city of harmony and peace.

Second Point. Actions.

"Consider how Satan summons together innumerable devils, how he disperses them to different cities,
throughout the whole world, not omitting a single
province, locality, class, or person."—"Satan summons," imperiously,—"disperses," violently,—"innumerable devils," an almost countless host of fallen
angels that slavishly obey through fear and hatred,
—"not omitting a single person." Each man has a
demon to tempt him, to lead him astray, to destroy
him body and soul. How great is our danger!
Every suggestion of self-complacency, of vanity, of
pride, of envy, of resentment, of impatience, of sensuality, is either prompted or fostered by that evil
genius. How this fact should help to keep us humble.
But unfortunately our heart may be so addicted to
these vices, that we do not notice the continual working of our infernal attendant. There is not enough
habitual opposition between our own soul and that
foul spirit.

Again, "consider how the Lord of the whole world
chooses out so many persons,— apostles, disciples, and
so forth,— and sends them all over the earth to diffuse His sacred doctrine through every class and condition of men."—"The Lord chooses," by the grace of
Vocation,— what an honor for such persons, since
they are given the same office as the Holy Angels,
—"and sends them," with all kindness. We too have
been sent by Him, to this particular locality. By the
omission of "men" on the side of Satan and of

" angels " on the side of Christ, St. Ignatius probably intended to emphasize the fact that ours is a spiritual combat, a warfare with the powers of darkness, as pointed out by the Apostle St. Paul. "For our wrestling is not against flesh and blood, but against principalities and powers, against the rulers of the world of this darkness, against the spirits of wickedness in the high places." (Eph. 6:12.) However, just as we should not ignore the fact that the Angels are sent by God to protect, assist, and save us; so we must not overlook the other fact, that many men are aiding the Demons in their work of deception and enthralment; namely, all those whose lives are governed by the love of riches, pleasures, and honors, in one word, the followers of the world. It is such people as these that manage our yellow dailies and spicy magazines, that write our salacious novels and immoral plays, that own our disreputable dance-halls and infamous pleasure-resorts, that support our irreligious schools as well as our temples of error, superstition, and atheism.

Third Point. Tactics and Aims.

" Consider the address which Satan makes, and how he commands them to lay snares and chains; telling them how they are first to tempt men to covet Riches,— as he is wont to do in most cases,— that thus they may more easily come to the vain Honor of the world, and then to unbounded Pride; so that the first step is riches, the second honor, the third pride; and from these three steps he leads them to all other vices." This behest of Satan not only displays his despotic character but also reveals his deep cunning and deceitful malice. His plan is to work first on our inborn leaning towards the objects

which minister to our earthly existence, under pretext
that these things are indifferent, or rather that they
are good; — for, in the words of Holy Scripture,
" God saw all He had made, and it was very good "—
that accordingly they may contribute to our happiness; and hence that there is no reason why we could
not make a right use of them. What renders men
particularly liable to deception in this matter is to
fancy that they have no inclination towards wealth
and distinction. True, as long as these things seem
entirely beyond our reach, we may experience no
positive desire for them; but how differently we
begin to feel about them the moment we perceive
a favorable occasion to indulge our natural craving.
Besides, have we no repugnance for poverty and contempt? Of course, we all have. Then we also love
riches and honors in exactly the same degree. This
is our weak spot, and Satan takes care to attack it
from every side. Just as he strives to make us desire
the goods and honors of the world on the false as-
sumption that they are indispensable for our happiness, our health, or our usefulness; so he strives to
make us dread poverty and contempt, mortification
and humiliation, by picturing these to us as incompatible with our happiness, our health, or our usefulness. But let us not be alarmed by these bugaboos.
The Saints were not only the happiest but also the
most efficient men that ever existed, and on the whole
they lived longer than tepid Religious and sinful
Worldlings. All tenderness and heroism, it has well
been said, goes with poverty and privation, not with
wealth and comfort. Again, while Satan promises
peace and happiness which he cannot give and indeed
would not give even if he could, he intends only to
render us miserable here and hereafter; and how

well he succeeds we know by our own experience and
by what we see daily going on in the world.

The Snares of Satan, consequently, are the possession, the use, or the desire of things pleasant, whether
superfluous or necessary, but indulged in without regard to the Will of God, simply in compliance with
our natural inclinations, and hence inordinately; likewise the removal, the avoidance, or the fear of things
unpleasant, without regard to the Will of God, simply
in compliance with our natural aversions. In other
words, every Inordination is a Snare of Satan.

This is no doubt an important discovery; but what
is far more important for us is not to allow ourselves
to be caught by our crafty foes. A few additional
reflections may help us to be ever on our guard.
We certainly need health and strength, rest and
recreation, food and drink, lodging, conveniences, and
clothing, learning and books, personal appearance
and social influence. We are already inclined,
through the corruption of our nature, to esteem and
seek these things independently of the Adorable Will
of God, as it is manifested to us by Commandments,
Counsels, Rules, Superiors, Inspirations. Now Satan,
through the suggestions of his demons and the seduc-
tions of his followers, is ever urging us on in the
same direction under plea that these things are all
good. Hence, we are constantly in danger of at-
taching ourselves to the various objects that may supply our needs, and of satisfying these needs more
abundantly than is consistent with the Divine Will
or conducive to our sanctification. The essential question for us is not whether these things are
good in a general sense, but whether they are good
in our particular circumstances, whether they help
us here and now to Sanctify and Save our soul, by

Praising, Revering, and Serving God. For instance,
we need sufficient clothing and footwear; but it is
neither necessary nor expedient that it should be as
fashionable and elegant as possible, or that our supply
should be so abundant as to obviate any further recourse to Superiors for the next two or three years.
On the contrary, we should wish and strive to have
at any time as scanty and poor a supply as our Superior will permit and sanction. We may need certain
little articles; for instance, stationery, soap, a match-
box, a pocket-knife, a watch, cuff-buttons, a note-
book, a pair of scissors; but anything beyond what is
cheap and useful is out of keeping with our Religious
Profession, a hindrance to our efficiency, and an obstacle to our sanctification. We need rest and recreation, food and drink; but no more and no better
than is required to do our work, to perform our
duties, to accomplish the Will of God. Perhaps we
need learning and books; but this does not mean that,
even with permission, we can freely indulge in the
reading of newspapers and novels, or turn our room
into a private annex to the library. All this is as
plain as daylight; yet our inordinate tendencies are
so strong and our enemies so persistent that we have
to exercise constant vigilance in order not to be led
astray. It is not without good reason, then, that the
Church exhorts us to pray daily: "Holy Michael, be
our Safeguard against the Wickedness and Snares of
the Devil."

Finally St. Ignatius bids us "consider the address
which Christ our Lord makes to all His servants and
friends, whom He sends on this expedition, recommending to them that they desire to help all, by guiding them first to the highest degree of Poverty of
Spirit, and even to Actual Poverty, if it pleases His

Divine Majesty and He should deign to elect them to
it; leading them, secondly, to a desire of Reproaches
and Contempt, because from these two Humility results, so that there are three steps; the first, poverty,
opposed to riches; the second, reproaches and contempt, opposed to worldly honor; the third, humility,
opposed to pride; and from these three steps let them
conduct men to all other virtues." These concise directions serve to put before us the Doctrine of our
Adorable Savior, as recorded in the Gospels, about
the value and use of the perishable goods of this
world. Nature, corrupted and blinded by sin, takes an
altogether different view. Just as we look almost instinctively for wealth and honor because of the gratification or exaltation they afford to the body and the
mind, so we quite spontaneously shrink from poverty
and contempt on account of the affliction or humiliation they entail for the body and the mind. How
different, by the way, the tone of our Lord's address
is from that of Satan's. "His servants and friends,"
by nature we are His unworthy servants, but by grace
we have become His friends, the friends of Jesus, the
Son of God. "Recommending to them," what condescension!—"that they desire," how this also reflects
the Gentleness of the Sacred Heart!—"to help all,"
this Religious do by their very Profession, their simplicity of dress, their austere mode of life, and they
may do so, besides, very efficaciously by conversation
or letter-writing, provided always their personal conduct be in close conformity with these fundamental
principles laid down by our Divine Lord.

The True Life is here pointed out by Christ; for
while yielding to our inordinate tendencies, our unruly passions, in conformity with the Deceits of Satan
our Enemy, means Slavery and Death; resisting them

in obedience to the Truth of Christ, our King, embodied in both His Doctrine and His Example, means Liberty and Life. Satan makes a perfidious alliance with our corrupt inclinations in order to ensnare and destroy us; but Christ teaches us how to check and overcome them, because He longs to bestow on us real happiness and everlasting bliss. Our Lord's first object, then, is to lead men to the highest degree of Spiritual Poverty; but gradually, of course, since there is question of the formation of good habits. The lowest degree of Spiritual Poverty is necessary for salvation, and consists in being so far detached from earthly goods, as for their sake or on account of their loss not to commit a Mortal Sin. Also this lowest degree includes a conditional acceptance of Actual Poverty, inasmuch as God might ordain circumstances in which Actual Poverty would be the only alternative. A very high degree of Poverty of Spirit would consist in being so completely detached from everything earthly, as not even for the sake of all the goods of this world, nor to avoid the utter spoliation of even the most indispensable things, to commit an Inordination. There are corresponding degrees in the love of contempt, which might not improperly be called " Obscurity of Spirit." Since practically there will always be room for advancement, the constant aim of our prayers and our efforts should be the very Highest Degree of Detachment from the Riches and Honors of this World. But we shall never make any progress until we are thoroughly convinced that on the one hand every Inordination, and all the more every Sin, being nothing but a concession to our morbid craving for earthly Goods and Distinctions, fosters and confirms the old habit of Pride; while on the other hand every

act of Self-Denial and Self-Conquest, every acceptance of Suffering and Insult, develops and strengthens
in our soul the supernatural habit of Humility.

These simple considerations should fill me with
intense gratitude for having been chosen by our Lord
to diffuse His Sacred Doctrine amongst my fellow
men, and for having been admitted by Him to a State
in which I am greatly protected from the Snares of
Satan, in consequence of the Vows of Poverty, Chastity, and Obedience. How difficult it must be for a
millionaire to have even the lowest degree of Poverty
of Spirit! Hence our Lord says that it is easier for
a camel to pass through the eye of a needle than for a
rich man to enter Heaven. Again, these same truths
should cover me with genuine confusion, seeing how
poorly I have corresponded till now to the grace of
Vocation for my own progress in Perfection, and how
little I have accomplished as yet for the Salvation
of my neighbor, because, instead of leading him to the
love of Poverty and Contempt, I have fostered his
natural craving for ease and show, for comfort and
applause.

But besides gathering from this Meditation lively
sentiments of gratitude and confusion, we should exert ourselves to reap in rich measure its precious and
manifold Fruit. First, Two Standards should not
only animate us with a real Dislike and Fear of Riches
and Honors, of pleasures and comforts, of distinction
and independence, of anything that may feed our
self-love and self-conceit, as the instruments abused
and disgraced by Satan to deceive and destroy us; but
also inspire us with a sincere Esteem and Desire of
Poverty and Contempt, of suffering and discomfort, of
slights and dependence, of anything that calls for
self-denial and self-humiliation, as the instruments

used and ennobled by Christ our Lord to sanctify
and save us. Secondly, Two Standards should communicate to us a certain Moderation and Circum-
spection in the use of those goods of this world which
we need to sustain our life or to keep up our name;
together with a decided Preference and Eagerness
for opportunities of privation and suffering, obscurity
and humiliation. Thirdly, Two Standards should
cause us to pray earnestly and continually for these
opportunities, every such petition being one of the
many acts of this kind which we shall have to make
in order gradually to acquire an actual leaning towards Poverty and Contempt. Fourthly, Two Standards should make us pass on from unremitting and
fervent Prayer to what most effectually fosters the
formation of the habit of Humility, namely, daily and
persevering Practice.

These several applications are after all but the
logical development of what we learned already in the
First Week. For even in The Foundation we understood the absolute necessity of counterbalancing our
unruly passions by contrary habits, to be formed and
confirmed by a lifelong succession of acts. Here, in
Two Standards, the injunctions and machinations
of Satan as well as the directions and tactics of our
Divine Lord furnish us with additional and powerful
motives for undertaking this momentous task. From
the present Meditation we carry away the solid conviction that, while to serve God and to save our soul
is practically impossible unless we offset our inordinate tendencies towards Riches and Honors by opposite inclinations towards Poverty and Contempt,
this can be accomplished only by frequent acts of
mortification and humiliation performed under the
influence of Heavenly Grace, in obedience to our Ador-

able Master, out of reverence for His Infallible Authority, and — as we shall consider more fully later on — in imitation of His most Admirable Example. It is evident that the stronger these supernatural inclinations grow in our heart, the safer we shall be against the Snares of the Devil, and that their strength will depend on the number and energy of the corresponding acts.

Though we can never be perfectly safe whilst we are in this life, it is only in so far as we have formed these inclinations calculated to weaken, restrain, and neutralize our innate tendencies towards Riches and Honors — which give support and furnish fuel to our Pride — that we shall possess the habit of Humility. Since this virtue prompts us to acknowledge our own vileness and our complete dependence on God, it also renders us submissive and conformable to His Holy Will, wherever and in whatever way manifested, and thus implies all other forms of moral rectitude. Consequently, those who have acquired the Virtue of Humility can easily be led to the explicit exercise of every other Virtue. On the contrary, the unbridled desire for Riches, the unmortified love of Honors, and especially the consummate vice of Pride, the three concupiscences, will lead a man readily into every kind of Sin.

In conclusion, our Adorable Master has now pointed out to us the only Practical Program for attaining the End of our Existence and for promoting the Extension of His Kingdom. Its items are few and clear: we are to esteem, desire, implore, seek, embrace, and bear Poverty and Contempt. Relying, therefore, on the help of grace, merited for us by our Blessed Savior and promised to us by our Heavenly Father, let us resolve to conform our entire conduct, even in its smallest details, to this Divine Program. The sooner we carry out this transformation, the more we shall advance in true humility and real happiness, and the better we shall succeed in bringing other men to the knowledge of Christ and the enjoyment of Heaven.

Triple Colloquy.— I will pray first to our Lady that she may solicit for me these graces from her Son and Lord, concluding with the Hail Mary; then to our Savior that He may obtain for me these same graces from the Father, finishing with the Anima Christi; and lastly to the Father that He may grant me these graces, saying at the end the Our Father. I will give fervent thanks for having been received under the Standard of Christ our Lord; acknowledge with deep shame and great sorrow that I have so often proved a useless servant, perhaps even a perfidious traitor; and beg for perfect detachment from worldly goods and honors by being frequently made to suffer privation and pain, slights and disappointments, criticism, derision, and insult.

FIFTH DAY

SPECIAL PATRON : St. Francis Xavier.

MOTTO: " He that is not with Me, is against Me."—
Luke 11 :23.

SPIRIT: Abhorrence of the goods of this world,
Comforts and Distinctions.

READING: Imitation; Bk. I, C. 9, 25.
　　　　　　　　Bk. III, C. 11, 13, 15, 17, 26,
　　　　　　　　　　34, 54, 55.
　　　Rules and Customs.

Examine carefully in what particulars you have
failed to observe the Rules, the Customs, the Orders
of your Superiors, the Duties of your Office, and the
Inspirations of Divine Grace. Take such practical
Resolutions as will insure your thorough amendment
of past faults, and such others as the Holy Ghost
will suggest to you for your future progress towards
complete self-denial and self-abjection.

THE THREE CLASSES OF MEN

Introductory Remarks.—Already in the First Week of these Spiritual Exercises, we should have conceived a thorough and, as it were, instinctive abhorrence of all inordinate actions and of their source, our inordinate affections. In the Second Week, we should get more and more convinced of the impossibility of our affections being other than inordinate as long as we of our own free will retain or use the objects on which they feed, the goods of this world. For, on the one hand, we have a very strong leaning to enjoy these goods for our own selfish gratification and, on the other hand, the Devil is ever cunningly urging us to seek, use, and acquire them, without regard to the Divine Will. Hence, if we are really anxious to serve God, to reach holiness, and to save our souls, we must be determined to flee from these goods as far as we can consistently with the claims of obedience and charity. This desire of self-spoliation, this dread of worldly goods, not only of their possession but also of their use, will be the more real and efficacious, the more intimate and vivid our appreciation is of the danger and deformity of inordination. In this respect, men may be divided into Three Classes, on which St. Ignatius directs us to meditate at this stage of our work, in order " to embrace that which is best." We will center our attention on three persons selected so as to be fairly representative of these Three Classes.

Subject of this Meditation.—Three individuals

have each acquired a large sum of money, say a million dollars, but inordinately, that is, not purely for the love of God. They all find, of course, in their affection to this money a hindrance to their actual peace and their eternal salvation, and they should like to rid themselves of this difficulty.

Composition of Place.—" To see myself standing before God our Lord and all His Saints, that I may desire and know what is more pleasing to His Divine Goodness."— Why standing, one might ask, and not prostrate? To remind me that I should always keep ready to carry out the Holy Will of God.

Petition.—" To choose that which is most for the glory of the Divine Majesty and for the good of my soul."— No one can fail to notice the close similarity between the grace asked for in this Petition and the disposition pointed out by St. Ignatius in the concluding words of The Foundation: " Desiring and Choosing only those things which are most Conducive to the End for which we were created."

First Point. The First Individual would like to shake off the affection he has for the money, so as to find in peace God our Lord, and so as to know how to save his soul; but he Takes No Means even up to the hour of death.

This person, then, does nothing, makes absolutely no effort, but puts off his amendment, his conversion, indefinitely. What folly, what slavery, and what risk! Folly, because these worldly goods cannot satisfy our heart and will abandon us anyhow sooner or later. Slavery, because they tie us down to this earth and fill us with anxiety. Risk, because they are recommended by Satan and repudiated by Christ. If my

case be that of this First Individual, I must remember
that not to advance, not to wish to advance, means to
go back, and that my unmortified attachments will
surely lead me into sin.   But no, I must not put off
my amendment, my conversion, any longer.   I must
take action, I must earnestly pray for help; I must
put in practice the teaching of Christ, my Savior; I
must apply myself to mortification and humility.

Second Point.   The Second Individual also desires
to shake off the affection for the money; but he wishes
to do so in such a way as to retain its possession, and
he Does Not Resolve, even if this should be better,
to Leave the Money in order to Go to God.

This person has only a velleity, but no energetic
wish to set himself right.   He would like to practise
Spiritual Poverty without having a conditional desire of Actual Poverty.   But this is a gross illusion
and a palpable contradiction.   He wants to remain
in the Snare of Satan but without feeling its inconvenience and danger.   He would wish to get matters
arranged according to his own whims and would like
God to connive at his inordinate attachment.   This
person, evidently, is not determined to make the greatest possible progress, which we saw was the one Indispensable Disposition for entering on the Retreat; he
has utterly failed to realize the Wonderful Predilection of our Divine Savior in his regard, to which alone
he owes his preservation from eternal perdition; he has
not conceived any real abhorrence of Sin and Inordination; he has not ratified the Unreserved Offering
of himself in The Kingdom of Christ; and as a willing
captive he is already passing over to the Standard of
Lucifer.

Third Point.   The Third Individual also wishes to

shake off the affection, but without any desire either
to retain or not to retain the money. He does not
even intend to wish for it except in so far as it shall
seem better for the praise and service of the Divine
Majesty. The Greater Glory of God our Lord is the
only thing that will move him either to take or to
leave the money, but meanwhile he wants to consider
that he Has actually Left it All.

This person is really in earnest. Being as yet ignorant whether or not he will be called upon to renounce the money, he strives to make himself perfectly Indifferent in its regard. Thus he corrects as
far as he can the inordination committed in acquiring
this fortune, and may confidently expect that God
will cure him of his attachment. Once the cause
has been removed, the rest is sure to follow with the
help of grace.

In this Meditation, then, I am forcibly reminded
that I must do something, that I cannot remain satisfied with inefficient half-measures, but should resolve
to take the most direct and practical means to overcome my difficulties and to advance in the love of
Poverty and Contempt. Those who are already leading the Life of the Counsels ought to make the application to all attachments not wholly based on God
as well as to all repugnances not purely inspired by
God; for instance, regarding a certain employment,
in a certain House, with certain companions, under
a certain Superior; or touching certain recreations,
comforts, studies, pursuits, regulations, customs.

In such cases, a Religious of the First Class will
say: "Oh! God has placed this book at my disposal "
— or "given me this opportunity of recreation
through my Superiors "—" and why should I bother
my head about the matter? 'Never ask for any-

thing, and never refuse anything.' I guess as long
as I don't commit a sin it will be all right." Indolent
and lukewarm, he is satisfied to remain caught in the
Snares of Satan, nor will it be long before he wears
the Devil's Chains.

A Religious of the Second Class will argue thus
with himself: " Well, I am ready to give up this thing,
whenever God, through His Providence or through
my Superior, should desire to take it away. But
meanwhile, I will strive to use it only with a pure
intention for His Service and Glory." This, however,
he cannot do, because he neglects to take the obvious
and only means. He may perhaps fancy that he is
indifferent, but his readiness is nugatory and he is
deluding himself with a false security, while in reality
he is deceived and entrapped by Satan.

A Religious of the Third Class, if he can rid himself
at once of the object, as a book for instance, will
do so right away. If there is question of something
more important that cannot be given up so promptly,
an office, let us say, he will at least beseech our Lord
most earnestly to take it from him, unless its reten-
tion should be for His Better Service and His Greater
Glory. But if his attachment is very strong, he will
without delay write or speak to his Superior begging him, if it can possibly be granted, for the very opposite of what he would naturally wish to have. Only
such a one is actually faithful to his Vocation and
really striving after Perfection.

A great truth to be kept in mind is, that God is not
going to help us — and hence that it is no use to pray
for such help — unless we first avail ourselves of the
means which He has already placed within our reach.
So in striving to get rid of an attachment, our prayer
to that effect should be earnest and is indispensable,

but it will remain fruitless if we neglect to give up, as far as circumstances will permit, the object to which we are unduly attached. We should either surrender it at once, or ask our Superior to take it away if he sees good, or at least implore our Lord to deprive us of it if not detrimental to His glory.

A few additional illustrations may serve to render this matter still clearer. Three Religious, for some reason or other, took a dislike to a certain charge with which they had been entrusted. They thought it proper to expose their difficulties to the Superior, but he only listened to them kindly without taking any action or even making any promises. The First still continues to feel discontented and discouraged. The Second says now and then a half-hearted prayer for resignation, and is meanwhile casting about for an opportunity to bring up the matter once more before his Superior. The Third offered himself at once to be kept in the same office as long as it might please his Superior, and then went to implore the help of grace till he had completely vanquished his dislike.

Three Religious Teachers are overfond of attending the scholastic games. During the Retreat they become aware of their trouble. Says the First: " Yes, I have been a trifle inordinate in this matter. But what can I do? A man needs a little recreation at least once or twice a week. But, of course, I will only go when I can do so without neglecting any of my duties." Says the Second: " Surely, I have become somewhat attached to these games. But in future I will go only when there is a general permission. Besides, I will first make a visit to the Blessed Sacrament, and ask our Lord for the grace of going solely in order to please Him and of doing all the good I can by my conversation and behavior." Says the Third:

" I will not go any more; no, not even when I am allowed, but only when I am positively sent by my Superior.   But I will take the first suitable occasion to
tell him about my overfondness for those games.   In
fact, I am determined to do everything in my power
to prevent myself from going again, except my conscience tells me that it is for the Better Service of
God.   However, even in that case, I will pray earnestly for the Divine Help and mortify my fondness
as much as possible."

Three Religious, let us suppose, to whom the use of
tobacco has been recommended by the physician and
who have received the requisite permission of Superiors, are gradually becoming a little addicted to
smoking.   Each of them happens to get a box of
Havanas from a friend or relative, and without consulting the Will of God obtains leave to keep the
cigars for his own use.   Shortly afterwards they make
their annual Retreat and wish to sanctify themselves.
They find the cigars to be a hindrance to their project inasmuch as they are unduly attached to them.
They also become aware that this attachment has
made them commit several faults for which as yet
they have felt no sincere sorrow.   One of the First
Class simply does nothing.   One of the Second Class
resolves to make a good intention before smoking.
One of the Third Class takes the box without delay
to the Superior.

In this Meditation, therefore, I should diligently examine whether I do not belong to the First or the Second Class, by only pretending or fancying that I wish
to advance in the Love of Christ and in Holiness of
Life without taking the indispensable measures, mortification, humiliation, self-conquest; or by putting
conditions to the Grace of God with regard to my

cooperation, saying as it were to Him, "Lord, I am ready for this, but not for that; I will go so far, but no further;" or by deceiving myself, praying perhaps oftentimes a day for opportunities of suffering, and meanwhile neglecting to embrace the occasions actually present or to use the means I have in my hand. I should earnestly ask myself: "What is there that keeps me back? Is it any creature outside myself to which I am unduly attached or for which I foster an inordinate repugnance? Or is it some unruly tendency within my own soul; a preference of my will and judgment; a clinging to my whims and fancies; a dislike to open my heart to those given me by God for my guidance; a lurking resentment at perhaps not having been treated fairly; a distaste for total dependence on Superiors in asking permissions, in stating expenses, and so forth; a shirking of the constant labor and watchfulness required for sanctification; or a dread of this very thing I am considering, this absolute self-spoliation and perpetual self-conquest?"

How is it, we may often have asked ourselves, that some Religious make very good Resolutions and yet fail to advance in Perfection? The present Meditation supplies the answer. It is either because they do not sincerely intend to carry out their Resolutions, as is evident from the fact that they never take any means to do so — and these belong to the First Class — or because, in forming their Resolutions, they deal only with secondary difficulties and superficial trifles, not with their real obstacles and fundamental needs, — and these belong to the Second Class. Again, some one might put himself this query: "But persons that seek everywhere their greater humiliation and continual mortification, are they not inclined to be towards others somewhat stern, harsh, severe, un-sympathetic, uncharitable?" On the contrary, the only obstacle to true, gentle, tender, and self-sacrificing charity, is inordinate attachment to self. We shall be charitable only in proportion as we become unselfish, self-forgetful, and self-denying. Religious that are content to stay in the First or the Second Class will never learn to practise charity.

"The same three **Colloquies** as were made in the preceding contemplation of Two Standards." To this direction St. Ignatius adds a very important note, in which he lays down a principle that is of almost constant application in the Spiritual Life. "It will greatly help us," he says, "towards the up-rooting of any inordinate affection or repugnance we may feel, to beg and beseech our Lord that He may take away the object to which we are attached or to send us the very thing to which we are averse, provided only it be for the service and praise of His Divine Majesty." Since we have all a great and last-ing antipathy to poverty, suffering, and contempt, it is evident from this principle of St. Ignatius that, if we really wish to see Grace triumph in our heart over Nature, we should make it our habitual practice to pray fervently for opportunities of bearing these af-flictions. But what concerns us more especially just now is to know how we are to apply the Saint's advice at the conclusion of the present Meditation. By this time we are supposed to have discovered to what objects during the past year we felt an attraction which we did not resist and to what other creatures we experienced an aversion which we did not over-come; or again, what particular charge we should be delighted to get for the coming year and what other

status we would receive with misgiving and disgust.
Now, if we have at all profited by the consideration
of The Three Classes of Men, we should forthwith
take up the work of our thorough reformation on all
these points.   In those things which depend on our
own initiative, we should with the help of Grace
proceed to act at once in a manner diametrically opposed to our unmortified passions; while in those
matters over which we can exercise no control, we
should with great earnestness beseech and conjure
in succession the Immaculate Virgin, our Blessed
Lord, and our Heavenly Father, to dispose them in
a way directly contrary to our natural tendencies,
always understood, of course, in so far as this will
not be detrimental to the Divine Glory.

THE TEMPTATION IN THE DESERT

Subject of this Meditation.— After Christ our Lord had received the baptism of penance, He went to the desert, where He fasted forty days and forty nights. Then He was thrice tempted by Satan, who said to Him: " If Thou be the Son of God, command that these stones be made bread;" and again: " If Thou be the Son of God, cast Thyself down, for it is written that He hath given His angels charge over Thee, and in their hands they shall bear Thee up, lest perhaps Thou dash Thy foot against a stone;" and lastly: "All these I will give Thee, if falling down Thou wilt adore me." Then the Devil having left Him, Angels came and ministered to Him.— Matt. 4 :1-11.

Composition of Place.— Mount Quarantana, or some other lonely and barren mountain in the desert between Jericho and Ephraim; and about fifteen miles to the west, Jerusalem with the Temple, which in spite of the distance we can distinguish by its gilded roof and snow-white pinnacles.

Petition.— A more intimate knowledge of Christ our Lord, Who permitted the temptations of Satan for my sake,— for my instruction by His conduct, and for my benefit by His victory,— that I may love Him henceforth more generously and follow Him more closely.

First Point. The First Temptation.
Our Divine Lord, to prepare Himself for His pub-

lic ministry, had withdrawn, under the impulse of the Holy Spirit, to a wild mountain region, and there spent forty days in prayer and fasting. Penance and Prayer, these are the two principal weapons, especially of those who are called to the duties of an apostle, but in general of all those who desire to labor for the salvation and sanctification of their neighbor, in union with Jesus, the Son of God. I can see my Adorable Savior there on the bleak and weird mountain, prostrate in a cave on the hard ground, imploring His Heavenly Father to bless His great Work, the Conquest of souls, the Conversion of sinners, the Redemption of the whole race of Adam; and through the very intensity of His supplications omitting for forty successive days to attend to the ever-increasing exhaustion of His Sacred Body. It is worthy of remark, that in like manner many Saints, docile to the promptings of the Holy Spirit, forgot to take their meals for one or more days, through the fervor of their meditation. Accordingly, this prolonged fast, this severe mortification and profound humiliation, was undergone by my Lord and Master, not only to atone for my acts of self-indulgence in eating and drinking, but also to teach me how I ought to join earnest occupation about my eternal interests to moderate disregard for my bodily comforts. An easy or lounging posture in performing my Spiritual Duties is surely not conducive to humility and devotion. Union with God demands detachment from creatures and implies power over self.

But there is a limit to even the most heroic abstinence. "When He had fasted forty days, He was hungry;" that is, He allowed His Blissful Soul, no longer wholly wrapt in prayer though always intimately united to God, to realize more keenly the pangs of natural hunger. Satan had evidently been watching his opportunity, and now judged that at last it had come. He considered that our Lord must be weakened by the long fast and wearied by the complete solitude. Let us remember that our Infernal Foe is always going about seeking to profit by every occasion, in order to bring our souls to destruction, and that we must not wonder if, even immediately after a more than usually devout Meditation or fervent Communion or successful Retreat, we find ourselves beset with violent Temptations. This earthly life is a perpetual conflict with our own Passions and with our spiritual Enemies. We can never afford to be off our guard even for one moment. The Tempter, then, approached our Divine Master with affected compassion, and pointing to the stones scattered on the ground, " If Thou art the Son of God," he said, " command that these stones become bread."

We may note that his lofty intellect is so darkened by Pride as still to make him doubt the Divinity of Christ. His words, though apparently a well-meaning suggestion, are in reality nothing but a subtle appeal to that reliance on earthly goods, which we have already considered in the meditation on Two Standards. " You have been fasting, my friend, it is proper that you should take some nourishment, you have a right to it, or rather it is your duty, in fact, unless you do so, you will not be able to accomplish the mission for which you are preparing." Is it not thus more or less that the Devil at times tempts also Religious? What he proposes at first is not a sin, but only an inordination, just a slight indulgence, a little relaxation, taken without regard to the Will of God, as manifested by our Rules, our Resolutions, our Superiors. It sounds so plausible, it seems so innocent, but in reality it is nothing but a piece of cunning deceit. This First Temptation, then, is one to Sensuality and to Distrust.

How does our Lord meet the tempter? With humble submission to the truth of the Sacred Scriptures, that is, to the Guidance of the Holy Ghost, and with boundless confidence in the Providence of the Eternal Father. "It is written," He answered, "man liveth not by bread alone but by every word that cometh from the mouth of God." (Deut. 8:3.) It is well worth our while to consider this answer, in order to understand and practise the great principle involved. There are two kinds of life; the one, natural, physical, inferior, which is sustained by earthly food; the other supernatural, spiritual, superior, which in the accomplishment of the Divine Will is sustained by Heavenly Grace; and this higher life we have to foster, if necessary, even at the expense of the lower. "Man liveth not by bread alone." In how many circumstances I could apply this truth: in weariness, hunger, privation, sickness! These and similar hardships may afflict my lower life, but at the same time are certain to benefit my higher life, because they are ordained for that purpose by the Adorable Will of God. Again, stones are not intended to be turned into food. To wish to anticipate the time and manner and means by which the Lord intends to come to our assistance by an act of His Almighty Will, shows disbelief in His Infinite Power and distrust in His All-Loving Providence. It is precisely under the most trying circumstances that we should practise the most child-like abandonment. As the Most High daily provided the Israelites in the desert with manna, so He can supply our need, if He pleases, even by a miracle. But Jesus had come to be like one of us, and He did not wish to exert His Divine Omnipotence in order to relieve His bodily exhaustion.

Second Point. The Second Temptation.

"Then the Devil took Him up into the holy City and set Him upon the pinnacle of the Temple, and said to Him [with feigned veneration], 'If Thou be the Son of God, cast Thyself down, for it is written, that He has given His angels charge over Thee, and in their hands they shall bear Thee up, lest perhaps Thou dash Thy foot against a stone.'" Christ, the King of Glory, permits Himself to be transported by Satan, the Prince of Darkness. What a humiliation voluntarily submitted to for my sake! I must, then, not become alarmed and disheartened if the temptation grows more and more violent, even if my body, my imagination, my very senses, should seem to be under the power of the evil spirits. For, as long as my will remains united to God in humble prayer, I have nothing to fear from all the assults of the enemy. It is worth observing that the Devil in quoting the ninetieth psalm omits a very important clause, namely, "to keep Thee in all Thy ways," which limits the application to any person that is acting in obedience to Providence and not going outside his appointed sphere. Cunning and deceit form the characteristic traits of the fallen angels.

This Second Temptation is one to Presumption and Vanity. "Cast yourself down from this lofty pinnacle; you will not receive any hurt since God has promised you His special protection; and the multitudes gathered down below in the courts of the Temple will instantly recognize you as the Messias." It is a common maneuver of Satan, when he is foiled in some temptation, to change suddenly to the contrary one.

So here, after first endeavoring to provoke distrust, he now strives to instil presumption.   But his other aim is to induce our Lord to an act of vanity, to a display of power that would attract public applause.   Love of the empty honors of the world, according to the usual tactics of Satan, follows after love of the perishable goods of the earth, as St. Ignatius points out in the meditation on Two Standards, and as any one can verify by observing what continually engrosses the hearts and minds of men.   Even Religious may experience this temptation, especially under the form of human respect.   " Do not run away from these visitors at the first sound of the bell," the Tempter will whisper, " they won't know what to make of you."   Or again : " Do not break off this recreation so suddenly, be a little more condescending, make yourself sociable."   Other Religious, subject to vanity, may be inclined to force themselves upon the public notice by advertising their doings, their plans, or their theories, preferably with a smiling photo the better to arrest attention.   But also temptations to presumption are not unusual among Religious.   " Why should you give up this reading?   Don't be so fidgety, you must learn to brave the danger, you have to acquire a knowledge of these things some time, and for the rest trust in God."

The answer of our Adorable Master is another act of humility by quoting once more the words of Holy Writ : " It is written, thou shalt not tempt the Lord thy God."   The Devil had invoked the authority of the Sacred Scriptures, and it is by this same authority that our Lord confounds the cunning of the tempter and lays bare his malice.   This may well remind us that we must fight our enemy with his own weapons ; what he suggests to render us vain we ought to turn to our Humiliation; what he holds up to make us impatient we must embrace as a welcome Cross; what he offers us to indulge our gluttony we must abstain from for our Mortification.   So also, the more he engages us to show ourselves before men on account of our growing knowledge or advancing age, the more we must seek to remain in the background; and the more he wants to discourage us by enfeebled health from laboring for the salvation and sanctification of souls, the more we ought to put forth all our energy of body and soul in union with our Divine Master.

"Thou shalt not tempt the Lord thy God."   (Deut. 6:16.)   Also to Religious our Blessed Lord addresses this admonition, particularly to such as wish to live within the sacred walls of the convent, without making progress, without striving after Holiness.   These surely are tempting God, by refusing Him that special Service for which He called them to this lofty State and bestowed on them so many graces.   But also those may be said to tempt God, who wish to become holy without using the means placed at their disposal; who do not apply themselves to prayer, obedience, self-conquest, and charity; who do not seek in all things their greater Humiliation and continual Mortification. Again, such also would be tempting God, who pray for the grace of rectifying their inordinate attachment to some creature without giving it up as far as they can; or who expect to derive lasting fruit from the annual Retreat without striving to get a clear Knowledge of the obstacles which up to this have kept them back on the road to Perfection, and without making such practical and generous Resolutions as are most likely to insure their advancement for the future.

Third Point.   The Third Temptation.

Again the Devil led our Lord to a high mountain —

probably the top of Mount Quarantana — and there represented to Him in an instant the kingdoms of the world in all their earthly splendor, saying to Him, " All these I will give Thee, if falling down before me Thou adore me." This last temptation, made without any deceitful reference to Holy Scripture or any pretended sympathy for our exhausted Savior, bluntly proposes a most grievous sin of idolatry. Satan knew from experience how far men will go when inflamed by the desire of earthly goods and worldly honors. Those who are determined to satisfy these inordinate cravings, not wishing to acknowledge and worship God, the Infinite Goodness, will degrade themselves so far as to give adoration to the very Demons of Hell. In this temptation, then, the Devil unmasks himself, he shows his ultimate purpose, the unbounded, consummate Pride of the wretched soul that has allowed itself to be ensnared and enchained by his empty promises. Let us well consider these awful chains riveted on so many men, and be on our guard against the impudent deceptions and ceaseless machinations of our Infernal Enemy.

Though Satan had obtained nothing in his preceding attempts, he does not hesitate to propose now a most horrible crime in an abrupt and insolent manner. It looks like an explosion of malice; he is no longer able to conceal or restrain his fury. Thus the Devil may often act with fervent souls that do not permit themselves to be caught in his Snares. Hence, once more, we must never be frightened, but bravely resist, putting all our trust in God. The very fierceness and magnitude of a temptation is a sign that our enemy is getting desperate, because he has been worsted in his carefully laid plans and cunningly disguised attacks.

Jesus answers by a renewed profession of humility:

"Begone, Satan, for it is written, the Lord thy God shalt thou adore and Him alone shalt thou serve." (Deut. 6:13.) To the overt temptation Jesus opposes direct resistance; the blasphemous pretension of the Fiend He meets with the holy scorn of a soul united to God. "Begone, Satan." No hesitation, no reasoning. It is thus that I too must reject all evil proposals, with firm and calm reliance on God, always falling back for my defense on His Divine Word, that is, on His Adorable Will, in whatever way manifested, the Commandments, my Rules, my Resolutions, the injunctions and wishes of my Superior, the directions and counsels of my Spiritual Guide, to whom my conscience should be ever wholly open.

Then the Devil withdrew for a time, and the Angels came and ministered to Jesus. After temptation, peace and consolation. But even during the combat, the Heavenly Spirits afford us protection and stand by our side. Yes, indeed, the words of Holy Writ, though referring principally to Christ our Lord, may be applied secondarily to every fervent Religious: "God has given His Angels charge over thee, to guide thee in all thy ways." And this supernatural consolation is only a faint foretaste of the inconceivable reward laid up in Heaven for those who here on earth have shared in the hardships and conflicts of their Lord and King. However, it consists not so much in spiritual sweetness as in spiritual progress, more Light, more Strength, more Love.

Colloquy with Jesus, the Conqueror of Hell; imploring abundant grace that I may bravely labor and struggle under His Standard; that I may promptly and energetically resist every kind of temptation after His Example; that I may frequently experience cold, hunger, weariness, and often bear slights, reproaches, insults, for Love of Him. Again and again I will promise Him with all the earnestness of my soul, to seek everywhere my greater humiliation and continual mortification, that thus I may be enabled to come off victorious in all the assaults of the evil spirits, instead of being disgracefully worsted, as has happened so often in the past. I will also give most fervent thanks to Christ my King, because, though He had no need of such special preparation, being hypostatically united to the Eternal Word, yet, for my instruction and encouragement, He not only lived for thirty years in poverty and lowliness, but, just before His encounter with Satan, humbled Himself most profoundly by receiving the baptism of John, and then persevered in prayer, solitude, and fasting, for the space of forty days. Accordingly, with firmer confidence than ever, I will appeal to His Sacred Heart for the grace of following Him henceforth more closely and more steadfastly in the Conquest of Souls. — Our Father.

THE TRIPLE FRUIT OF HUMILITY

Not a few spiritual writers maintain that one of the most remarkable phenomena in asceticism is the undeniable fact, that several Saints, at the very time when they had already reached a high degree of perfection, occasionally declared themselves the worst sinners on earth. But what really seems much more remarkable, is this other undisputed fact, that all the Saints, without exception, habitually treated the persons with whom they came in contact as their betters; or, which comes to the same thing, they habitually treated themselves as worse than all the rest. Indeed, for a man to call himself the worst, the weakest, the dullest individual of the human family, is after all a comparatively easy matter; since hardly one soul out of a thousand will believe him, while the remaining nine hundred and ninety-nine,— with the exception, perhaps, of half a dozen simple folks that will mistake his words for a proof of Humility,— will prefer to think that he does not believe it himself. But to act invariably, on all occasions, towards all other men, as their inferior, is something diametrically opposed to the most potent tendency of our nature as well as to the most deep-seated prejudice of mankind, and, consequently, extremely difficult.

Supposing, however, a person sincerely and constantly acts as everybody's servant, we need not be surprised that he should now and then declare himself such; for this would only be repeating in words what he has been emphatically asserting all along by deeds. Surely, if a virtuous man, not to say a Saint, treats everybody else as better than himself, we must conclude that he really looks upon all others in that light, and if he does look upon them as his betters, it follows logically that they truly are such — for else his virtue, his sanctity, would be based on an erroneous judgment; a conclusion which is inadmissible — that they are such, not possibly, or probably, or conditionally, but actually, certainly, and categorically. The only thing we need not grant, is that they are such in every sense or from every point of view. In what sense, then, and from what standpoint, can we truly and positively deem and call ourselves worse than all the rest of men, and consequently treat them as our betters?

The only satisfactory answer to this query is furnished by St. Thomas (2-2, q. 161, a.3) and runs thus: "By considering in ourselves only what is our own," namely, our utter nothingness and profound sinfulness, "while considering in all others only what is God's," that is, the gifts they have received from Him in the natural and the supernatural order. But, some will say, of what practical use is this? In this sense, of course, every man is worse than all the rest. A child knows that. Quite so, this statement of the Angelic Doctor requires no proof; in fact, we might call it a mere truism. But just let us try to act upon it sincerely, habitually, constantly; and it will soon assume for us an altogether different aspect.

Yet, if we wish to become humble, that is exactly what we have to do. For Humility, according to the same authority, inclines us always to take our proper place with regard to God and whatever represents God. Now God is infinitely exalted above all created being and perfection, while we, as we are of ourselves, are placed at the other extremity, infinitely below all created being and perfection. This also is plain enough even to a child; in fact, it is the same truism as the one just mentioned, only in a slightly altered form. But always to take that place, at least inwardly if we cannot do so outwardly, never to lift up ourselves unduly before God or anything that represents God, there lies the difficulty and there also lies the virtue of Humility as practised by the Saints. They treated themselves and wished to be treated as worse than all sinners, simply because they recognized in even the greatest sinner some limited participation in the Adorable Perfection of the Most High — a participation which they, the Saints, would not and could not find in themselves as their own.

On the other hand, as St. Thomas also teaches, Humility does not require that a man, taken precisely for what he is of himself, should lower himself beneath any other man, also taken precisely for what he is of himself; much less does Humility require that a man, considered as divinely endowed with various gifts, should lower himself beneath another man, considered without any such gifts, as a mere sinful nothing. Either would be an absurdity, while Humility is but the practical embodiment of a truth so simple and evident, that we may well style it a truism.

But why is it not sufficient to acknowledge and praise God personally, as the Supreme and Absolute Perfection? Why must we, besides, recognize and honor that Perfection in all creatures? Because they all bear an essential relation to Him and hence necessarily represent Him; in other words, because He placed us in the midst of creatures, precisely in order that we might have an ever-present opportunity of ex-

hibiting towards Him that profound veneration, un-
qualified submission, and supreme love, which are due
to His Infinite Excellence.

This indirect but continual worship would have
been indispensable, even if we had been born in original justice; how much more so now in our fallen condition, now that we are naturally so full of pride that
it pervades, like a virulent poison, our entire being
and infects, so to speak, the very marrow of our bones?
Pride is the very antipode of Humility, or to borrow
St. Augustine's forcible expression: "As Humility
is the love of God to the contempt of self, so Pride is
the love of self to the contempt of God." Again, just
as Humility presupposes a most plain and palpable
truth apprehended by the mind, so pride has for its
intellectual prerequisite, not mere ignorance, but
falsehood, a gross and glaring falsehood, by which we
pretend to be something of ourselves, apart from God,
and fancy that our proper place is somewhere between
the infinitely high and the infinitely low, but not
indeed at the very bottom of the abyss of nothingness
and sin. In fact, Pride goes so far as actually to
usurp the throne of the Most High. Instead of wor-
shiping God made Man, it worships man made god.

Saturated, as we are, through and through, with
this hellish venom, which is ready to break out in our
every thought, word, and action, true reverence
towards God is a sheer impossibility, unless we labor
incessantly at counteracting this loathsome disease,
this desperate madness, this monstrous perversion of
truth and order and justice; by casting ourselves beneath every one of the numberless beings that surround us, in so far as each, in its own more or less
limited way, represents to us the Supreme Majesty of
God; by shutting our eyes, as it were, to all that is

weak, defective, and hurtful in other creatures, in order to observe in them only what is powerful, perfect, and beneficial; and, on the other hand, by being blind, so to say, to whatever goodness we ourselves may possess through the Divine Liberality, in order to rivet our gaze only on what we are by our own birthright and achievement; namely, negation, corruption, and degradation.

And in this we can never go too far. For Humility is not a matter of sentiment, nor does it admit of exaggeration; but it must ever remain in strict accordance with the truth and perishes immediately on being severed from the truth. It is, in fact, a Practical Love of Truth, yea, the Only Genuine Love of Truth, for it is the love of a truth that is most distasteful, most abhorrent to our fallen nature, a truth that knocks down and dashes to pieces the phantastic idol of our inordinate self-esteem.

To obtain Humility, we must get wholly possessed of this truth; namely, that apart from God we are nothing and worse than nothing; we must identify ourselves with it; we must act upon it with unwearied energy and a holy, unconquerable obstinacy; act upon it continuously, in spite of the engrossment of duties, the cares of business, or the distractions of recreation, in spite of the buoyancy of health or the languor of indisposition, the elation of success or the depression of failure, in spite of the tumult of passion, the onslaught of temptation, the bitterness of spiritual dereliction, or the sweetness of heavenly delights. And if we happen to notice something wrong, something deficient, something imperfect in any other creature, we must invariably take it as a most useful object-lesson, teaching us unmistakably what we are of ourselves, and reminding us emphatically of our own unlimited capacity for evil. In this way, we shall neither be disturbed nor disheartened by our own failings, nor be surprised or scandalized at our neighbor's faults, but all our knowledge will conspire to make us despise self more heartily and revere God more profoundly, in accordance with St. Augustine's loving prayer: "Grant me, O God, to know myself and to know Thee, that I may despise myself and love Thee."

Now, the benefits we derive from Humility are many and varied. This lowly virtue makes us less liable to error and protects us against fraud and imposture; it cures us of the baneful habit of criticising and ridiculing whatever happens to be at variance with our pet ideas and selfish aims; it frees us from the incubus of self-consciousness; and it renders us a welcome friend to all men, even to the proud. But leaving these minor advantages to future consideration and personal experience, let us for the present concentrate our attention on the Three Principal Fruits of Perfection produced by Humility; namely, a Life of Loving Prayer, a Life of Constant Mortification, and a Life of Ardent Charity.

First Fruit of Humility: a Life of Loving Prayer.

Evidently, it is only in proportion as we are penetrated by a keen sense of our own utter helplessness, that we feel prompted to have recourse to God, to place in Him our entire trust, and to pour out before Him urgent and incessant petitions for His All-Powerful Assistance. But if we do so, since the Lord hears us whenever we pray to Him with Humility and Confidence, He will gradually flood our soul with His supernatural light and reveal to us our numberless miseries ever more distinctly, whilst He will in the same measure sustain our spirit with His heavenly grace and encourage us to renew our entreaties with ever greater fervor and frequency.

Besides, Humility, by causing us to refer to God alone all the perfections we notice in any of His creatures and all their imperfections to ourselves, enables us truly to live, according to the maxim of the Saints, as if the only two beings in this world were God and Self. Thus we are not only kept persistently in His Adorable Presence, offering Him a perpetual sacrifice of praise, abandoning ourselves entirely to the rule of His Never-Failing Providence, and directing all our actions solely to His Greater Glory; but we are also continually borne up from the consideration of these creatures, on the wings of a most child-like and self-forgetful admiration, to Him, the Inexhaustible Source of all perfection and beauty, ever exclaiming in spirit with the Royal Psalmist: "O Lord, how wonderful is Thy Name throughout the universe! As often as I behold the firmament, the work of Thy Fingers, and contemplate the moon and the stars which Thou didst fashion, I am lost in astonishment that Thou shouldst be mindful of man and shouldst visit the son of man in Thy Mercy."

But when reflecting how this infinitely Great God not only condescends to be mindful of man and to visit him in His Mercy, not only vouchsafes to labor, as it were, for man, in all His creatures, but even has deigned to come down from His realm of endless bliss, in order to be mocked and calumniated, to be trampled and spit upon, to be scourged and crucified for man, and actually goes so far as to conceal every vestige of His Sovereign Majesty under the lowly appearances of food and drink, from sheer excess of goodness toward a being so wretched, so despicable, so ungrateful; then the humble soul seems no longer able to contain herself, she is pierced with rapturous grief, she is merged in torments and yet would not part with them for all the joys of earth, though she does not even think of this, but only adores and loves. And just as worldlings are ever looking for amusements and distinctions, and hankering after affection and esteem; so this soul is wholly bent on trials and humiliations, and thirsts for hatred and contumely, because she cannot bear, or rather wholly abhors, to be treated better or to be more respected than her Lord and Savior, Jesus Christ.

Second Fruit of Humility: a Life of Constant Mortification.

As soon as we come to realize, on the one hand, God's Supreme Majesty and Incomparable Holiness, and, on the other, our own utter nothingness and manifold sinfulness, we cannot suffer that there should remain in us any danger of future disobedience or any trace of former rebellion; and hence, while waging an implacable warfare with all the corrupt tendencies of our nature, we feel an urgent need of paying, by this very means, even the last farthing of that immense debt we have contracted by our sins towards the Divine Justice.

Again, the thought of God's Astonishing Goodness and Mercy towards men, of His Labors and Watches, of His Passion and Death, of His Apparent Annihilation in the Holy Eucharist, fills the humble heart with such an overwhelming sense of the heinousness of even the smallest deliberate venial sin, that no penance appears too hard or too long, no tears too constant or too copious, no contrition too intense, to atone for such black ingratitude.

Besides, we are conscious that as long as our soul

is marred by any stain of guilt or punishment, there can be no question of that intimate friendship, for which the continual contemplation of God's Ineffable Beauty and Perfection makes us long and yearn with the utmost vehemence. Spurred on, by this loving shame and burning with a holy hatred of self, we invite all creatures to avenge on us the outrages we have committed against the Most High, and thank every being that brings upon us pain, distress, or contempt, for thus fitting us for a closer union with our Adorable Master, a sweeter foretaste of the beatific vision. In fact, this very desire of purgation and atonement imparts to our hearts a marked resemblance to the Sacred Heart of Jesus, ever Radiant with Absolute Purity yet ever Consumed with Insatiable Longing to blot out our sins by the unspeakable tortures, anguish, and ignominy of the Cross.

Third Fruit of Humility: a Life of Ardent Fraternal Charity.

True Humility not only inclines us to give to all the preference in everything and sincerely to esteem them as our betters, but it also makes us acknowledge, revere, and cherish in every one God our Lord. Hence, just as Humility leads us unerringly to the love of God in Himself, so it leads us necessarily to the love of God in His image, wherever and in whatever degree that image may be found, but especially where that image is shining forth, or at least is intended to shine forth, with transcendent brightness and beauty, as in man.

Again, since Humility indirectly renders man subject and conformable to all Divine Order, Law, Counsel, and Example, the mere recollection of the Son of God expiring on the Cross for the salvation of the world, a simple glance at the Crucifix, is sufficient to inflame the humble Christian with efficacious zeal for procuring the good of his brethren, the conversion of sinners, the advancement of the just, the exaltation of the One, Holy, Catholic, and Apostolic Church.

Moreover, for a Spiritual Being, whether Divine, Angelic, or Human, love is an imperative necessity, so much so that St. Catherine of Genoa declares that hell would not be hell, were it not that the reprobate are forever deprived of love. "To love and to be loved," says St. Augustine, "is the soul's incessant craving." Consequently, as soon as the obstacles to holy love are removed by Humility, the soul is kindled with this celestial fire and transformed by it into the likeness of the Infinite Goodness, God. And as the Divine Goodness is essentially communicative, actually benefiting every creature to the full of its capacity, this supernatural likeness renders us at once efficient instruments of blessing to other beings, so that the higher we rise in heavenly favor, the deeper we lower ourselves again as the devoted servants of all, striving to bestow on each, according as circumstances will suggest, esteem, affection, encouragement, care, comfort, assistance, whatever good, in short, Providence may have placed at our disposal. However rude, however degraded, or however perverse our neighbor may be, we cherish him with a love far more tender and far more operative, than we ever felt naturally for our dearest friends. We embrace the whole world, we desire to toil and suffer for our charges, for our Community, for our Country, for the entire Church, and whether living or dying we long to become, in union with our Adorable Master, victims for the salvation and sanctification of souls.

In connection with this, the end of our holy Institute, let us never lose sight of the grand principle laid

down by St. Paul: " The foolish things of the world
hath God chosen that He may confound the wise, and
the weak things of the world hath God chosen that He
man confound the strong, and the base things of the
world, and the things that are contemptible, hath God
chosen, and the things that are not, that He might
bring to naught the things that are, so that no flesh
should glory in His sight." This is the one absolutely
indispensable preparation for the great work before
us; to become foolish, weak, base, contemptible, and
hateful, in our own sincere conviction and inmost appreciation. Without this preparation, no talent, no
learning, no experience, no polish, no influence will be
of any avail for the propagation of the Kingdom of
Christ. But, if we are thoroughly humble, gentle,
and meek, our various ministries and our very lives
will be blessed with a wonderful efficacy for winning back sinners and leading men to Heaven.

Such, then, are the admirable effects of Humility:
**Love of God, Love of the Cross, and Love of our
Neighbor.** Surely, it is well worth the trouble to
pray and labor for this virtue with all the energy
of our being. True, our Pride is a vice most difficult
to eradicate. Yet what would be utterly impossible
to merely human efforts, becomes not only possible
but even easy and delightful with the help of Grace.
Day after day, then, through the all-powerful mediation of Mary, Mother of God, the most lowly Virgin of
Nazareth, I must keep imploring real and solid Humility from the Sacred Heart of Jesus, the Supreme
Pattern and Prolific Fountainhead of every Virtue.
Moreover, relying exclusively on His light and
strength, I will unflinchingly descend into the dark
abyss of my origin; I will diligently explore the foul

recesses of my vices; I will persistently strive to
bring both my interior and my exterior into exact
conformity with the truth; I will unhesitatingly embrace every lawful means to remain completely hidden, unnoticed, and ignored, or else, to be known
for what I really am and despised to the full of my
deserts; I will eagerly seize upon every opportunity
of lowering myself beneath other men and other
creatures; I will everywhere claim, as my special
privilege, to be allowed to render others the most
laborious and most menial services; I will inwardly
abase myself whenever any one bestows on me even
the slightest attention or the most trifling benefit;
and I will sincerely rejoice at the certain prospect
that, sooner or later, all my vileness shall be revealed
before the whole world on the day of the General
Judgment, the day of the triumphant vindication of
the Rights of God, the day of the endless exaltation
of the Divine Goodness.

What, indeed, would be the use of cajoling ourselves with dangerous illusions, of wasting the precious time in attempting to effect an impossible com-
promise between Grace and Nature, and of squander-
ing our energies in fruitless endeavors to rear a lofty
structure of Sanctity before we have laid deep and
solid the foundation of Humility? God unceasingly
demands our total and absolute surrender, as the one
condition to raise us to real Holiness and inconceivable Glory. "Every one of you," says our Divine
Master, "that does not renounce all he possesses, cannot be My disciple." And again: "Unless you become as little children, you shall not enter the Kingdom of Heaven." Our corrupt nature, on the
contrary, unceasingly clamors for a recognition and
independence which inevitably leads to unutterable

woe and infinite disgrace. This absolute surrender of ourselves, this mystic renunciation of all we possess, this total abandonment of our false pretensions, this complete subjection of our inborn lawlessness, is Humility.

Humility is the root of Sanctity, the measure of Sanctity, the safeguard of Sanctity; Humility practically is Sanctity. Hence, the first, the chiefest, and the only thing we have to do is to humble our own self. We must break off with this perfidious rebel, we must drive this wretch back into his native nothingness, we must confound this arrogant monster with his blunders and misdeeds, we must scorn the fantastic notions and morbid desires of this maniac, we must make this proud demon forswear all pretense to even the slightest share in whatever good there may be either in our body, or in our soul, or in our labors, or in our connections, or in our nationality, or in our Institute.

Yes, even in our holy Institute, for though this our beloved Mother, thanks to the Divine Favor, has ever done and is still doing great things for the salvation and sanctification of souls, and though it be the bounden duty of every true child of hers to take a deep interest, a noble pride, an intense delight, both in her grand past and in her promising future; yet, as soon as a member begins to look upon this work with self-complacent satisfaction; as soon as he refers to it with uncalled-for frequency and emphasis; as soon as it tends to lessen his esteem for any of his fellow men; as soon as it no longer sends to his brow the blush of shame and indignation for still falling so far short of the lofty perfection put before him by his Saintly Founder; as soon as it does not rouse his whole being to more faithful imitation of his

Spiritual Ancestors and Brothers, to more strenuous exertion along the path of virtue and in the Lord's Vineyard, to more continual practice of Self-Denial and Self-Abasement; that moment he proves a traitor to his Order, a destroyer of its widespread Influence, a profaner of the heroism of its Confessors and the blood of its Martyrs. Every Religious Society was founded on Humility, and in Humility lies all its strength, its beauty, its glory, its efficacy, and its very life.

THE TEMPEST ON THE LAKE

Introductory Remarks.— With regard to temptations many Religious fall into two mistakes. On the one hand, they make too little of self-complacency, vanity, disobedience, uncharitableness, resentment, criticisms, and complaints; while on the other hand, they make too much of thoughts, imaginations, or emotions contrary to chastity. They readily yield to the former and feel little or no sorrow for doing so; but about the latter they get deeply disturbed and sorely vexed, instead of calmly resisting them with prompt and fervent prayer. Whence this difference? Temptations against chastity make us realize more vividly that our wretched soul is imprisoned in a corruptible body and thus they shock our pride. But instead of humbling ourselves, we begin to fret and worry to no purpose, except to render the temptation more persistent and violent. Consequently, the remedy is to apply ourselves more earnestly to the practice of Humility, Obedience, and Charity.

Subject of this Meditation.— Christ our Lord, after having fed an immense multitude with five loaves and two fishes, ordered His Disciples to retire to the boat and to go before Him across the lake, whilst He dismissed the people and went up into the mountain to pray. A violent storm arose and the boat was being tossed about on the waves, when Jesus came to His Disciples walking on the waters. As they thought that it was an apparition, He said to them, " It is I, fear ye not." Peter, at His command, came to Him, walking upon the water, but becoming alarmed began to sink. Our Lord, however, saved him saying, " O thou of little faith, why didst thou doubt? " And when they had entered the boat the wind ceased.— Matt. 14 :22-32.

Composition of Place.— The lake of Gennesareth swept by the storm, and the boat of the Apostles at the mercy of the waves.

Petition.— From the various details of this occurrence, to gain a more intimate knowledge of our Lord, so that I may love Him more fervently and follow Him more generously.

First Point.   The Disciples on the Lake.

It is the evening after the multiplication of the loaves, by which Christ had given such a striking proof of His Divine Power and foreshadowed the mystery of the Holy Eucharist. And now, almost immediately after His Apostles had filled twelve baskets with the fragments left of the bread, precisely now that the people aroused by this stupendous miracle, insist on proclaiming Jesus their long-expected Messias, their King, He is putting the obedience and confidence of His privileged Disciples to a most severe test. Without allowing them to watch and direct the course of this popular enthusiasm, so congenial to their national aspirations and their personal ambition, He simply bids them go before Him across the lake. He does not even tell them when or how He will rejoin them. Just now, when the prospects of their beloved Master look so fair, they must leave Him. So it may happen likewise to Religious, that, precisely when the circumstances seem most favorable for doing their work, either individually or collectively, they are suddenly removed from their sphere of action. Let us always humbly and lovingly adore the dispositions of Providence, especially in the arrangements of Superiors; but for this purpose it is evidently necessary that we should keep ourselves thoroughly detached from every creature.

The wind is contrary, the sky is overcast, the day is waning, yet the Disciples obey. This lake on which they are ordered to embark, may well symbolize the present world with its many dangers and sudden storms. It would, no doubt, have been much more agreeable for them to stay with Jesus on the safe shore or even to retire with Him up on the lonely mountain to some place of rest; but the moment Superiors ordain otherwise or Providence disposes differently, we must sacrifice all our personal views and natural inclinations with a holy joy and eagerness. Then, whatever difficulties turn up in our new career, we may count on the Divine Assistance that the waves will not overwhelm our skiff, that the waters of tribulation will not submerge our soul. But we must take care to have a pure intention in setting out. For, if our heart is not exclusively fixed on God, if we start out with a view to some personal advantage, then even the lightest breeze of adversity is sure to upset us. Such, perhaps, was the case in the past when, on account of some trifling ailment, we importuned the Superior to be relieved from our charge or even to be recalled from our post.

The Disciples, therefore, set out together, a little band, united by the ties of charity, bound for the same port, and pledged forever to mutual assistance. In this respect they may remind us of a Religious

Community. How closely united all its members ought to be as true brothers by supernatural love, animated with the sole desire of pleasing their Heavenly Father and of rendering one another, for His sake, every possible service. Am I such a Religious? Do I at least pray daily, during the Holy Mass and in my Holy Communion, for my Superiors as well as for the other members, for the sick and suffering, particularly for those detained in Purgatory?

But as the night advances they are being tossed about upon the billows, unable to make any headway against the fierce tempest. A faithful picture of what happens to us in the Spiritual Life. We pushed from shore full of energy, our first exertions made us get on fairly,— such was probably our noviceship,— but then darkness began to fall and to grow thicker, a contrary wind arose and waxed stronger, we were no longer capable of making any progress, soon we were drifting at the mercy of the waves, we felt our courage vanishing and feared every moment to go down. God permits these periods of trial and temptation, of desolation and failure, in order that we may learn experimentally to distrust our own weakness and may thus be urged to place our entire reliance on Him. Yet, all the while, we seem to be alone and abandoned.

Jesus had remained on shore. After dismissing the excited multitude, He had withdrawn to the mountain to pray. Do I too have recourse to special prayer, when either I myself am tempted or some other member is afflicted, when the welfare of the Community is threatened by adversity or contradiction, when it seems to me that fervor is yielding to relaxation and zeal is lapsing into indifference? Meanwhile our Lord is fully aware of the critical situation of His cherished Apostles, He is spiritually present in their midst, He diligently watches over their bark, and it is especially for them that He pours out His most ardent supplications. So now in Heaven, He is ever pleading for each of us the infinite merits of His Sacred Wounds. So, again, He remains ever with us, the Spouse of our souls, in the Adorable Eucharist. No doubt, the Apostles on their part thought of their loving Master; though, perhaps, some felt inclined to murmur at having been thus exposed to imminent danger of death. How foolish, how ungrateful, it would have been for them to entertain such a thought. I must, then, never think that I am really alone and abandoned in my difficulties and hardships. At the very hour when Jesus appears to be farthest away, He intercedes for me most efficaciously with the Eternal Father, and the moment I seem on the point of perishing is just the one at which He will show Himself again to restore me to safety and peace. "Let not your heart be troubled nor let it be afraid," neither in darkness nor in danger, neither in desolation nor in death.

Second Point. Our Lord Comes to His Disciples. About the fourth watch of the night, that is to say a little before dawn, Jesus comes down from the mountain and goes across the waves towards the boat. He walks on the water, thus showing that He is the Sovereign Lord of all creation, and that He rules everything by His mere Will. Let us adore Him in this manifestation of His Infinite Majesty; let us beg to be wholly immolated in body and mind to His Divine Glory. How eagerly the lower creatures offer Him their miraculous support and protection! So they often did also in the case of His Saints.

What confidence, therefore, should be ours as long as we are acting under the orders of our King, combating under the Standard of our Captain, toiling and suffering in affectionate subjection to our Superiors? Really, our confidence should be unlimited, no less than our devotion.

As the Disciples see our Lord advancing towards them, they take Him for an apparition and cry out for fear. Under the stress of tribulation we too find it sometimes difficult to recognize our Divine Master. We are full of alarm through lack of Faith, we fail to see God in whatever befalls us through the agency of His creatures, and especially in what is imposed or entailed on us by Holy Obedience. But we are also full of fear through lack of trust in the Wisdom and Goodness of our Heavenly Father. How displeasing, how offensive, such diffidence and cowardice must be to His Sacred Heart. But our Blessed Savior quickly reassures His frightened Apostles saying: "Be of good heart; it is I, fear not!" Thus, when Jesus deigns to reveal Himself to our troubled mind and to let His sweet voice resound within our afflicted soul, He treats us so lovingly and inspires us with so much courage, that all apprehensions vanish at once. And then we feel able to brave even worse tempests.

No sooner had Jesus entered the boat than, by a mere act of His Will, the wind ceased, and in another moment they found themselves landing on the desired shore. So when Divine Grace descends into our soul, it stills the most violent disturbances, and though, while the trouble lasted, we were apparently making no progress whatever, yet now, of a sudden, we can notice a considerable gain. Let us, then, not be disheartened because the trial is prolonged or because we cannot perceive any spiritual improvement. During the storm we are unable to estimate how much headway we are really making; and even, if we had not made any at all, Jesus, by a mere act of His Will, can cause us to reach in an instant the object of our lifelong prayers and endeavors. Let us, therefore, never slacken in our longing nor grow despondent in our striving after Holiness.

Third Point. Our Lord and Saint Peter.

When Jesus had said, " It is I," Peter cried out, " Lord, if it be Thou, bid me come to Thee upon the waters." And our Savior answered, " Come." What was it that urged Peter to make such a bold proposal? It was undoubtedly his strong faith and his ardent devotion, the desire of being as soon as possible with his Beloved Master. Let us imitate the Apostle in these his characteristic virtues. Let us, if possible, anticipate in the chapel the hour for meditation, office, examen, and visit. Jesus did not blame Peter's request; on the contrary, He granted it approvingly. We are thus reminded that it is praiseworthy to aspire after the closest union with Christ our Lord and to offer ourselves to walk the unknown paths of Supernatural Prayer. According to the testimony of the Saints and the teaching of the Doctors, nothing is better calculated to cleanse the soul from all earthly dross than the graces communicated to it in Mystical Contemplation. While we must never attempt anything beyond what is common, without an explicit call, an authentic invitation of our Adorable Spouse, we should diligently prepare ourselves for this immense favor by unwavering fidelity and great generosity.

Will Peter, consequently, reach Jesus safely? Yes,

but Jesus will also test the confidence and the humility of His Apostle. There comes a violent gust of wind; Peter too is now getting alarmed and begins to sink. But at once he cries out for help: " Lord, save me, I perish." Why does Peter sink? Because, in spite of the word of Jesus, he doubts of his own safety. So it may often go with us in the outward temptations to which we are exposed in consequence of the arrangements of Holy Obedience, or in the inward trials that come upon us on the road to sanctity through the permission of Divine Providence. But let us always do like the Apostle: let us call on Jesus, our Compassionate and Gracious Lord. Surely, if Peter had continued to doubt he would actually have gone under. But the very imminence of the peril gave him a deeper sense of his own nothingness and made him appeal with greater earnestness to his Loving Master.

Especially in those moments of difficulty or danger, when we find our confidence upset and our resolutions shaken, we should, with the utmost ardor, implore the mercy of our Heavenly Spouse. It was in order to comply with the Call of God that we entered the Religious State, and that we bound ourselves by the three Vows to bend all our energies and devote our whole life in striving after the Perfection of Charity, after the most Signal Service of our Adorable King, after the most Generous Imitation of Jesus our Lord. Let us, then, not get frightened by the thought of failure, or at the view of the obstacles, or by the length and severity of the contest. Far from it. But let us persist in appealing to our Divine Master, with a sincere acknowledgment of our past shortcomings and with a fervent prayer that He may deign to reach out His hand to us, as He did to Peter, and may enable us to enjoy at last His intimate Friendship, His holy Familiarity. " O thou of little faith, why didst thou fear? " Why so fainthearted, why so pusillanimous? All such apprehensions about the reality of our Vocation, all such misgivings about our ultimate success, are to be utterly discarded. Without trials, where would be the merit of faith, where would be the very possibility of progress?

Colloquy with Christ our Lord, begging Him to give us courage in the correspondence to His Call, in the accomplishment of His Will, in the practice of Religious Obedience. We will confess to Him our shame and sorrow for having on so many occasions yielded to lassitude and despondency; and we will fervently beseech Him to pardon our diffidence and cowardice. And then, with renewed trust in His Power, Wisdom, and Love, we will implore Him not to spare us any trials or afflictions that may advance us ever so little in His Holy Service or fit us in any degree however small for His closer Imitation.— Our Father.

SIXTH DAY

SPECIAL PATRON: St. Francis of Assisi.

MOTTO: " My God and my all."

SPIRIT: Esteem and Desire of Evangelical and Religious Perfection.

READING: Imitation; Bk. II, C. 9, 11.
              Bk. III, C. 6, 7, 12, 23, 31, 32,
                      35, 38, 43, 59.

Continue the work of yesterday, writing down your Lights and Resolutions, and reviewing the Notes of your previous Retreats. Consider also what subject you ought to take for your Particular Examen, and study out the details of your plan of campaign.

THE CONVERSION OF MARY MAGDALEN

Subject of this Meditation.—While Christ our Lord was at table in the house of Simon, the Pharisee, Mary Magdalen entered carrying an alabaster vase of perfume. Placing herself behind our Lord at His feet, she began to bathe them with her tears and to wipe them with her hair, and having kissed them repeatedly she poured out on them the precious ointment. As Simon, in his inmost heart, disapproved of all this, Christ spoke up for her, saying; " Many sins are forgiven her, because she hath loved much," and then turning to Magdalen He added; " Thy faith hath saved thee, go in peace."— Luke 7 :36-50.

Composition of Place.— The dining-room in the house of Simon.

Petition.— An intimate knowledge of my Lord, receiving the homage and penance of Mary Magdalen, that I may love Him more ardently and follow Him more closely, after her example, even to the foot of the Cross.

First Point. Persons.— While our Blessed Savior is at table, with Simon, the Apostles, and other invited guests, Mary Magdalen enters carrying in her hands an alabaster vial.

We may first contemplate our Dearest Lord reclining with perfect composure on the couch, according

to the Oriental custom, partaking modestly of the
food provided by His host, and striving by His
heavenly conversation to enlighten the minds and
touch the hearts of these prejudiced Pharisees. What
ardent zeal shines forth in his whole Person!
Though He had not been received with even the
ordinary marks of respect and kindness, customary
in those times among the Jews, though He had not
been offered any water for the almost indispensable
washing of the feet, nor the kiss of friendship equivalent to our more usual shaking of hands, and much
less any special token of esteem as the perfuming of
the head with some fragrant essence, yet our Divine
Master, full of humility, meekness, and love, would
seem only the more intent on procuring the happiness
and the sanctification of His ungracious host. Hence
we should learn not to lose heart if, in our visits
to the Blessed Sacrament, in our assistance at Holy
Mass, and even in our reception of the Adorable
Eucharist, we are at times so listless, so distracted, so
cold. Jesus knows our weakness, our misery, and if
only we humble ourselves sincerely and lovingly, He
will surely bestow on us the same graces as He would
have given us had we been recollected and fervent.
But how should I feel under similar circumstances?
How do I act when slighted or ignored?

But now, to the surprise and disgust of Simon, Mary
Magdalen unexpectedly enters the dining-room. She
was well known to all present as a sinful woman,
and she keenly felt all eyes, except those of our
Divine Savior, fastened on her person. What confusion! especially as she went straight to where our
Lord was reclining, knelt behind Him at His sacred
feet, and thus made a public avowal of her wicked
past, not only before the good and simple Apostles,

but also before the haughty and sanctimonious Pharisees, and before the numerous lookers-on, her own
townspeople. But she relished all this confusion,
for it gave some relief to the burning contrition that
filled her soul ; it was like a sweet balm to her crushed
and broken heart. Oh! why cannot I imitate her?
When I enter the chapel and come into the Presence
of my Divine Lord, why cannot I stir up similar
sentiments of confusion and contrition, considering
how inordinate and how sinful, perhaps, my life has
been during so many years? And when I am in the
company of my Brethren why cannot I realize more
vividly my utter unworthiness to associate and to sit
at the same table with them, or even to render any
service to these dear friends of my God and Savior?

Second Point. Actions.— Mary Magdalen kneels
down at the feet of our Lord, behind His adorable
Person; bathes them with her tears, wipes them with
her hair, covers them with kisses, and pours on them
the fragrant contents of the alabaster vase. Let me
study in detail these successive manifestations of her
humble and contrite love.

She kneels down behind the Person of our Lord,
as unworthy to meet His gaze or to occupy His attention; at His feet, bending down in the attitude of a
servant and a suppliant. How well it would be for
me, if I were to make it my custom thus to approach
my Divine Master, with interior and exterior abnega-
tion, when I begin by Prayer and, more especially,
when I am about to receive Him in Holy Communion.
There is no better preparation for this inestimable
favor than sincere Humility and fervent Humiliation;
and on our part it is the only preparation He looks
for, provided it be joined, as in the case of Mary

Magdalen, to a boundless Confidence, an exclusive
trust in the Goodness, the Mercy, the Love of Jesus
our Lord. In fact, these two virtues, Humility and
Confidence, always go together, for the less we rely
on self, the more we rely on God. We are often, perhaps, dry in our Meditation, at Holy Mass, or in Holy
Communion, because we do not approach our Lord
with these essential dispositions of Humility and
Confidence. We look sometimes too much for sensible devotion; or, what is worse, we go about these
sacred functions in a humdrum, routinary, superficial, indolent manner. Yet it is so easy to practise
Humility and Confidence. Is not our very motion
of kneeling down an expression of our lowliness, an
act of self-humiliation? And what prevents us, in all
our dealings and relations with Superiors, companions, pupils, and outsiders, from making ourselves,
in very truth, their humble and devoted servants?
Oh! if we only knew how rapidly this would advance
us in the sweet familiarity of Jesus, how anxious we
should be not to miss a single of these golden opportunities!

She bathes the feet of Christ with her tears. O
blessed tears of contrite love! I too should shed
them oftener, if I realized better the ingratitude and
malice of worldliness and sin, especially in a Religious who has been so highly favored by Heaven, has
been the object of such wonderful predilection on the
part of God, and is still being loved by Jesus with
such extraordinary preference and such tender solicitude, in spite of all my shortcomings and infidelities.
Oh, could I only blot out my whole wicked past with
floods of burning tears! But if I cannot weep outwardly in humble prayer, at least inwardly my heart
should bleed with deep contrition, and if my eyes

yield no tears of penitent love, my body should bear the marks of sharp atonement.

As her tears fall more abundantly on the feet of our Lord, she strives to wipe them away, again and again, with her long, flowing hair. It was the symbolic dedication to Jesus of all she held most dear, of her entire person. That which had been the object of so much care, and the subject of so much vanity, and perhaps the means of gaining so much unlawful affection, now she turns to the most lowly and repugnant use, namely, that of wiping the dust and moisture from the feet of a guest treated with such scant courtesy by the master of the house, Simon. Oh! but what use could, in reality, be more noble and glorious than this: to cleanse and comfort the sacred feet of Jesus, the All-Beautiful, the Son of the Eternal God! What have I got to dedicate to the Personal Service of my Lord and Savior? I have my limbs, my senses, my strength, my faculties, my talents, and these I will, henceforth, consecrate entirely to Him. But above everything else He wants all my affections, my whole and undivided heart.

Then she kisses the feet of Jesus. Contrition, humility, confidence, and love, are all inseparable. If we wish to love our Lord ardently, if we desire to taste at times the wonderful effects of Divine Charity, let us ever be intent on humbling ourselves sincerely, inwardly before Him and outwardly before all those who represent Him, not only our betters and our equals, but especially the haughty, the insolent, and the unsympathetic, the ignorant, the helpless, and the sinful. What greater happiness on earth than, for the sake of Jesus generously to embrace poverty, privation, weariness, pain, neglect, and contempt. Accordingly, she kisses only His feet; for even in the expression of our love we must be humble, waiting for the blissful moment when our Heavenly Lord will deign to admit our soul to the holy intimacy of a Spouse. Yet she actually covers them with her kisses. So should we ever be animated with child-like fervor, never ceasing to testify our affection to Jesus by a thousand little practices of self-denial, self-conquest, and self-abjection. Besides, every exterior action, done thoughtfully and deliberately, intensifies our interior disposition.

Lastly, Mary pours out the fragrant contents of the alabaster vial. It was probably a souvenir of some former acquaintance, an object, besides, which she had prized very highly for its own intrinsic value. But these are the very reasons why now she longs to make of it a complete holocaust to her Divine Master, in atonement for her past faults, in token of her detachment from created goods, and in recognition of His supreme Excellence and Loveliness. So should we ever strive to make to our Heavenly Spouse the generous sacrifice of every natural inclination or aversion, the unreserved offering of every object toward which we feel some undue attraction, the total renunciation of everything except His grace and His love. How sweet-scented an oblation this would add to the priceless immolation of Himself in Holy Mass! Only when every creature shall thus have been turned out of our soul, will Jesus be able to dwell in it as our only Good, our All. Oh! why should we ever hesitate to make such an advantageous exchange, of the Infinite, Eternal, All-Beautiful Creator, for a finite, perishable, and shadowy creature?

Third Point. Words.— Our Lord defends, consoles, and dismisses Mary Magdalen.

All this while the Master, filled with the tenderest compassion, had allowed Magdalen thus to manifest her faith, her contrition, and her love. But Simon, the Pharisee, did not understand how a prophet, a holy man, could permit himself to be approached and touched by a sinful woman. In fact, his soul was too full of indignation to allow him to speak, but he had silently come to the conclusion that Jesus could, after all, not be the true Messias. Any dislike or disesteem we may feel towards others, on account of their vices or defects, comes not from Grace but from Nature, not from God but from Satan; and hence its immediate effect on our soul is to darken the light of the understanding and to extinguish the fervor of the will. Our Lord, by kindly manifesting that He knew what was going on in the mind and heart of Simon, gave him a delicate but powerful confirmation of His own Holiness and Divinity. How gentle are all the ways of our Dear Savior! How do I proceed in the exercise of works of zeal? in striving to correct the mistaken notions of non-Catholics or in endeavoring to recall sinners to the practice of their religion?

But Jesus also wished to bring His host to an acknowledgment of his inferiority as compared with this notorious woman, and thus to cure his pride. So our Lord called the attention of Simon to the fact, that the various acts of service and kindness which he as host should have shown to his invited guest, had been performed most lovingly and lavishly by this repentant sinner, whom he despised on account of her past misconduct. " Simon, do you see this woman? When I entered your house, you gave me no water for my feet, but she has washed my feet with her tears and wiped them with her hair. You gave me

no kiss, but she, since she came in, has not ceased to
kiss my feet. You did not refresh my head with
perfume, but she has poured attar over my feet."
And then Jesus drew, from this different behavior, a
most remarkable conclusion. "Hence, I tell you,
many sins are forgiven her, because she has loved
much. But to whom less is forgiven, he loves less."
She had committed many sins, no doubt, but they
were now forgiven her completely, not only as to the
guilt but also as to their temporal punishment and
their moral effects on the soul. In fact, who can
doubt that Mary Magdalen by her contrition had
obtained pardon of the guilt even before she entered
the dining-room? But now, on account of the deep
humility and the great love she has shown, the temporal punishment also is remitted and the moral consequences are destroyed; all the evil is entirely
undone, canceled, and obliterated. Not so, however,
with Simon. For though the sins he had committed
are fewer, yet they are not forgiven him completely,
because he has loved less. Consequently, Simon is
now actually more sinful than Magdalen. Thus it
may also happen among Religious, that those who are
conscious of grievous faults committed in the past,
show greater generosity and fervor than others who
were preserved, by a most extraordinary mercy and
a most gratuitous predilection on the part of God,
from falling into mortal sin; so that the former are
now more pure and holy than the latter. Let us
examine ourselves, whether we are like Magdalen or
like Simon, or perhaps like neither, inasmuch as having led very foolish and wicked lives before in the
World, we are still leading very imperfect and tepid
lives at present in Religion.

But we should also learn from this incident, that

even our former infidelities may greatly help us to advance in humility and charity. At any rate, whatever may have been our past, let us act, henceforth, in such a way as soon to receive from our Divine Lord the sweet assurance of His complete pardon: "Thy sins, my child, are forgiven thee." We have to get it anyhow before we can enter Heaven; why, then, not strive to get it while yet on earth? O blissful moment! let us make the firm resolve to hasten its arrival by our constant longing, by our unremitting fervor.

These last words of our Lord made some of the invited guests wonder, because they still lacked Faith in His Divinity. Faith is the foundation of all supernatural virtue. Hence our Blessed Savior turning once more to Mary Magdalen, who was still kneeling at His feet in humble contrition and grateful love, said, "Thy faith has saved thee, go in peace." Thus also in our own case, if we wish to become holy and perfect, we must strive to actuate, practise, and increase our Faith; seeing God in the Holy Eucharist, in our Superiors, in our Rules, in our companions, in our pupils, in all men, in all creatures, and in all the workings of Providence. Unless a Religious labors to lead a life of faith, a life every moment of which is animated and energized by faith,— not governed by natural likes and dislikes, not shaped by foolish whims and impulses,— he will ever be in danger of losing his Vocation. But above all let us ponder on the goodness of Jesus towards Mary Magdalen, when He told her, "Go in peace." For the words of God effect what they signify, and the peace of the Lord surpasses all understanding.

Colloquy with St. Mary Magdalen, and with our

Divine Savior. We will beg this Holy Penitent to obtain for us the grace of never ceasing to shed tears and to do penance for our many sins, of eagerly availing ourselves of every opportunity to humble our pride and mortify our senses, and of employing each moment of our existence to accumulate at the feet of Jesus the practical tokens of our love. Then we will, after her example, prostrate ourselves before our Adorable Master and conjure Him, by all He has done and suffered for us, to render also us deserving of His complete pardon and to grant us likewise the favor of accompanying Him daily, through the whole course of His bitter Passion, even to His Death on the Cross.— Our Father.

THE THREE DEGREES OF HUMILITY

Introductory Remarks.— In this Exercise St. Ignatius puts before us the only really safe disposition for ever acting, henceforth, in full accordance with the Holy Will of God, and no longer being led astray by the impulse of passion or by the cunning of Satan. This disposition, which he calls the Third Degree of Humility, he shows to consist in a fixed determination to imitate as closely as possible Jesus Christ Crucified; and his main purpose, consequently, is to make us strive, by prayer and practice, for the acquisition of so momentous a grace. This magnanimous disposition, in fact, embraces all that is most perfect; it embodies the genuine doctrine of the Saints; and it marks the climax of the Spiritual Exercises.

Throughout this Meditation, Humility is considered, not as a passing act, but as a habitual disposition, a supernatural virtue, in three successive stages of development, initial, advanced, and final. In so far as every habit, whether good or bad, may be more or less firm, it goes without saying that each of these three stages, modes, or Degrees of Humility, admits of an unlimited number of gradations.

Another point to be noted is this. Since Humility is by definition a virtue that makes us take our proper place with regard to God and whatever represents God, it consequently causes us to shape all our thoughts, desires, and actions, in entire conformity with the Divine Will, as manifested by Commandments, Superiors, Rules, Circumstances, and Inspirations; nay, more than this, it renders us docile to the Teachings and Counsels of Christ our Lord, and eager to imitate and resemble Him, our Adorable Savior, not only inwardly but also outwardly, by actually welcoming, for His love and reverence, poverty, suffering and contempt.   Now, in explaining the Three Degrees of Humility, St. Ignatius takes the virtue, not in its primary sense, but in this secondary or derived meaning.

Evidently, it is only after one has acquired to some extent the more obvious and less difficult Degrees of Humility, that he can begin to appreciate and practise the highest Degree, which transforms the soul truly into a living image of Jesus Crucified. But since Religious, by the grace of God, are resolved to strive after real Holiness, and by the Vows have entered the State of Perfection, they are without exception positively called to this Third Degree of Humility.

Subject of this Meditation.— The three Degrees of Humility.

Composition of Place.— To see myself standing before God our Lord and all His Saints, that I may desire and know what is most pleasing to His Divine Goodness.

Petition.— Light to understand thoroughly and strength to practise generously the doctrine of the Saints, as contained in the Third Degree of Humility.

First Point.   In What the Three Degrees of Humility Consist.
" The First Degree of Humility," says St. Ignatius, " is necessary for eternal salvation.   It consists in

submitting and humbling myself, as far as I can, in all things to obey the law of God our Lord, so that even to secure the possession of this whole earth or to save my own temporal life, I would not enter into deliberation about breaking a commandment that binds me under mortal sin." This disposition implies an intense abhorrence of Mortal Sin, such as ought to have been conceived in the First Week and intensified all along in the Second. But even so, a person in this First Degree of Humility being mainly actuated by fear, may sometimes give way under the onset of passion or the stress of temptation, and hence, unless he strives to advance to something higher, his Salvation still remains very uncertain. As yet he has acquired only the lowest degree of spiritual poverty and obscurity.

"The Second Degree of Humility," says St. Ignatius, "is more perfect than the first. It consists in finding myself in such a state as in no wise to be more inclined towards riches than towards poverty, or to be more desirous of honor than of dishonor, or to prefer a long life to an early death, when the service of God our Lord and the salvation of my immortal soul are equal; and, consequently, never to enter into deliberation about committing a venial sin, not even for the sake of the whole world or for the avoidance of a most painful and shameful end." This disposition evidently supposes that one has so completely mortified his unruly passions as to be totally Indifferent to plenty or privation, to esteem or contempt, to health or sickness, and so forth; in other words, that one has humbled himself so thoroughly and conformed himself so entirely to the Holy Will of God, as habitually to shun every Inordination and effectually to minimize the danger of Venial Sin. It is

this intense horror of Venial Sin and Positive Inordination which we labored to obtain already in the
First Week and afterwards strove to strengthen
throughout the Second Week. Evidently this Second
Degree of Humility postulates a correspondingly high
degree of spiritual poverty and obscurity, and indicates a considerable progress towards real Holiness.
The main motive is no longer fear but justice. Yet,
owing to our extreme weakness and fickleness, even
this Second Degree by no means eliminates all un-
certainty of Salvation; and hence we eagerly pass
on to the consideration of something still more noble
and arduous.

" The Third Degree of Humility," says St. Ignatius,
" is the most perfect. Including the First and Second
Degrees, it consists in my being habitually so disposed that whenever equal praise and glory will ac-
crue to the Divine Majesty, in order to imitate more
closely Christ our Lord and to become actually more
like to Him, I desire and embrace poverty and contempt, with Christ poor and contemned for my sake,
rather than riches and honors, and I choose to be
deemed useless and foolish in this world for the love
of Christ, Who was first held to be such on my account, rather than to be considered wise and prudent."
Here we view the very summit of Evangelical Perfection: " If thou wilt be perfect, take up thy cross
daily and come follow Me." Here we also discover
the highest degree of spiritual poverty and obscurity.
Humility seems now only another aspect of Charity.
For the predominant motive by which a soul is sustained in the practice of this Third Degree is an
ardent personal love of Christ Crucified. She longs
to share in His hunger, His thirst, His poverty, His
obscurity, His torments, His insults, His abandon-

ment, and His death, provided only she does not go counter to the Divine Will. Nothing can keep her from embracing on every occasion the Cross of Suffering and Contempt except the knowledge that such a course would be detrimental to the Glory of her Savior and her God. However, though the strongest impulse is supplied by love, other motives are by no means excluded. Hence, in our endeavors to acquire the Third Degree of Humility, we may be greatly assisted by the desire of canceling our debt of temporal punishment, of destroying the moral stains left on our souls by past sins, of becoming efficient instruments in saving and sanctifying our neighbor; for thus also, surely, we shall better imitate Christ our Lord and more closely resemble Him in His Innocence, His Holiness, and His Zeal.

Second Point. How the Successive Degrees of Humility are Mutually Related.

We may begin by asking ourselves what would be the import of the Zero Degree of Humility. It would denote the state of a soul in which the restless cravings for riches, pleasures, and honors, hold absolute sway, without any fear of God, or any sense of duty, or any love of Christ, to keep them within bounds. This, therefore, is the Degree of the Genuine Worldling; whose every thought and desire is bent on self-aggrandizement, self-indulgence, self-worship; whose heart is wholly taken up with food and drink, exercise and amusement, business and sport, politics and intrigues. Is my habitual condition in any way akin to this?

In the First Degree, these unruly tendencies, though not yet completely controlled, are already somewhat checked by reason and faith. Hence, in this state of the soul, mortal sin, but not venial, is at least habitually excluded. It is, consequently, more or less the Degree of the Ordinary Christian.

In the Second Degree, the earthly inclinations of our corrupt nature are exactly counterbalanced by the opposite effects of supernatural grace. The soul, therefore, is theoretically in a moral equilibrium which, as long as it is not disturbed, prevents her from falling into inordination and sin. Practically, no one can keep himself so nicely balanced; but making due allowances for human instability, we may call it the Degree of the Fervent Catholic.

Lastly, in the Third Degree, the love of Christ Crucified has taken complete possession of the soul, so that its inordinate leanings towards wealth, enjoyment, and distinction, are now entirely outbalanced by the contrary aspirations to share in the privations, afflictions, and insults of the Son of God. Such a soul is just as eager for opportunities of mortification and humiliation, as the worldling is for occasions of gratifying his sensuality and pride; and hence what is despised and abhorred by the one is esteemed and embraced by the other. " The world is crucified to me and I to the world." This, evidently, is the Degree of the Saint.

To sum up, then, the Zero Degree is the habitual state of Sin, the First Degree is the habitual state of Grace, the Second Degree is the habitual state of Fervor, and the Third Degree is the habitual state of Heroism.

Third Point. Every Religious Should in dead Earnest Take Up the Practice of the Third Degree of Humility.

To look upon the Third Degree of Humility as

something fanciful, visionary, or ideal, not intended to be practised and mastered by the chosen followers of Christ our King, by those who have embraced the Evangelical Counsels, would stand on a par with removing the Crucifix from the churches, schools, and homes, as was done by the so-called Reformed Christians of the Sixteenth Century. The Third Degree is just as appropriate and indispensable for a Religious, as the Crucifix is for a Christian. A Crucifix should not merely be a work of art made for exhibition in a museum, and so the Third Degree should not merely be an interesting speculation, a piece of sublime perfection reserved for Canonized Saints. Let it be clearly understood, however, that there is no question of longing for poverty, obscurity, pain, and contempt in themselves, or of praying for afflictions and humiliations for their own sakes. In fact, this would hardly be possible, since we cannot desire what we necessarily fear and shun, but even if it were possible, there would be neither profit nor merit in such unnatural self-hatred. But we should long and pray for these things, inasmuch as Christ our Lord bore them for love of us and on our account. As such we should eagerly embrace them in spirit; but even then we have no business to embrace them in reality, unless they come to us through Holy Obedience, from Divine Providence, or with the recommendation and approval of our Rules, Customs, or Confessors.

Again, it is very needful in this matter, to set aside all fictitious pictures and empty fears. When we pray for temporal favors, do we expect that God will right away lavish on us all the wealth of the world? Of course not. In fact, we always pray to Him with the implicit condition, " as far as it may promote our real well-being " or " provided it will tend to Thy greater glory." Hence we must not imagine that in consequence of our prayer for suffering and contempt, God will suddenly overwhelm us with an avalanche of affliction. Since to suffer with Christ and for Christ is the greatest of all blessings, the most precious of all favors, we may, on the one hand, rest assured that it will be bestowed upon us only in a limited measure, and that we shall have to correspond earnestly and pray ardently before we get any more. On the other hand, "God is faithful." In His fatherly Love and tender Solicitude, He will never allow any affliction to befall us, without giving us also abundant grace to bear it patiently and generously. Unfortunately, to many men the indispensable trials of their earthly existence come as bitter remedies; and not a few, having utterly neglected to make the necessary preparation, bear them reluctantly, impatiently, and sinfully. But to faithful and fervent souls, these same trials come as the extraordinary distinctions, the loving caresses of their Heavenly Spouse, which fill them with the deepest peace and sweetest happiness.

Indeed it is difficult to see how any person can truly love Christ our Lord without sincerely wishing and ardently praying to suffer with Him and for Him. If I realize who I am, a despicable sinner, and Who Christ is, the All-Holy Creator, how could I ever cease longing and striving to be treated and afflicted after the manner He was treated and afflicted for love of me, and in expiation of my numerous and shameful offenses, committed precisely against Him? Suppose I had a dear friend, lying dangerously ill and suffering excruciating pain, or unjustly cast into prison and inhumanly tortured, could I meanwhile go and enjoy myself? But if he should undergo all those afflictions through my fault, and to ward off from me the just punishment of my perfidious crimes, perpetrated against his own fair name, against his very life, and I had still left in me any remnant of gratitude, one spark of human affection, what else could I do but spend night and day in tears and groans, amid every kind of discomfort and every mark of contempt? Yet, in the actual case, we have not two human beings more or less equal, but the Lord of Infinite Majesty and a mere sinful nothing.

Therefore, if we really wish to advance in the love of Jesus, our God and Savior, let us daily, with great confidence, beg for the Third Degree of Humility, for the grace of sharing in His Cross. Union with Christ Crucified, is the ultimate goal of our Vocation on earth, the means most conducive to the Divine Glory, the highest form of true devotion to the Sacred Heart, the most indispensable preparation for a fruitful Apostolate. Two kinds of acts will infallibly lead us to this habitual union: Prayer and Practice. We must begin by sincerely and earnestly begging for suffering and contempt, in order to become more like to our Divine Master, Who willingly bore even the most poignant ingratitude and the most revolting injustice and the most cruel torments and the most bitter outrages for love of us, in our behalf and on our account. In the next place, we must strive to accept joyfully every opportunity of mortification and humiliation, in hunger and thirst, heat and cold, ailments and accidents, reproofs and penances, disappointments and misunderstandings, slights and insults, or anything else from which we naturally shrink and flee, whether it come to us in the observance of our Rules, or in the discharge of our Duties, or through the disposal of Providence, or through the action of Superiors, or with the permission of our Confessor, or from the thoughtlessness of our fellow Religious, or by the malice of our Enemies. And if our repugnance seems too strong to master, we must not cease imploring the help of grace till we are heard. Thus little by little, in spite of many failures, notwithstanding our utter weakness, by dint of prayer and practice, we shall acquire that habitual union with Christ Crucified, in which consists the Third Degree of Humility. This, then, is to be our resolution for the future; but, as to the past, we should stir up in our hearts feelings of lively shame and deep regret for having misused so many valuable opportunities of sharing in the Cross, when we were impatient under affliction or resentful under humiliation. We should also examine whether we have sincerely forgiven all those who were in any way the cause of these trials, and whether we are now animated towards them, precisely for that reason, with affectionate gratitude, often beseeching God our Lord to shower down upon them in return, His choicest gifts and graces.

Colloquy.— At the conclusion of this important Exercise, St. Ignatius advises us again to address a Triple Colloquy to the Blessed Virgin, to Christ our Redeemer, and to the Eternal Father. Let us make it with the utmost fervor and generosity of which we may be capable under the action of the Holy Spirit, remembering that the Third Degree of Humility is the most precious grace with which the soul can be enriched during her probation for Heaven.

THE HOLY EUCHARIST

Emmanuel, God-with-us, that is the Holy Eucharist. Hence it is the life and center of the Catholic Church, the sum and substance of the Christian Religion, the pledge and prelude of the everlasting Bliss of Heaven.

The Real Presence.

Who is present in this tabernacle? Jesus Christ, the Second Person of the Ever-Blessed Trinity, true God and true Man, born at Bethlehem some nineteen hundred and fifteen years ago, of the Immaculate Virgin Mary. He is present here with that very Body which was scourged and crucified for my sins, with that same Blood which was shed for love of me, with that identical Soul which was crushed under intolerable anguish in the garden of Gethsemane, with that incommunicable Personality which is ever receiving the loving adoration of myriads of celestial Spirits. He is here, my Creator and my Redeemer, my Sovereign Lord and my Supreme Judge, my Heavenly King and my Eternal Spouse, hidden under the appearances of bread and wine; His Sacred Humanity being present, after the manner our soul is in the body, whole and entire in every part of the consecrated Host. I do not understand this, but I know it to be a fact with far greater certainty than if I did grasp it fully with my own mind, because I believe it on the word of God Himself, conveyed to me by His Holy, Apostolic, and Infallible Church. But do I sufficiently realize this wonderful mystery, do I strive to bring home to myself what my faith teaches, so that this supernatural conviction may sanctify my entire conduct and inflame my soul with the most ardent devotion? Do I recognize how it is His personal love for me that causes Him to abide here with me in the tabernacle?

I am, then, continually living under the same roof with the God of Infinite Majesty and Holiness. What a privilege! What person in the world, be he ever so pious and virtuous, enjoys such happiness? This is truly the House of God, not merely inasmuch as it is dedicated to His special Service, not simply because it is owned by nobody except by His supreme Vicar, but also, in the far truer sense, that He has fixed here His personal and permanent Abode. Oh! how pure and holy ought to be this House of God, how careful we ought to shun every sin, every inordination even, in the immediate presence of this infinitely Perfect and Loving Master! How can we presume to profane these Sacred Precincts, to insult this most Gracious Lord, by yielding voluntarily to our base passions, to self-love, self-complacency, self-worship, faultfinding, aversion, envy, impatience, sensuality, or sloth? Oh! how much more hateful and shameful sin appears in a Religious, living as he does night and day in the actual company of this Adorable Friend, to Whom he has sworn everlasting fidelity! Is this the way we repay the measureless love and ineffable condescension of our Great God? If our passions are strong and our temptations importunate, is He not here purposely to assist us in our trials, to defend us against our assailants, and to give us the victory over all our enemies?

Visits to the Blessed Sacrament.

We know all this, and yet, such is our lukewarmness, such our ingratitude, that it is too much for us to take now and then a few minutes from our favorite occupations, to go and speak to this Loving Master and expose to Him our many miseries and obtain the countless graces He is so desirous of pouring out on our souls. Some Religious have plenty of time for taking exercise, for recreative reading, for unnecessary conversation; in fact, they have time for almost anything and everything except for making now and then an extra Visit to our Lord in the Blessed Sacrament. Have we at least settled on a certain number of extra Visits? At what hours of the day? And are we faithful to these resolutions? When in bodily suffering, in mental distress, or in spiritual desolation, do we ever think of having special recourse to our Divine Consoler? Oh! think of the pain we give Him by this coldness and forgetfulness. Let us not measure the fathomless love of Jesus by our own shallow affection. His Sacred Heart is ever consumed with an unspeakable longing for our happiness here no less than hereafter. But He knows that happiness is inseparable from holiness. It is because He wants us to be happy, constantly happy, intensely happy, that He desires to make us holy and yearns for us to come to Him, the Only and Inexhaustible Source of all Holiness and Happiness.

But even at the ordinary Visits, made in common, how many distractions we indulge in and how little we seem to appreciate what we are doing! Those few precious moments, during which we might treasure up so much light and strength, so much solid consolation and heavenly joy, pass not seldom like a dream, and it is only when we get up from our knees

that we realize where we are. Oh, could we but realize our loss! Is not our behavior sometimes such
that it might be justly considered a worthless piece of
routine, an act of sham adoration, a cruel insult? O
infinite patience and meekness of the Heart of our
Savior and our God! How is it that Jesus can toler-
ate all this from those who have come purposely to
live with Him and to draw others to His service,
from those who for years already profess themselves
His faithful followers and devoted companions?
Can we not possibly take some efficacious means, can
we not adopt some suitable method, to prevent such
irreverent conduct for the future? But no means nor
method will prove of any lasting benefit, unless we
cherish a personal Love for Jesus in the Holy Eucharist. Love is the only infallible remedy. And
genuine Love springs from a lively Faith.

It is plain that the more profound our inward
veneration is for the Adorable Sacrament, the more
intense also will be our outward reverence in the
chapel or sacristy, the more diligent our care of whatever pertains to the altar or the tabernacle, and the
more exact our observance of all liturgical prescriptions. In ornamenting the sanctuary we should avoid
whatever savors of gaudiness or display, and rather
strive to combine grave simplicity with substantial
grandeur. Everything on or about the altar should
be kept scrupulously neat and clean. Faded or
wilted flowers should be promptly removed, even if
no fresh ones can be supplied. But especially in the
matter of music and singing, the authoritative directions of the Holy See should be punctually and energetically carried out. It is sheer folly to think
ourselves obedient, as long as, under any pretext
whatever, we fail to comply with the express wishes,

nay, the positive injunctions of the Sovereign Pontiff. Where there is a will there is a way. Even if we cannot immediately carry out every prescription to the letter, we should at least make a start by doing all we can.

Holy Communion.

Our Divine Lord instituted the Blessed Sacrament not only to remain with us till the end of time, but also to renew, day after day and hour after hour, the holocaust He made of Himself on the Cross. This is another privilege of the Religious Life, to be able to assist every day at Holy Mass. Truly, an inestimable privilege! For what is the Mass but the same offering that was made on Mount Calvary, of the same Victim and by the same Priest, Jesus Christ, the Incarnate Son of God? But while just as true and real a Sacrifice, it is unbloody and mystic. The Divine Victim, though substantially present, is no longer in the usual condition and the ordinary form of a mortal man, but under the foreign appearances of bread and wine. By His death on Calvary Jesus merited infinite grace for all mankind, and this grace is applied to us individually in the Mass, especially through Holy Communion. Having consecrated ourselves anew, during that August Sacrifice, to the Adorable Will of God, God, on His part, never outdone in liberality, communicates Himself to us. As if His love could brook no delay, in expectation and in token of that fuller communication which He intends to make of Himself in Heaven, and by which we shall share in His own Infinite Beatitude, He longs to give Himself already now to us by anticipation in Holy Communion. " Lo! the Divine Nourishment of the Blessed Angels has become the Food of Mortal

Wayfarers. O wondrous fact! The poor and lowly servant feasts on his Lord."

Our soul, then, is fed, so to speak, by Him Who becomes corporally present within us, our Adorable Savior. Just as common bread repairs, supports, and energizes the body, so this Heavenly Food, when received in due dispositions, refreshes, sustains, and inflames the soul, that is, the supernatural life of the soul, Sanctifying Grace. And as bread is transformed into our bodily substance, so we are transformed into Christ, the less noble into the more Noble. Transformed into Christ, so that we live by Him, inasmuch as by mutual love He abideth in us and we abide in Him, His Will being our only pleasure and our will no other but His. This spiritual transformation manifests itself by two special effects. One of these is to lessen and deaden in us that most dangerous inclination, the cause of all our misery and corruption, namely, our inordinate self-love and self-esteem, that monstrous pride which continually prompts us to rebel against God and to trample on our neighbor, that deep-rooted egoism which even here on earth can make our life a veritable hell. This effect is the healing grace of the Holy Eucharist. But there is another effect equally marked, which has been called its cheering grace and makes the soul break forth in vigorous and ardent acts of charity. Who is there amongst us that has not sometimes experienced this sudden outburst of fervor after a meditation full of aridity and drowsiness? Both these effects, however, depend for their intensity on the earnestness with which we prepare to receive our Divine Guest, on our recollection of mind, on our detestation of sin, and on our detachment from creatures.

How great, then, should be our care in preparing for Holy Communion, both overnight and in the morning! Overnight, before closing our eyes in sleep, we should call to mind once more the immense happiness, the priceless favor, that awaits us in the morning, and with ardent desire anticipate the hour of rising. On awaking during the night our hearts should at once go back to our Sweet Prisoner in the tabernacle, Whose most Affectionate Heart is ever pleading for us with unabating solicitude and tenderness. And in the morning, from the moment we hear the sound of the bell, rising immediately as at the voice of our Beloved, we should entertain no thought and form no desire, except to consecrate ourselves wholly to the service of our Divine Master, faithful to our resolution of living and breathing and laboring and suffering, only for love of Him, every moment of the day. This is of the highest importance if we wish to make a fervent and fruitful Communion; namely, to banish promptly and energetically all anticipations and recollections, all projects and regrets, from the time we awake till we have concluded our thanksgiving after Mass. On the other hand, how diligent we should be in renewing our determination to practise our Particular Examen, how careful too in observing all the so-called Additions, how energetic in applying our mind and heart to our Meditation, and how eager to assist at the Adorable Sacrifice!

And all the while, how we should long and sigh for the coming of our Dearest Lord, our Only Love! Yes, our Only Love, for this we have firmly settled long ago and forever, that Jesus shall be our Only Love, and that we will not love creatures, ourselves included, except for Him and in Him. But as the blessed moment draws near, oh! how fervently we shall repeat our humble protest that we will never again offend Him, never in the least displease Him, never deliberately violate any of our Rules, never wilfully discard any wish of our Superiors, never admit even for an instant any impatient motion, any improper imagination, any uncharitable feeling, never hesitate one second to make any sacrifice that may be acceptable to Him. Not content, however, with our own weak endeavors, we shall earnestly implore our Holy Patrons and all the Glorious Saints, our Guardian Angel with the other Blissful Spirits, and conjure our Heavenly Mother Mary, to come to our assistance, to join their burning supplications to our lukewarm prayers, to communicate to our hearts some of that profound humility and consuming love which unites them so intimately and so inseparably to God our Lord, to Jesus our Adorable Guest. Oh! could we but share in those perfect dispositions with which she, the Immaculate Virgin, awaited the coming of her Son and her Savior in the Holy Communion. With what modest gravity and intense devotion we would approach the altar, and how we would annihilate ourselves, as it were, in adoration and love, at the moment He deigns to enter our wretched hearts. Thus we should strive to make every Communion as if it were both our first and our last, each time receiving our Divine Spouse with such contrition, gratitude, and affection, as to make up, in some degree, for all our past distractedness, tepidity, and irreverence.

But as soon as we possess Him, let us adore, and love and thank with if possible still greater fervor, completely abandoning ourselves to the impulse of His grace. Next, let us beg with the utmost confidence for His favors. Is there anything He can refuse us, now that He has lowered Himself so infinitely as to descend into our soul, that soul yet so terribly disfigured in consequence of its former slavery to the spirits of darkness? But while ever ready to follow the motion of grace, we should nevertheless on our part have some simple method to spend these precious minutes of sacramental union with our Adorable Master, in a manner most conducive to our own sanctification and His greater glory. Hence we should be thoroughly familiar with a number of acts by which our soul can properly express her appreciation for the visit of so great a Guest. They should be made, not with the lips, but rather with the heart; and if we find in them anywhere sufficient matter to occupy us in sweet converse with our Heavenly Spouse, let us delay there till we are fully satisfied. Acts of faith and adoration, of hope and gladness, of love and consecration, of contrition and reparation; acts of gratitude also, inviting once more our Immaculate Mother, Mary, the Blessed Joseph, our Holy Angels and Patron Saints, and the whole Court of Heaven, to help us in rendering thanks to our Divine Lord for His incomparable mercy; and lastly, acts of petition, recommending to His Sacred Heart, not only ourselves, but also our Superiors and fellow Religious; our relatives, friends, and charges; the parish and its Pastor; the diocese, the clergy, and the Bishop; the universal Church and especially our Holy Father the Pope; the conversion of sinners, the return of our separated brethren, the cessation of persecution, the success of foreign missions, the relief of the Souls in Purgatory. Some method like this may often prove very useful, yet we should never adhere to it so rigidly as to hamper or destroy the action of grace.

St. Aloysius, being allowed as a rule to communicate only on Sundays, used to devote the first three days of the week to thanksgiving and the last three days to preparation. Since we are incomparably more privileged in being permitted Daily Communion, we should strive to keep thinking of our Adorable Visitor, with humble and loving gratitude, all during the morning hours, whilst during the latter half of the day, amidst our various occupations, we should begin to long and hunger for His next coming. This spiritual appetite is, after all, the best preparation and the indispensable disposition for the reception of the Holy Eucharist, for the eating of this true Bread from Heaven.

THE LAST SUPPER

Introductory Remarks.— We now enter upon the Third Week of the Exercises. "While excluding joyful thoughts as of the Resurrection and of Heaven," says St. Ignatius, " I should strive to excite myself to sorrow, grief, and anguish, frequently recalling to mind the labors and afflictions which Christ our Lord bore from the moment of His Birth to the mystery of the Passion on which I am going to meditate."

Subject of this Meditation.— Christ our Lord, having sent two of His Disciples from Bethany to Jerusalem to prepare the Supper, went there Himself towards evening with the other Disciples, and, after washing their feet, gave them His most Holy Body and Precious Blood, speaking to them long and lovingly while Judas was gone to sell his Divine Master.

Composition of Place.— The road from Bethany to Jerusalem, and also the supper-room or cenacle.

Petition.—" To feel sorrow, affliction and confusion, because for my sins our Lord is going to His Passion."— This confusion will dispose us to conceive greater grief and anguish in meditating afterwards on the principal events of the Passion.

First Point. The Adorable Person of our Lord.
While about to meditate on the Passion, we should consider not only what Christ is going to suffer but also what He wishes to suffer in His Sacred Human-

ity. " With desire I have desired,"— that is, I am
consumed with desire,— He said to His Apostles as
they were about to begin the legal supper, " to eat this
Pasch with you, before I suffer."   And already several months previously He had told them, " I have a
baptism wherewith to be baptized and how I am
straitened until it be accomplished."   So great was
this eagerness of the Sacred Heart that even in the
midst of the most cruel torments He was ready to
suffer more, if such could have been pleasing to His
Heavenly Father or beneficial to us poor sinners.
This, in fact, was the opportunity for which He had
been longing ever since the first moment of His Incarnation.   This was the precious occasion of manifesting His gratitude to the Adorable Trinity for all the
wonderful graces and favors lavished upon Him, as
Man, with such incomparable liberality.   This was
the acceptable hour to satisfy the justice of Almighty
God for all the countless offenses committed by mankind, from the disobedience of our First Parents
down to my own Personal Sins.   This was the final
conflict for delivering His brethren from the tyranny
of Satan, from the slavery of their passions, from
the awful danger of eternal damnation; and this the
loving holocaust to merit for each of us all the
graces we should need to advance in Holiness and to
obtain everlasting Bliss.   It is to this burning zeal of
Jesus our Lord, it is to this vehement longing of His
Sacred Heart, that I in particular owe my merciful
preservation from the unquenchable flames of hell,—
perhaps, even from the horrible guilt of mortal sin,—
together with all the heavenly favors that have enabled me, in spite of my many faults and my excessive
weakness, to enter a Religious Institute and to em-

brace the State of Perfection. Should not, then, also my heart be animated with a sincere desire, with an ardent longing to suffer with Christ and for Christ, in the accomplishment of the Divine Will, in my efforts to advance in Sanctity, in my labors for the benefit of my fellow men, in my practice of Prayer, Penance, Charity, and Obedience?

"Consider also," says St. Ignatius, "how, during the Passion, the Divinity conceals Itself"; — that is, how the Divine Personality, hypostatically united to the Sacred Humanity, could destroy the enemies of Christ yet does not do so, but on the contrary allows Him to suffer so cruelly. It is especially during the Passion that we fail to notice any manifestation of the Godhead; no miracles, no transfiguration, no not even, perhaps, the habitual majesty in the personal appearance of Christ our Lord, which inspired all who beheld Him with respect and veneration. Why does the Divinity remain thus, as it were, hidden? It is out of delicate regard for the ardent wishes of the Sacred Heart of Jesus. It is to give Him the long desired opportunity of showing His gratitude towards God and His charity towards sinners. It is also to give men a Supreme Model for their imitation in the trials and hardships of this present life, that they may learn how they can best thank their Heavenly Father for His Singular Predilection by their loving obedience to His Adorable Will. Only the intimate union existing between the Divinity and the Humanity in the Person of Christ our Lord, can explain this admirable condescension, this temporary concealment. Consequently, how completely mistaken we are if in our sufferings or temptations or tribulations, from whatever source they may arise, we get discouraged and disheartened because God does not immediately and manifestly come to our assistance, either by checking those who afflict us or at least by making us feel His sensible Presence. He will assuredly do so in His own good time, but meanwhile concealing Himself, as it were, He enables us by His grace to bear our afflictions with patience and even with joy, and makes us see in them a precious opportunity to atone for our sins, to practise virtue, to accomplish something for the sanctification and salvation of souls, and to acquire another trait of resemblance to our Crucified Lord and Savior.

Lastly, I should consider that He is going to suffer all these tortures and all these insults for my Sins, and consequently what I in turn ought to do and to suffer for Him. Of all the aspects of the Sacred Passion this surely is the most wonderful, that He, the Holy One, the Son of God, the Lord of Infinite Majesty, should suffer such extremes of pain and anguish and ignominy, in order that I, His rebellious creature, might not be condemned to that everlasting torment and infamy which I had so justly and so often merited by my Iniquities. This, indeed, surpasses all created understanding; this should cause me to die of shame and grief and love. How could I ever bewail and detest my Sins sufficiently? Have I done so in the past? Must I not, at least, begin to do so now? And what labors ought I not to undertake for Him, or rather what afflictions ought I not to bear for Him in return? Is there any duty that could be too hard for me, in view of such amazing love? No, indeed; nor can I rest satisfied with mere exertion of body or mind however strenuous; I must suffer for Him, and suffer for Him all I can, never saying enough, but even when at its worst exclaiming, "More suffering, O Lord, and more love!"

Second Point. The Words of Our Lord.

At the Last Supper, our Adorable Savior exhorted His Apostles repeatedly to mutual Charity, and then solemnly implored His Heavenly Father to bestow upon them the grace of perfect Union. " I give you a new commandment," He said, " that you love one another, as I have loved you, that you also love one another. By this shall all men know that you are My disciples, if you have love one for another." (John 13 :34-35.)   Again He said, " This is My commandment that you love one another as I have loved you. Greater love than this no man hath than that he lay down his life for his friend. You are My friends, if you do the things that I command you." (John 15 :12-14.)   And lastly, " I pray that they all may be one as Thou, Father, in Me and I in Thee, that they also may be one in Us, so that the world may believe that Thou hast sent Me." (John 17 :20-21.)   The practice of Fraternal Charity, the imitation of the most Loving Heart of Jesus, that is after all to be the distinguishing mark of every true Christian and, consequently, the chief virtue of every sincere Religious. While, on the one hand, it is precisely in the ceaseless exercise of Fraternal Charity that we shall find the opportunity and the grace of bearing fatigue, hardship, anguish, and contempt for the sake of our Divine Lord; so, on the other hand, the more eagerly we embrace poverty, suffering, and humility, the more faithfully also we shall comply with this farewell commandment of our Adorable Master: to love one another even as He has loved us, ready to sacrifice not only our convenience, our time, our rest, our health, but even our very life, for the good of our neighbor. Yet we must bear in mind that the love which consumes the Sacred Heart of Jesus is Supernatural

Charity, Apostolic Charity, Zeal for Souls. In the midst of our works of mercy, corporal and spiritual, we must never lose sight of our ultimate object: to free souls from the slavery of Satan, from the corruption of sin, from the darkness of unbelief, from the seduction of the world, from the danger of eternal perdition; to bring them to the knowledge, love, and service of God our Lord here on earth, and thus to the enjoyment of everlasting Bliss in Heaven.

Third Point. The Actions of our Lord.

Washing of the Feet.— What a wonderful spectacle of humility and love: Jesus Christ, the Son of God, in the attitude of a slave, kneeling at the feet of His Apostles and rendering them this lowly service with the tenderest affection. The Almighty Creator washes the feet of His sinful creatures. Can we ever admire this sufficiently? Oh! if Jesus, my Savior and my God were thus to come to me, what would be my confusion on seeing Him about to perform so loving and lowly a service for a being so wretched and so vile. Would I not exclaim with Peter: " Lord, dost Thou wash my feet? Thou shalt never wash my feet." Yet this is precisely what our Divine Master does for me day after day. For who else but God serves me in my manifold helplessness and attends to my numerous needs? It is true, He does so through other men, through my fellow Religious, through my Superiors, but does He, therefore, do it less Himself? Does He not give them the faculty of rendering me service, out of pure affection for me? Does He not actually cooperate with them in these acts of humility and charity? Or does He perhaps serve me less, because He deigns to associate with Himself instruments that derive all their efficiency from Him alone, and deigns to employ them not from any need on His part, but from sheer liberality, that they may share in His Divine slavery of love? Hence, on the one hand, what should not be my interior confusion on receiving such services,— for admit them I must no less than Peter, if I wish to remain in the friendship of our Lord,— and, on the other hand, how eagerly I should seize every opportunity of serving my Companions, my fellow men, while holding myself utterly unworthy of such an honor. Indeed, how Divine it is to serve, and how Human it is to be served. To serve is the privilege of the more godlike in strength and goodness, to be served is the lot of the weak and helpless. Whatever gifts were bestowed upon me by God my Creator and Lord, natural or supernatural, were intended not simply for my own private benefit, but more especially for the service of my brethren. " I have given you an example," said our Adorable Savior after performing His lowly task, " that as I have done to you, so you do also. If then I being your Lord and Master have washed your feet; you also ought to wash one another's feet." Humility, humility! when shall we grasp its paramount importance, when shall we give ourselves to its earnest practice? Only thus shall we be able to love one another, even as Christ has loved us; only thus can we all be one, even as He is one with His Eternal Father.

Institution of the Holy Eucharist.—" As He had loved His own," says St. John, " He loved them to the end "; that is, He loved them so as to exhaust for them the resources of His Infinite Power; and so as never, even to the end of the world, to leave them without His Sacred Presence, without His Divine Sacrifice, without His giving Himself for the nourish-

ment of their souls in Holy Communion. "Greater
love than this no man has but that he give his life for
his friend." Yes, no man can do more than that;
but God can; He can give Himself. And this He did
precisely when He was about to suffer the most painful and shameful death for my sins. "The Lord
Jesus, the same night in which He was betrayed, took
bread, and giving thanks, broke, and said: 'Take ye
and eat: this is My Body which shall be delivered for
you: this do for the commemoration of Me.' In like
manner also the chalice, after He had supped, saying:
'This chalice is the new testament in My Blood: this
do ye, as often as you shall drink, for the commemoration of Me'" (1 Cor. 11:23-25.) How have I till now
corresponded to so prodigal a love? What is my
devotion towards our Lord in the Adorable Eucharist?
How do I prove to Him my gratitude by Visits, at
Holy Mass, before and after Holy Communion? Am
I careful in whatever belongs to the cult of the Blessed
Sacrament? the linen, the vestments, the adornments,
the sanctuary lamp, the candles, the music? Am I
punctual in the observance of all the rubrics that regard the celebration of Holy Mass, the administration
of Holy Communion, and the conduct of Public Worship? Again, since He has loved and still loves each
one of us with such excess of love in this August Sacrament, can I ever think of having done enough for
Him in my exercise of Fraternal Charity? Was it
not immediately after the Institution of the Holy
Eucharist that He inculcated His new commandment,
to love one another as He loved us? How sincere,
then, how tender, how generous, how self-forgetful,
and how untiring should be my Fraternal Charity!
What intimate union there should reign among those
who daily receive Him, in the same chapel and at the

same hour, in Holy Communion! Lastly, has He not instituted this Adorable Sacrament precisely to enable us to love Him in return for such wonderful, excessive love of His, and to give us abundant grace that we might do what is so utterly impossible to human nature, namely, to embrace everywhere suffering and contempt, to seek in all things our greater humiliation and continual mortification, in compliance with His Teaching and in imitation of His Example, simply that thus we might more truly resemble Him, our King, our Savior, and our God?

Colloquy.—"To finish," says St. Ignatius, "with a colloquy to Christ our Lord, and then to say an Our Father. Or if devotion urge me, three colloquies, one to the Mother, another to the Son, and a third to the Father, in the same form as that laid down in the meditation on Two Standards and in the note which follows the meditation on The Three Classes." Let us endeavor to pour out our hearts in ardent sentiments of humility, contrition, gratitude, and love, as well as in urgent petitions for light and strength to confirm us in our practical Resolutions.

A. M. D. G.

SEVENTH DAY

SPECIAL PATRON: St. Mary Magdalen.

MOTTO: " I live in the faith of the Son of God, Who loved me and delivered Himself for me."— Gal. 2:20.

SPIRIT: Longing for the evils of this world, Hardship and Contempt.

READING: Imitation; Bk. II, C. 12.
　　　　　　　　　　Bk. III, C. 19, 50, 56, 57.
　　　　　　　　　　Bk. IV, C. 2, 4, 8, 9, 10, 15.
　　　　Fourth Gospel; C. 18, 19.

Strive to confirm all your Resolutions by the ardent love of Jesus Crucified, beseeching Him earnestly for a share in His sufferings and humiliations. Determine the subject of your Particular Examen.

THE AGONY AND THE BETRAYAL

Introductory Remarks.— During the whole of this Third Week of the Exercises, and particularly during each successive Meditation on the Passion, we should make every effort to obtain the precious grace — that grace which gives the initial impulse toward genuine Sanctity — of desiring and embracing poverty, obscurity, hardships, and humiliations, for the love of Christ Crucified. We should not cease begging and beseeching our Divine Master, through the intercession of our Blessed Mother, till we feel certain that we have been heard, that is, till we are positively resolved, in our innermost heart, to accompany Him on the royal road to Calvary. To be a Religious, if it means anything at all, means this, to follow Christ; not in empty words or poetic fancies, but in downright truth and solid reality. By His excessive afflictions He merited for us abundant grace to do so; and, therefore, instead of cowardly shrinking from this glorious task as if above our strength, we should take it up at once with the utmost confidence. Our Lord did not redeem us by His discourses and miracles, but by His Passion and Death; and hence the only thing that will gain Holiness for ourselves and Salvation for our neighbor, is not our appearance, or our talents, or our office, or our achievements, but our actual union with Him on the Cross of suffering and contempt. It was by meditating on the Sacred Passion that the martyrs obtained the grace joyfully to

bear their horrible and shameful torments.　Similar
trials may await us, trials that involve the loss of
comfort, country, liberty, and life.　Are we ready for
them?　We do not know; but if only we meditate as
they did, we too shall come out victorious, however
fierce the combat.

Subject of this Meditation.— After instituting the
Holy Eucharist, Christ our Lord went down with His
Apostles to the valley of Josaphat.　On entering an
olive orchard, called Gethsemane, He left eight of the
disciples near the gate and the remaining three a little
further.　Then He betook Himself alone to prayer
and suffered such anguish as to sweat copious drops
of blood.　When the hour had come, He went forth to
meet Judas, who betrayed Him with a kiss, while the
other Apostles fled in various directions.　Being arrested like a criminal, our Savior was dragged up the
slope of the hill to the palace of the High Priests.

Composition of Place.— The garden of Gethsemane,
the road leading up to Mount Sion, and the palace of
the High Priests.

Petition.—" Affliction with Christ filled with affliction, anguish with Christ overwhelmed with anguish,
tears and grief on account of the terrible sufferings
Christ underwent for my sake " in the garden of Gethsemane and during the betrayal.

**First Point.　The Agony in the Garden of Geth-
semane.**

Our Blessed Redeemer, after celebrating with His
Disciples the Jewish Passover and instituting the
Holy Eucharist, spoke that wonderful farewell dis-
course on our obligation of loving one another even as

He has loved us, and then went down to the valley of
Cedron. This stream, skirting the eastern portion
of Jerusalem, divides Mount Moriah, the hill on which
the Temple stood, from the opposite hill, the Mount
of Olives. At the foot of this latter hill, near the
ravine formed by the torrent, lay an olive orchard,
called Gethsemane, where our Lord was wont to pass
the nightly hours in watching and prayer.

It must have been about ten o'clock when Jesus with
His Apostles reached this spot, and the full moon,
rising slowly from behind Mount Olivet, left the
garden of Gethsemane wrapped in darkness. Scarcely
had Jesus entered the gate, when He allowed Himself
to be seized upon by a most vehement sense of desolation. " Sit ye here," He said to a group of His Disciples, "while I go yonder to pray." And going on
with only three of them, Peter, James, and John, He
led them under the obscurity of the olive trees, toward
the gloomiest corner of the garden. Never before had
the Apostles seen their Beloved Master plunged in
such sadness as this; He appeared to be wholly over-
powered by terror and dejection. The God-Man
paused a moment. " My soul," He groaned, "is sorrowful even unto death. Wait you here, watch and
pray." Then withdrawing from them about a stone's
throw, He sank upon His knees and gradually bowing
His head till His brow touched the very earth,
" Father," He prayed, " Father, all things are possible
to Thee, Oh! take this cup away from Me!" And He
added, " But Thy will, not Mine, be done."

After a more or less prolonged interval, He would
repeat the same prayer in similar terms, till at last
rising with difficulty, He returned to where He had
left the three privileged Apostles. But there was not
one friend to watch with Him, not one human heart to

sympathize with Him in His bitter distress. Weariness and sorrow had oppressed them with sleep. "Simon," our Lord said gently to Peter, "so thou sleepest? Couldst thou then not watch one hour with Me?" And then He uttered a loving warning for all: "Watch and pray, that you enter not into temptation, for the spirit is willing but the flesh is weak."

Again He withdrew from them, and casting Himself down in the dust, He abandoned Himself once more to this frightful agony, while repeating over and over again the same petition as before: "Father, if this cup cannot pass except I drink it, Thy will be done." And now that beautiful countenance, the delight of the Holy Angels, pale and worn, was flooded with tears, that majestic frame, the glory of manhood, quivered from head to foot, like a broken reed, while through every pore of that innocent body, there issued a sweat of blood, which saturated the garments of the Son of God and trickled down in heavy drops upon the ground.

What was the cause of this overwhelming anguish, this awful agony, borne by Christ my Savior? First, the clear foreknowledge of His approaching torments and affronts, and from this I can gather how excessive they must have been when He suffered them in reality the next day. Secondly, the heinousness of the sins of men, which He had taken upon Himself thus to expiate; and here I should call to mind my own sins, considering how by themselves they would have been sufficient to crush the Sacred Heart of Jesus and yet how little penance I have done for them till now. Thirdly, the ingratitude of almost countless millions and millions of souls who, in spite of His bitter afflictions, in spite of His Boundless Love, would deliberately rush into eternal perdition; but especially the ingratitude of so many Religious, His chosen companions and privileged friends, who would be content to lead lives of lukewarmness and routine, of inordination and sin. I also was present to my Divine Redeemer in the garden of Gethsemane; but while He was praying I was asleep, while He was weeping I was dissipated, while He was agonizing I was looking for enjoyment. Yes, I was present to Him, and He offered His mortal anguish to atone for my resistance to the promptings of grace, for my impatience under affliction and contempt, for my murmurings against the orders of Superiors, for my remissness in Meditation and Examen, at Mass and Communion.

Second Point. The Betrayal.

It was now near midnight. The full moon, standing high in the heavens, was flooding the valley with her silvery light. The most profound peace reigned over all nature. "Rise, let us go," said Christ to His Apostles, "behold, he who will betray me is at hand." Judas was bringing up an escort, placed at his disposal by the High Priests and the Sanhedrin, a veritable mob made up partly of military guards of the Temple under one of their officers, and partly of hired watchmen whose duty it was to prevent disorder in the city during the night. They were armed with clubs and swords, and provided also with lanterns at the suggestion, it seems, of the traitor. The police were to lead away the Prisoner, while the soldiers would see to their protection against any violent resistance on the part of His Disciples. Judas had led the way to the entrance of Gethsemane, intending to surprise the Apostles and not expecting to find himself at once face to face with his Master. But at that very moment, our Lord, going before His three favorite Disciples, reached the spot where he had left the other eight at the beginning of His Agony. This sudden meeting caused the traitor to become confused; he hastily stepped forward and, perhaps, without knowing very well what he was doing, took Jesus by the hands, as was the custom, and kissed Him, saying, " Hail, Master."—" Friend," whispered our Lord into his ear, " why art thou come? " And putting him gently away, He added, " Judas, dost thou betray the Son of Man with a kiss? "

Here we see the terrible results of inordination. Judas started on his downward career when, having charge of the alms contributed for the support of the Apostolic Community, he became gradually attached to money. Now he is so completely blinded and hardened by his passion for wealth that, for the paltry sum of thirty shekels, he has engaged to deliver his Adorable Master into the hands of the High Priests. Having lost all supernatural faith, hope, and love, the subsequent realization of his foolish and criminal bargain will only serve to seal his everlasting doom by driving him to a horrible suicide. Have not some Religious Vocations ended in a similar catastrophe! Well may we take to heart the warning words of Christ: " Watch and pray that you enter not into temptation: the spirit, indeed, is willing but the flesh is weak."

Though grieved beyond measure by the base betrayal of Judas, our Lord advanced calm and majestic to meet His enemies. " Whom seek ye? " He asked in a clear voice. They sneeringly answered: " Jesus of Nazareth."—" I am He." The moment His answer reached their ears, they were overmastered by a mysterious force and fell backward to the ground, Judas with them. For a few moments they remained

as if paralyzed, then they rose up full of wonder and
fear, while the traitor tried to sneak away in the
crowd. Christ repeated His question: "Whom seek
ye?"—"Jesus of Nazareth," they replied in a sub-
dued tone. "I have told you that I am He," our Lord
said, "if therefore you seek Me, let these go their
way." And so speaking He pointed to His Disciples
who were standing in a group at a little distance,
some indignant and angry, others sad and frightened,
but all aware that their own lives, as well as that of
their Beloved Master, were at stake.

Here we can admire both the irresistible power of
our Divine Lord, which He is ever willing to exert if
need be in behalf of His servants, and his watchful
solicitude for the safety of those faint-hearted
Apostles. Hence we should learn that God will never
allow us to suffer beyond our weakness, and that,
whatever temptation He may permit to fall upon us,
He will always provide abundant grace that we may
resist and conquer.

The men now drew near to Jesus and prepared to
lay hands on Him. At sight of this some of the
Apostles cried out, "Lord, shall we strike?" And
without waiting for an answer, Peter rushed into the
crowd and with a random blow cut off the ear of a
man called Malchus. This unexpected display of
boldness caused the mob to recoil for a moment and
our Lord took the occasion to calm the excitement of
His Disciples. "Let them alone," He said, "and put
up again thy sword into its scabbard. The chalice
which my Father hath given Me, shall I not drink it?
Thinkest thou that I cannot ask My Father, and He
will give Me presently more than twelve legions of
Angels?" Then stooping down to Malchus, who was
lying in the dust, He touched his ear and healed the

wound; while the Apostles abandoned their Divine Master and scattered in various directions.

As the action of Peter had caused some delay, the Priests came up to see what was the matter, and Jesus addressed to them this terrible rebuke: "You are come out, as if I were a robber, with swords and clubs to apprehend Me. I sat among you daily, teaching in the Temple, and you laid not hands on Me. But this is your hour and the power of darkness." But they received His words with a scornful smile. At the command of the Tribune, the Temple guards surrounded Jesus, and the henchmen of the Sanhedrin bound His hands; after which they hurried Him off, with blows and kicks, across the wild torrent and up the steep slope, to the palace of the High Priests on Mount Sion.

The behavior of the Apostles teaches us the inconstancy, smallness, and selfishness of our own hearts, in contrast with the steadfastness, generosity, and charity of the Sacred Heart of Jesus; while the obduracy of the Priests shows us to what depths of wickedness we may descend, if we fail to check the first motions of ambition, envy, or pride. But throughout this Meditation our main concern should be, by humble endeavor and fervent supplication, by ardent contrition and tender compassion, to take a real share in the crushing sadness and manifold affliction which our Divine Lord longed to experience in order to ransom us from the thraldom of Hell and bring us to the possession of Heaven.

Third Point. What Christ is Going to Suffer and Wishes to Suffer in His Sacred Humanity.

As this is one of the special points recommended by St. Ignatius to our diligent consideration whenever we meditate on the Passion, let us strive to bring home to ourselves the inward eagerness, the holy impetuosity, with which the Son of God now allows Himself to be pushed and dragged like a dangerous impostor or odious malefactor who is rushed into the presence of the Magistrates to hear the public condemnation and to receive the just penalty of his crimes. It was all because of His Measureless Love for us, mere nothings and wretched sinners. Yet we, far from imitating our Adorable Savior, far from gladly bearing with Him harsh and contemptuous treatment, how often have we not acted even worse than the well-meaning but timorous Apostles? Full of sympathy, they grieved and wept at seeing their Cherished Leader at the mercy of His powerful and pitiless enemies. We, on the contrary, not only refused to accept our little share in the afflictions of Christ our Lord, but even strove to drown His very remembrance in the sinful gratification of our sensual appetites. Painful as was to the Faithful and Generous Heart of Jesus the cowardice of those chosen Disciples, bitter as was the treason of Judas Iscariot, has not also our conduct on many occasions been such as to cause yet greater pain and bitterness to this most Affectionate and most Devoted Friend? And what consolation have we given Him till now to atone for our base ingratitude? Even if we were to shed a torrent of tears every day of our life, even if we were moreover to chastise our sinful flesh with every instrument of penance, and to subdue our unruly passions with every practice of mortification, and to afflict our foolish pride with every kind of humiliation, it would all be as nothing in comparison to the wrong we have committed against Him, our Savior and our God. The Apostles ever afterwards spent themselves in ceaseless labors, amid innumerable hardships, appalling dangers, and stubborn persecution, for the Adorable Name of Jesus; till finally they followed their Divine Master even to prison, to torture, and to death. But where are our works of expiation, what has been our return of love, during so many years since our conversion from the world? Alas! how perfunctory has been our contrition, how shallow our amendment, how distracted our prayer, how lax our poverty, how imperfect our chastity, how half-hearted our obedience, how defective our observance, how sluggish our zeal, and how cold our charity! But if such has been our conduct towards Jesus in the past, it certainly shall not remain the same for the future. This we promise Him, while putting our entire trust in those infinite treasures of grace which He purchased for us by His Sacred Passion and Death. Henceforth we will prove to Him our love, not only by the tears we shall daily shed for our sins and by the satisfaction we shall constantly make for our offenses, but also by joyfully bearing with Him and for Him every opportunity of mortification and humiliation with which He may vouchsafe to honor us as His poor servants and lowly companions.

Colloquy with Jesus in anguish and agony, with Jesus betrayed and abandoned, with Jesus arrested and maltreated, for love of me and on my account; continuing to implore the grace of sharing in His sufferings and humiliations, till I actually feel that my petition has been heard.— Anima Christi.

THE SCOURGING AND THE CROWN-
ING WITH THORNS

Subject of this Meditation.— Pilate, in order to gratify the hatred of the High Priests ordered Jesus to be scourged, after which the soldiers mocked and maltreated Him as a would-be King of the Jews.

Composition of Place.— The inner courtyard of the fortress Antonia or Prætorium.

Petition.— Affliction with Christ filled with affliction, anguish with Christ overwhelmed with anguish, tears and grief on account of the terrible sufferings Christ underwent for my sake during the scourging and the crowning with thorns.

First Point. The Scourging or Flagellation.

Pontius Pilate, the Roman Procurator of Judea, had already more than once proclaimed our Savior innocent of all the malicious and absurd charges laid against Him by the Jewish High Priests. Nevertheless, through a most cowardly, unjust, and heartless condescension to the envy and rancor of these degenerate sons of Abraham, he delivered his Divine Prisoner to the soldiers to be scourged. The Scourging, or Flagellation, amongst the Romans, was a punishment reserved for aliens and slaves, and was inflicted with such severity that not seldom the sufferer would not only faint but actually die under the lash. But

the Son of God longed for our sakes, for the sake of
each one of us, to be humiliated like the vilest outlaw
and to be chastised like the worst criminal.

Jesus, accordingly, was led to a marble column that
stood in the center of the courtyard of the Prætorium,
the fortified residence of the Roman Procurator.
There the soldiers rudely stripped Him of His garments, tied His wrists to a ring in the top of the pillar,
so as to stretch His body to its full length, and then
strapped also His feet, which barely touched the
ground, to the base. Upon this one of the executioners came forward, holding in his hands the terrible
lash made of several strips of rawhide about eighteen
inches long. Sometimes these were moreover gar-
nished with bits of bone or points of metal. The man
took his stand behind the Humble Victim, on a large
stone step so as to aim his blows more surely. For
a moment there reigned silence around that fatal
column, while everybody was waiting for the word to
strike. Jesus alone was praying. Let us meanwhile
make an act of the most intense and profound adoration.

At the command of the officer in charge, the execu-
tioner began to strike slowly and heavily, spacing the
blows on the quivering flesh from the shoulders down
in such a way as to leave no spot untouched. Hissing
the scourge went through the air, and wherever it came
down there it left one or more ugly wales. Soon the
skin was all torn and the lash dripping with blood.
Every one of the now rapidly succeeding blows en-
larged the gashes already made, so that after a while
the whole back seemed but one open wound. The sides
also of our Adorable Savior were cruelly cut by the
sharp ends of the thongs, and even the remotest parts
of His Body got their share of torture. His head was

drooping backward; His breast was heaving irregularly; He was about to swoon away.

It is universally admitted that the more delicate a man's nervous system and bodily organization is, the more sensitive also he is to suffering. Now there had never been such a perfect specimen of manhood as our Divine Lord, and this very perfection of soul and body gave to each of the blows He received an efficacy of which we cannot even form a faint idea. Indeed it would be difficult for us to realize what an ordinary person would have endured under this barbarous punishment. It is a well known fact, that where this penalty is still sometimes inflicted, though the number of blows is very limited, even the most robust men are liable to faint.

Yet this physical torment was only the smallest portion of the afflictions borne by Jesus during the Scourging. The deep confusion caused by the exposure of His Virginal Body to the unholy gaze of the bystanders, and still more the crushing anguish arising from the foulness and malice of the particular kind of sins He was thus expiating, these were mental torments entirely beyond the reach of our human understanding. There is, indeed, abundant reason for thinking that this frightful Flagellation was intended and undergone by the Son of God as a special expiation for transgressions of the Sixth and Ninth Commandments, for sins of sensuality, immodesty, and impurity. For, on the one hand, these sins are most degrading, inasmuch as they subordinate the immortal soul to the corruptible body and subject the free spirit to the brute animal; and, therefore, Jesus, in offering Himself as a Victim for man thus dishonored, wished to be treated after the manner of a slave. On the other hand, the sin of impurity, whether commit-

ted in thought, in word, or in act, implies a certain
worship given to the flesh; and hence Christ, in atonement for this idolatry, willed His Sinless Flesh to
be so deeply humbled and so cruelly lacerated.

But at last this horrible scourging had come to an
end and the soldiers loosened the ropes that bound
our Lord to the pillar. His Sacred Body, all covered with wounds and completely exhausted, sank to
the ground in a pool of blood. This, then, was the
awful price paid by Jesus, my God and Savior, for
the carnal vanity, wanton immodesty, and sensual
indulgence of mankind, for those heinous offenses the
mere recollection of which — if I ever had the misfortune to commit them — should cause me to die of
shame and grief. He Who is Essential Purity and
Absolute Holiness, was here publicly handled like the
most vicious scoundrel and the most contemptible
wretch; that thus He might, in our stead, make adequate reparation to the outraged Majesty of the Most
High. Whoever at any time fell grievously, can say
in very truth: "This excruciating torture and anguish was all the work of my hideous sins; every blow
was struck and every insult was inflicted by my shocking violations of the Divine Law. It was for me that
Christ suffered all this; for me, the real criminal; for
me, most wicked sinner; for my sake and on my account. But what have I as yet done or suffered for
Him, or rather for myself, to expiate on my part
these unmentionable excesses? How can I bear to see
Him, my Innocent Redeemer, my Adorable Master, in
such torment and ignominy, whilst I, His guilty
creature, His faithless servant, remain in ease and
comfort? What, then, am I going to do and to suffer,
henceforth, in penance for my shameful iniquities and
in return for His Boundless Love?"

Second Point.   The Crowning with Thorns.

Our Divine Savior, with a great effort, was just rising to His knees in order to resume His garments. He was surrounded by a group of idle soldiers, who had been present at the Scourging and were now taunting Him with coarse and cruel jests, while they were waiting for the further orders of Pontius Pilate. Suddenly one of these men got a wicked inspiration. He remembered that Jesus had proclaimed Himself a king, but that as such He had already been ridiculed by Herod, who had sent Him back to Pilate clothed in the white robe of a candidate for office, and that He had actually been rejected by His own people, who even now were clamoring in the square outside, in front of the fortress, to see Him crucified.   While the Roman Procurator was still deliberating on his future course of action, it occurred to this man that he and his fellow soldiers might divert themselves with this strange Jew, by subjecting Him to a sham investiture of royalty.

The suggestion met with general approval. At once they summoned all their comrades, some five hundred in number, to take part in the entertainment, and having slipped a rope about the hands of our Adorable Savior they dragged Him just as He was, into a large hall or portico, opening on the inner courtyard.   There some of them threw over his bare shoulders an old military cloak instead of a royal mantle, made Him sit down on a block of wood as on a throne, stuck a piece of bamboo, for a scepter, between His fettered hands, whilst others, out of the thorny branches used for the fire, fashioned something like a cap to serve as a kingly crown, and, amid the noisy acclamations and insulting jeers of the whole crowd, pressed this violently down over His bleeding

brow.— Here again let us make an act of most humble
and fervent adoration.

The ceremony of coronation being thus concluded,
those brutal soldiers formed a large circle around our
Lord, and organized a procession of inauguration.
Slowly they passed before Him, each one in turn bending the knee in mock veneration, whilst saluting Him
with a derisive " Hail, King of the Jews! " and then
getting up they spat upon His haggard and blood-
stained countenance, and inflicted blows and kicks
upon His wounded Body, or snatching the reed from
between His hands they drove the crown of thorns
deeper and deeper over His drooping Head. Every
now and then, the procession would get disorderly;
several of the men were, or pretended to be pushed on,
and fell clumsily over their agonizing Victim, Who
was thus more than once trampled under foot and
well-nigh stifled in the crowd. Yet above all the
tumult of laughter and abuse, there constantly re-
sounded the insulting cry: " Hail, Jesus of Nazareth,
King of the Jews." Our Lord, however, bore everything with unbroken silence and unalterable meekness; only His tears bespoke the excess of His sufferings.

Man had sinned through pride; I had sinned
through pride,— through self-complacency, vanity,
human respect, ambition, stubbornness, disobedience,
— and for this pride Jesus desired to atone by submitting to this atrocious buffoonery, this inhuman cruelty.
Yes, we are all permeated with this venom of Hell;
every one of our sins is an effect of this detestable vice,
and if we wish to make our salvation certain, if we
wish to cancel the faults committed in the past, if we
wish to serve God more faithfully in the future, if
we wish to persevere in our sublime Vocation by

steadily advancing towards Holiness, we must strive
by all means to become thoroughly and profoundly
humble. Being made the sport and plaything of
these insolent soldiers, the Son of God says to each
of us with urgent emphasis, " Learn of Me, because
I am meek and humble of heart." But woe to us
Religious if we neglect or discard this supreme lesson of humility; woe to us if we can behold our Adorable Master subjecting Himself to this disgustingly
outrageous treatment, on account of our very pride,
and do not resolve, with the help of His grace, lovingly to welcome and patiently to bear every slight,
every rebuke, every insult, every humiliation that may
come to us from His Divine Providence, through the
agency of any man, high or low, cultured or ignorant,
devout or wicked. " For if in the green wood they do
these things what shall be done in the dry? " What
will be the eternal confusion heaped upon a Religious
lost through pride?

Third Point. The Concealment of the Divinity.
This remarkable fact, to which St. Ignatius takes
care to call our attention from the very opening of
the Third Week, stands out vividly in the Scourging
and still more so in the Crowning with Thorns. The
Sacred Humanity of Christ was not only deprived of
the normal effects of the beatific vision,— though
this continued substantially unchanged,— but also
of every other form of assistance and consolation.
To the eyes of the bystanders there was nothing in
Jesus that could strictly be called godlike: He had
been completely abandoned to the savage fury of His
tormentors. Nevertheless, the human will of Christ,
ever perfectly united to the Divine Will, accepted not
only most patiently but even most eagerly every pain

and every indignity inflicted on Him by these ruffians, for the glory of God and the salvation of souls. "When He suffered He threatened not; but He delivered Himself to those that judged Him unjustly." (1 Pet. 2:24.) The Divinity sustained the Humanity only in so far as to enable our Savior to suffer the more and the longer, that thus He might satisfy more fully His boundless gratitude for all the favors of the Adorable Trinity, His burning zeal for the offended Majesty of the Most High, and His devouring thirst for the happiness of His brethren.

It is plain that, whatever we may do, we can never except very distantly approach such transcendent Holiness, or make any but a very inadequate return for such astounding Liberality. But surely, though it be beyond our strength to do all we may wish, we should at least do whatever we can with the help of Divine Grace. At the revolting spectacle of this wanton barbarity exercised against this Meekest and Humblest of men, in Whom by faith we clearly recognize the Almighty Creator, the Sovereign Lord, the Infinite Goodness, we will prostrate ourselves before Him in profoundest adoration and offer Him our irrevocable renunciation of human comforts and earthly distinctions, as far as permitted by His most Loving Providence. For the future, our satisfaction shall be to be deprived of what would gratify our senses and passions; our ambition, to be treated as the lowest and the least of mankind. Far from importuning our Heavenly Father to shield us from affliction or humiliation, we will henceforth thank Him for granting us these precious opportunities to do penance for our sins, to imitate the example of His Only-Begotten Son, and to prove our gratitude for His ineffable Mercy and Love.

Colloquy, with Jesus scourged and mocked for love of me and on my account. With what earnestness and confidence I should implore from Him an intense shame and burning contrition for any sinful indulgence contrary to modesty or purity, for any foolish unguardedness in the use of my senses or imagination, for any inordinate curiosity in reading or study! But I must also beg Him again and again, by this fearful Flagellation and this fiendish Mockery which He bore with such perfect Meekness, for my sake and in my stead, to bestow upon me the priceless grace of applying myself unceasingly to the acquisition of the Third Degree of Humility. Lastly, ought I not to promise Him, my Heavenly Spouse, that as long as my health permits, I will not only avail myself diligently of all common exercises of penance, but besides generously practise whatever self-affliction I may undertake with leave of my Confessor or Superior? How many Religious fast rigorously almost the entire year? how many abstain habitually from whatever might gratify their palate? how many discipline their bodies severely nearly every day? how many wear pointed steel chains like bracelets or girdles from the hour they rise till breakfast time? how many pass one or more nights every week sleeping on rough boards or on the bare ground? how many pray morning, noon, and night, for several minutes with arms extended? how many constantly volunteer to do the lowliest and hardest work about the house, laundry, refectory, kitchen, or scullery? All this and much more they gladly undertake — though not without permission of their Superiors — in order to make reparation for sin and to become similar to their Divine Master. Hitherto I have done very little indeed. But I will not rise from my knees till Jesus, my

Merciful Lord, has inspired me with some definite and efficacious Resolutions to follow Him from now on not merely in fancy but in very deed.— Our Father.

THE HOLY MASS

Of all devotional exercises calculated to advance us in grace and perfection, none can be more efficient than attendance at Holy Mass. For the Sacrifice of the Altar, in which Christ our Lord daily offers Himself in a mystic though real manner, through the instrumentality of the verbal Consecration, is the same as that which He offered some nineteen hundred years ago, through the instrumentality of the Roman soldiers, on the ignominious Cross of Calvary. But just as many of those who were present at that Bloody Immolation of the Lamb of God went away unchanged for the better, so even now many of those who assist at the Unbloody Immolation of Jesus Christ, derive from it but little benefit. The cause is not far to seek. It is our lack of spiritual insight. We do not appreciate at their true value the Sublime Mysteries so constantly enacted before us on the altar, we do not understand what part we are to take in this Divine Function, we do not see how we are to realize our part. Let us therefore, consider briefly; first, the Value of the Holy Sacrifice as shown by its threefold end; secondly, the Share we are to take in it, namely, our self-sacrifice in union with Christ; and thirdly, the Means of actuating this self-sacrifice.

The Threefold End or Purpose of the Mass.
The Primary and Essential Purpose of all Sacrifice is Adoration; namely, that practical recognition of

God's Supreme Excellence and Absolute Dominion which all intellectual creatures owe Him as their First Beginning and their Last End. Of all our duties this one is no doubt the most fundamental and the most indispensable. It is a duty the rapturous performance of which will engage us for all eternity in Heaven, singing in sweetest harmony with myriads of Blissful Spirits, "Holy! Holy! Holy! Lord God of Hosts!" For though an act of love and an act of adoration are formally different, yet they are materially inseparable, so that adoring love and loving adoration are one and the same motion of the soul. Now in Holy Mass we possess a most potent means of complying with this all-important obligation. For the Victim offered in acknowledgment of the Divine Supremacy is truly a Victim of infinite worth, the Man-God, Jesus Christ; and It is offered with the fathomless humility and the unspeakable love of His Sacred Heart. Let us, then, exert ourselves particularly during the solemn moments of Consecration, when our Blessed Savior is mystically renewing the unreserved Immolation of Himself once made on Calvary, to stir up similar sentiments in our own proud and selfish hearts. It is only thus that we can learn to value every creature solely in its relation to the Creator, that we can succeed in concentrating all our energies on the perfect fulfilment of the Divine Will, and that we can come to be wholly possessed by a burning zeal for the greater glory of the Sovereign Majesty, so as to live henceforth for nothing but the wider, more copious, more splendid manifestation of the Infinite Goodness and Beauty, God.

Another End of the Holy Sacrifice is Propitiation. For this we have the constant teaching of the Church, and the frequent references in her time-hallowed liturgy. Moreover, our Adorable Redeemer clearly indicated this End, when He first made the mystic oblation of His Body and Blood. "This is my Body," He said, "which is being given for you."—"This chalice, which is being poured out for you, for the remission of sins, is the new testament in My Blood." Now, this Propitiation consists in the application of the infinite atonement and merit of the Cross; and inasmuch as it is our Blessed Lord Who offers Himself for us in Holy Mass, its propitiatory, satisfactory, and impetrative effects are infallible, provided we assist at the Sacrifice with the requisite dispositions. Hence, practically, the fruits of justification and sanctification, the temporal and spiritual benefits, reaped from this August Function are exactly proportional to our actual purity and fervor of soul. If only we knew, therefore, how to profit by this stupendous grace, we might confidently expect to obtain not merely a daily more complete canceling of the guilt, penalty, and residue of sin, but also a rapid increase of virtue and a marked progress towards perfection, together with countless other favors for ourselves and our neighbor. And this should spur us on, when engaged in hearing Mass, most ardently to implore the Divine Liberality for our own necessities as well as for the interests of our Companions and the sanctification of our Superiors, particularly for the welfare of our Holy Father the Pope. Besides, we should pray earnestly for our pupils or other charges; for our relatives, friends, benefactors, and enemies; for Bishops, Priests, Religious, and Laymen; for sinners, heretics, schismatics, unbelievers, and idolaters; lastly, for all those who are in affliction, for those about to die this very day, and especially for the Suffering Souls in Purgatory. If we but reflect seriously for a few moments how the Sacred Heart of Jesus is, as it were, breaking under the strain of His passionate longing for the salvation and perfection of every single man, with what intense desire should we not be consumed to pray, labor, suffer, and die for the spiritual progress of our brethren and the eternal welfare of souls?

The Third End of Holy Mass is Thanksgiving. Just as we cannot adequately honor God without imploring His all-powerful help for our countless miseries and necessities, so we do not honor God worthily, unless we also render Him devout thanks for the inestimable blessings incessantly poured out on every creature and most of all on man. And here, in order that we may be able to share somewhat in that most humble and fervent gratitude which is ever bursting forth from the Heart of our Savior, let us briefly review, especially during the latter part of the Mass, the principal favors of which we have been the unworthy recipients. For convenience, we may arrange them under eight heads, like the eight notes of a celestial gamut, the exquisite melody of which is forever rising from the multitude of the Blessed to the throne of the Uncreated Goodness, the Most Holy Trinity. First, the Almighty Father loving me with an infinite, gratuitous love from all eternity and in time creating me man; secondly, the Adorable Word made Flesh for my redemption, laboring and suffering for my sake, and dying on a Cross to atone for my detestable iniquities; thirdly, Jesus, true God and true Man, dwelling with me under the same roof in the humble tabernacle, offering Himself anew for me on the altar at this very moment and at every hour of the day all over the world, and lowering Himself even so far as to become the Food of my soul in Holy Communion; fourthly, the Divine Spirit, continually descending upon me for my guidance and consolation, inspiring me with good thoughts and generous desires, purifying me more and more from sin and its consequences, and daily rendering my heart a less unbefitting temple for the Ever-Adorable Trinity; fifthly, Mary, the Immaculate Mother of God, truly also my Mother, ever watching over me with the most tender solicitude, my joy in affliction, my strength in temptation, my perseverance in weariness, and my unfailing refuge whenever I fall; sixthly, my Vocation to the Religious State in this holy Institute, and all its special means of sanctification, continually bestowed on me in spite of my utter worthlessness and numberless infidelities; seventhly, God, in His Admirable Providence, with unsearchable wisdom and unwearied love, at every instant of my existence, disposing everything, past, present, and future, every circumstance of my life from the most trifling detail to the most decisive event, to make me holy, perfect, entirely His; and lastly, Jesus, my Triumphant Redeemer, preparing for me, instead of the well-deserved, everlasting torments of Hell, an inconceivable, never-fading bliss in Heaven, a true participation in the very Nature of God. After thus recalling to mind this endless chain of most marvelous favors, we shall surely be forced to exclaim: "O infinite bounty, O inexhaustible liberality of my Creator, my Redeemer, and my Spouse! How have I been able to live so long without loving Thee? without sacrificing for Thee my whole self? without consuming all my gifts and talents in praising and serving Thee, and in inviting all creatures to thank and glorify Thee? Take, then, O Lord, take and receive all I am and all I have, only give me Thy grace and Thy love, to draw all hearts to the worship of Thy Blessed Name, to the experience of Thy Boundless Mercy, and to the accomplishment of Thy most Holy Will."

The Share we are to Take in the Mass.

Having thus briefly considered the triple end of Holy Mass, adoration, propitiation, and thanksgiving, — which may, not inaptly, be referred to the three Persons in the Indivisible Divine Substance, Father, Son, and Holy Ghost,— let us now examine what part we are to take in this daily oblation of the Incarnate Word. As we all know, the first point of difference between the Sacrifice of the Cross and the Sacrifice of the Mass is this, that on Calvary our Divine Savior was the sole Pontiff, while on the Altar He is offered not only by Himself as the principal and efficient Priest, but also by the Celebrant, as a true, though subordinate, and, we might almost say, ministerial Priest; and, besides by the entire body of the Faithful, as represented in the person of the Celebrant. Hence, in the Canon of the Mass, Holy Church directs him to pour forth the following prayer: " We, therefore, beseech Thee, O Lord, graciously to accept this oblation made to Thee by us, Thy Servants, and by Thy entire Household." In fact, already before the Preface, the Celebrant thus exhorts the Congregation: " Pray, brethren, that the sacrifice which is both mine and yours may become acceptable to God, the Father Almighty." However, from this we must not conclude that all the members of the Church offer the Mystic Sacrifice in exactly the same way. For while many do so only habitually,— those namely who, by their profession of Christianity, participate in the worship given to God all over the world according to the rites instituted by Christ,— others offer the Holy Mass also actually either by helping to procure what is necessary, or by serving the Celebrant at the altar, or by merely attending the Sacred Mysteries.

But from this first difference there follows another and very important one; namely, that in Holy Mass the Mystical Body of Christ, the Catholic Church, forms part of what is offered to God, while on Calvary Jesus was the sole Victim. For the outward sacrifice, that is, the action witnessed by the senses, derives all its meaning from the fact that it is symbolically expressive of the inward worship by which a man submits and devotes himself entirely to God. This flows from the very nature of a Sacrifice, and is confirmed by the explicit teaching of St. Thomas. It is this interior self-immolation which is referred to in the beautiful prayer made immediately after the oblation of the bread and the wine: " In a humble spirit and with a contrite heart we beg to be received by Thee, O Lord, and may our Sacrifice this day be such in Thy sight as to please Thee, O Lord God." Hence, in so far as the members of the Church really participate in the Eucharistic Holocaust of Christ, they necessarily also associate themselves with the Divine Victim, offering It as a substitute for their own persons and intending thus to express the feelings of unconditional submission and unreserved dedication with which they desire to be consumed for the honor of the Most High. The Church, then, in Holy Mass is joined to Christ not only as Offerer but also as Victim, she being the Mystical Body of which He is the Head. This is why our Adorable Savior wished to be immolated on the Altar under such appearances as would figure forth this Mystic Body, which He was to acquire by His Passion and Death.

In other words, the Species of bread and wine are symbols of the mutual union of the Faithful, inasmuch as the one results from the grinding of many grains and the other from the crushing of many berries. This is also why, even after the Consecration, which essentially constitutes the Eucharistic Sacrifice, the Celebrant begs God to look down upon the Oblation with a serene and propitious countenance, and to command It to be laid by angelic hands on the celestial altar in the sight of His Divine Majesty. For these and similar prayers, which might otherwise appear inexplicable and inadmissible, become full of meaning and devotion, as soon as we recollect that in Holy Mass the Church is both actively and passively associated with Christ our Lord.

We are therefore warranted to conclude that in order to derive from this August Sacrifice the full benefit intended, we must unite ourselves to the Sacred Heart of Jesus in a twofold manner: as offering and as offered. During this Sublime Function, our hearts should, like It, be wholly engrossed with the three great Ends, Adoration, Propitiation, and Thanksgiving: earnestly striving to relish and imitate the absolute purity of all Its intentions and Its devouring zeal for the exaltation of the Divine Glory, Its vehement detestation of even the slightest venial sin and Its insatiable thirst for man's salvation, Its perfect reference of every gift to the Eternal Goodness and Its burning gratitude for the numberless favors continually lavished on all mankind. However, not content with this, we should conjointly with our Blessed Redeemer also offer ourselves and all we are and have, for these same Ends for which He offers Himself daily on our Altars, in memory of His Sacrifice on the Cross. This, the most obvious and

most indispensable element of attendance at Mass, is
unfortunately the very one that is most commonly ignored and most completely overlooked. Reverential
postures, devout prayers, loving aspirations, though
all very good, are only accessories, whilst the principal thing is Self-Immolation in union with Christ our
Lord. From what has been said it is also clear, that
hearing Mass ought to be the special devotion, the
favorite exercise, not to say of every Christian, surely
at least of every Religious, since his very State is one
of complete self-immolation and his whole Life is to
be a continual practice of self-denial.

How to Actuate our Self-Sacrifice.

It only remains now to make a few suggestions
about the Means we have of actuating this Sacrifice
of self in union with Christ. For mere words will
not do, we must come to deeds. St. Paul in his First
Epistle to the Corinthians, in explanation of the Divine injunction, " Do this in commemoration of Me,"
adds, " For as often as you shall eat this Bread and
drink this Chalice, you shall announce the death of
the Lord." Now St. Basil makes on these words the
following beautiful commentary: " We announce
the death of the Lord when we die to sin and live to
Christ, or when the world is crucified to us and we
are crucified to the world." And this meaning, attached by a Holy Doctor to the text of the Great
Apostle, is by no means so far-fetched as it might
appear to some at first sight. For how, indeed, can
we more clearly announce the death of Christ, that
is, how can we more loudly proclaim that excess of
Divine Love which caused our Adorable Savior to
expire for each of us in unutterable shame and affliction, than by completely sacrificing ourselves, after

His example, by His grace, and for love of Him?
But there is no Self-Sacrifice possible, at least in this
present world, without suffering anguish and contempt. Not that anguish and contempt constitute
the Sacrifice, but they are its inseparable concomi-
tants, or rather its requisite instruments, the indispensable means for its execution; while the Sacrifice
itself consists in the interior abandonment and dedication of the soul to God, an act that necessarily
produces an increase of heavenly peace and supernatural nobility, and which forms the ceaseless occupation of Saints and Angels in Eternal Bliss. But,
here on earth, the perfection of our Self-Sacrifice will
be exactly proportional to the intensity of our affliction and the depth of our humiliation. Hence, the
more intimately we wish to participate in the Holocaust of our Divine Master, the more ardently we
must cherish the Cross, not only by generously bearing our actual troubles, but also by earnestly praying
for as much bodily and mental suffering as may be
compatible with God's Adorable Providence. Now
this we can do from three distinct motives; first, from
contrition for our sins, desiring to atone for them as
fully as possible by the application of the infinite
merits of our Blessed Lord; secondly, from zeal for
souls, embracing our trials in union with our Crucified Redeemer for the salvation and perfection of our
brethren; and thirdly, from pure affection, simply to
exercise and strengthen our love for Him, Who
has loved us so excessively from all eternity, our
Heavenly King.

As to the First Motive, however high we may have
risen in the spiritual life, we should constantly keep
in mind that devotion without contrition is sheer illusion. Not only the guilt of venial faults, but also

the unpaid penalty of past sins, and the evil tendencies they have fostered, are so many stains which, as long as they are not wholly removed by due atonement, render us displeasing in the eyes of our All-Holy Lover and prevent Him from admitting us on terms of intimate familiarity. Just as a person that has offended a dear friend or owes him a considerable sum of money, feels ashamed to appear in his presence, so the soul defiled by sin or its consequences dares not and cannot gaze on the blissful countenance of her Divine Spouse. And as after death, the redeemed but still imperfect spirit eagerly plunges itself into the cleansing fires of Purgatory, so already here on earth, the truly repentant sinner is ever animated with a holy hatred and sincere contempt of self, and longs to be despised and ill-treated by every creature of God. Now such a petition may be conveniently joined to the consideration of the First End of Holy Mass, Adoration, and thus engage us during the early part, for which the Liturgy prescribes various penitential prayers together with the Angelic Hymn or Greater Doxology.

As to the Second Motive from which we may beg for affliction and humiliation, namely, zeal for souls, it hardly needs any further development. Every member of an apostolic Institute should be able to say with St. Paul; "I fill up in my flesh what is wanting to the Passion of Christ, for His Body, which is the Church." For, though our Blessed Lord procured man's redemption at the price of His Blood poured out in an ecstasy of love, amid the direst torments and the bitterest ignominy, yet the effects of that redemption are still to be distributed all over the world and to be communicated to all succeeding generations by the Voluntary Crucifixion of the disciples and

companions of the Divine Crucified. According to
the admirable plan of God, men are to be saved and
sanctified, principally by Himself and secondarily by
one another, but in either case through the Cross. As
long as we are looking for our own satisfaction,
whether it be of the senses, or of the intellect, or of
the will, we are not laboring for souls. Our labors,
whatever they may be, will be fruitful for salvation,
only in as far as they are seasoned by mortification
and humiliation, by weariness and contradiction, by
loss of comfort, health, honor, liberty, and life. Not
that we are to pray, without a special inspiration, for
the rare privilege of being cruelly butchered by barbarous idolaters. But while in the Holy Mass the
Sacred Heart of Jesus is daily impetrating for us and
all men the fruits of His Priceless Passion and Death,
we too should beseech and conjure our Heavenly
Father for the grace of partaking more largely in
the measureless affliction of His Incarnate Son, and
of being more completely immolated by Obedience for
the salvation and perfection of our neighbor.

But even if we had neither sins to atone for nor
souls to save and sanctify, there would still be a Third
Motive from which to beg for pain and scorn, the
motive of pure affection for Jesus, our Adorable Master. For true love incessantly strives after a perfect
communication of goods, after the leveling of every
inequality and the obliteration of every distinction,
save only that of individuality and personality. The
Lover cannot bear to be better circumstanced or to be
more honored than the Beloved. Now, in our present
condition, we have no proper knowledge of God, the
Beloved of our souls, except only in so far as He
revealed Himself to us in His assumed Humanity,
poor, ignored, reviled, betrayed, mocked, scourged,

crowned with thorns, overwhelmed with infamy, and nailed to a Cross, dying the death of a recreant slave. It is precisely this sensible manifestation of God's Ineffable Goodness that so powerfully stirs the human heart, while the abstract consideration of His Adorable Perfections leaves it cold and barren. And hence no true love here below without pain, no life without death, no perfection without self-renunciation. God Himself has obeyed this supreme law, the Law of Love. For, as He found us sunk in wretchedness and degradation, He forsook the inaccessible splendors of His Majesty, and for our sakes took upon Himself the form of sinful flesh. His is a more than passionate love, an excessive love, a substantial love, a Divine Love; let ours be at least a human love, a passionate love, a love of soul and body, a love that energizes all our faculties, all our senses, a love that ever prays and strives and longs to become more and more similar to the Beloved, and to be clothed, for His sake and reverence, with the glorious livery of the Cross. This is a marvelous grace, and surely there can be no more appropriate time to implore it than when our hearts, refreshed and inflamed by Holy Communion, are united to the Sacred Heart of Jesus in offering to the Ever-Blessed Trinity a perfect Sacrifice of Thanksgiving.

These, then, are some brief suggestions regarding the realization of our Self-Sacrifice. Only let us remember that we cannot come to Jesus except through Mary, and that, if we desire to suffer with Him, none can teach us how except she, who standing till the end under the Cross of Calvary, had her Immaculate Heart transfixed with all a mother's agony of love, for our sins, for our sanctification, and for our Crucified God.

THE REJECTION AND THE CRUCIFIXION

Subject of this Meditation.— After the Crowning with Thorns, Pilate showed Christ our Lord to the people and the High Priests, but they continued to clamor for His Crucifixion. On being asked whether they wished to crucify their King, they positively rejected Him and proclaimed their subjection to Cæsar. Then Pilate yielded completely to their fiendish hatred and condemned Jesus to be crucified. This sentence was carried out on Calvary, where our Divine Savior remained for three hours hanging on the Cross before He expired.

Composition of Place.— The tribune or loggia over the gateway of the fortress Antonia, with the large hall adjoining it in the rear; and the Via Dolorosa, leading to Mount Calvary, a hillock beyond the western walls of Jerusalem.

Petition.— To bear affliction with Christ filled with affliction, anguish with Christ overwhelmed with anguish, to shed bitter tears and feel piercing grief, on account of the terrible sufferings which Christ underwent for my sake during the Rejection and the Crucifixion.

First Point. The Rejection.
From the top of the double flight of marble steps leading down into the courtyard, Pilate beckoned the

soldiers, who were still mocking and insulting our
Divine Lord, to bring up their Prisoner. At once
they made ready to obey. The Procurator slowly
passed through the hall towards the tribune which
was constructed over the arched entrance of the fortress Antonia. He was followed by a picket of legionaries supporting our Adorable Savior, Who was
utterly exhausted and faltered at every step. An immense crowd had gathered in the square below.
Pilate began to speak: " Look, I bring this Prisoner
here before you, in order you may know that I find no
cause in Him." And disclosing the Sacred Person of
our Lord, Who till then had been hidden from the
view of the people, he added in a loud voice, " Behold the Man."

The Procurator had counted on this unexpected
apparition to soothe the hatred of the Priests and to
surprise the populace into pity. Who, indeed, could
have resisted the sight of that bare and bleeding
Figure? That languid head surmounted by a crown
of thorns, that pallid face stained with gore, those
half-closed eyes, those shriveled lips, those mangled
shoulders only partly covered with a shabby mantle,
those fettered hands holding a bamboo scepter, that
whole Being immersed in an abyss of humiliation
though illuminated by an unearthly majesty,— was
not this enough to subdue even the hardest heart?
In fact, a few moments of silent awe followed the
sudden appearance of our Divine Lord. Then the
members of the Sanhedrin raised the cry: " Crucify
Him! Crucify Him!" Again there was silence, and
Pilate answered gruffly, " Take Him yourselves and
crucify Him, for I find no cause in Him." There was
in this reply disappointment, anger, and contempt.
What had it served him to treat these men with so

much consideration? It would have been better to
let them feel his authority. But now it was too late.
They were practically masters of the situation and
might easily stir up a rebellion. What was he to do?

But presently, the crowd having recovered from
their surprise, hurled at him, like a defiance, the
answer suggested to them by the Priests and the
Scribes: "We have a law, and according to that
law He ought to die, because He has claimed to be
the Son of God." On hearing these words, Pilate
became more afraid and embarrassed than ever, and
taking his Prisoner back into the hall he asked Him
with ill-concealed agitation, "Whence art Thou?"
But Jesus kept silent. "Speakest Thou not to me?"
insisted Pilate, "Knowest Thou not that I have power
either to crucify Thee or to release Thee?" Then
our Lord answered in a voice, full of gentleness and
dignity, "Thou shouldst not have any power over
Me unless it were given thee from above." And as
a last word of warning, that Pilate might not, through
an unjust sentence, abuse the power of which he had
been boasting, Christ added, "Therefore, he who
delivered Me to thee has committed the greater sin."
The Procurator understood both the instruction and
the admonition. The question was settled. Without
further delay he left the hall and announced to the
people that he had decided to set his Prisoner at
liberty. But meanwhile the members of the Sanhedrin, aware of Pilate's emotion at their previous statement that Christ had claimed to be the Son of God
and fearing some unexpected turn of affairs, had prepared the populace for this emergency. So, as soon
as Pilate had signified his intention, they all cried out
together, "If thou dost release this Man, thou art not

Cæsar's friend, for whosoever declares himself a king is a rebel against Cæsar."

The Procurator appeared as if struck by a thunderbolt. His face turned pale and for a moment he was lost in thought. When he regained himself, his decision had been reversed. Why should he run the risk of incurring the anger of Tiberius Cæsar, for the sake of this Jew who appeared so little anxious to save Himself? True, it was a disgraceful surrender for a Roman officer, but for this he would avenge himself on this howling mob and their crafty abettors. Pompously he mounted the steps of his tribunal and ordered our Divine Lord, Who had remained behind in charge of the soldiers, to be led forth once more. Then pointing to the Prisoner, still presenting the same harrowing spectacle of acute suffering and profound humiliation, he said to the crowd in a tone tinkling with irony, "Behold your King!" They at once understood Pilate's meaning and the word stung them into madness. "Away with Him!" they yelled savagely, "Put Him to death! Crucify Him!" But Pilate persisted, "Shall I crucify your King?" It was both a cruel and a dangerous whim, thus to associate Jewish royalty with the punishment reserved for slaves. However, he was gratified far beyond his wishes. Sealing their rejection of Christ with an act of unparalleled baseness, the High Priests, those very men who represented the old party of national independence, cried aloud, "We have no king but Cæsar." It was finished. Since the leaders of the nation had thus openly ratified their subjection to the Roman Emperor, Pilate no longer dared to refuse them the life of this innocent and godlike Man. Turning, accordingly, to our Adorable Savior he pronounced sentence in the customary form: "Thou shalt go to the cross."

Here let us pause to reflect. Priests clamoring for the condemnation of the Holy One and plebeians thirsting for the blood of the Beneficent One and magistrates sentencing to the cross the Innocent One, vividly exemplify to what horrible crimes men may be driven on by their unmortified passions. For though there could never be a more glaring instance of perverted justice than the condemnation of Christ our Lord, yet it is by no means a solitary one but has been repeated over and over again down to this very day. Even persons consecrated to the service of God and bound to the pursuit of Perfection, unless they keep a continual and stern watch over their mind and heart, may frequently fall into more or less grievous faults against Fraternal Charity. They may do so by entertaining rash suspicions, by harboring unkind feelings, by passing uncalled-for criticisms, by uttering offensive remarks, by exaggerating personal defects, by making false accusations, by discountenancing laudible projects, by thwarting good works, and in a hundred other ways. Worse still if such unmortified, uncharitable Religious assume the mask of outward decorum and effusive piety, and, though continually swayed by their prejudices and prepossessions, their aversions and sympathies, are ever ready to maintain that they are seeking nothing but the salvation of souls and the greater glory of God. It is an evil to which we all are more or less prone, because as yet no one is perfectly truthful and humble, no one utterly unselfish and detached; and it is this evil in particular which we should learn to abhor and uproot while considering the Rejection of Christ our Lord. For as often as we think, speak, or act, to the detriment of our brother, we are assisting the High Priests in their persecution and joining Pilate in his condemnation of the Son of God. "Amen I say to you, as long as you did it to one of these My least brethren, you did it to Me." But to abhor and uproot an evil that is within us, means to practise Self-Contempt and Self-Denial, and this in turn is certainly the fittest reparation we can offer for past offenses against Fraternal Charity as well as the best preparation we can make to obtain the grace of bearing opposition and injustice, after the example and for the sake of Jesus, our Heavenly King.

Second Point.   The Crucifixion.

It was now nearly noon.   The sky, bright all morning, began to darken, a thick haze seemed to be gathering from all around, like a veil drawn by a mysterious hand to hide from Heaven the crime about to be consummated on earth.   Not a breath of air was stirring and the heat was suffocating.   Dragged, rather than led, by the soldiers that formed the guard, and followed by the two criminals who had been designated to die with Him, our Divine Lord reached at last the bare and level top of the rocky mound, just outside the Gate of Judgment, called Golgotha or Calvary. It was situated right near one of the most frequented thoroughfares of the city and, on this account, had been selected for this solemn execution.

Simon, the Cyrenean, threw down the heavy Cross which he had been compelled by the soldiers to carry after our Savior; and the executioners made their final preparations to do their grewsome work. Amongst the Jews it was customary to give those about to be put to death, a drink of wine mixed with myrrh or some other narcotic, in order if not altogether to deaden at least to lessen somewhat the acuteness of their torments. Also on this occasion the usual cup had been prepared by some charitable persons, but our Lord, taking only a few drops to taste its bitterness, gently declined to avail Himself of this only means of relief. And now He was once more disrobed by the soldiers. It was indeed a pitiful sight, that delicate Body all bruised and lacerated by the scourge, now bleeding afresh through the violence with which His garments were torn off, and trembling from extreme weakness at the outrage He was thus made to suffer before the vast multitude.

But without uttering a word of complaint or waiting for a command, Jesus stretched Himself out on the instrument of His last and most terrible agony. The executioners briskly secured His arms and wrists with ropes to the crosspiece, then took their large-headed spikes, planted the points on the palms of the hands and, with a few sharp blows, nailed these to the wood. The blood gushed forth, the fingers bent inward, the knees drew up, the eyes filled with tears, and a soft moan betrayed the intensity of the pain. It was now the turn of the feet. A nervous shudder passed through the silent Victim, as the executioners forcibly extended the legs along the main beam of the Cross. But what did they care, accustomed as they were to such spasms? Whilst two of them held down the feet in the required position, the other two quickly drove in the remaining nails. Then they fastened to the top-piece the tablet bearing in Latin, in Greek, and in Hebrew, the inscription, "Jesus of Nazareth, King of the Jews." Their task was now really done, but they were not yet satisfied. That title, "King of the Jews," reminded them of the crown of thorns which, probably, had been removed to strip our Lord of His seamless undergarment. They picked it up and pressed it down upon His head, whilst He uttered that most sublime prayer: "Father, forgive them, for they know not what they do."

Jesus was now suffering all the frightful torment, all the horrible ignominy of Crucifixion, the full penalty demanded by the Divine Justice for our sins. His whole Body writhed in a natural effort to find a less painful posture on that awful Cross. The chest expanded to inhale air, the head fell forward, and in turn imparted a violent shock to the arms. Then the convulsion passed downward depressing the loins, bending the knees, and ending in the feet, whose contracted toes scratched the wood. The blood from the wounds in His hands ran in streams along His outstretched arms and down His mangled Body, till mingling with that which flowed from the wounds in His feet, it drenched the ground below. His heart palpitated irregularly, His brain was burning with the heat of fever, His entrails were consumed with thirst, deep sighs issued from between His parched and livid lips, whilst His tearful and wide opened eyes seemed to implore a little compassion.

Compassion! Not from the High Priests, His ecclesiastical superiors, who gloated to see the disgrace and agony of their Victim and even now assailed Him with bitter sarcasm; not from the fanatic multitude, His own people, who saw in Him That hung upon the tree, as they read in the Scripture, only the accursed of God; not from the Roman legionaries, His executioners, for they were too well inured to scenes of torture and bloodshed. Mary, His tender, loving Mother stood there under the Cross of her Innocent Son, but her presence could serve only to intensify the anguish of His most Affectionate Heart. And the

Eternal Father, the Adorable Trinity? Oh! Jesus
had offered Himself as a holocaust for our sins, and
He did not wish for any mitigation of the punishment,
which the Infinite Wisdom and Goodness desired Him
to undergo for the redemption of the guilty race of
Adam. Far from it. Even now His Sacred Heart
was yearning for more torture and anguish, if this
could be conducive to the glory of the Divine Majesty
or the salvation of mankind. Men had rebelled
against their Creator, and Jesus longed to reconcile
His brethren, longed to set them the example of submission and conformity to the most Holy Will of God,
by becoming obedient even to the death of the Cross.
And thus He hung there for three, three long hours,
an outcast, mocked, reviled, abandoned, and cursed.
"My God, My God, why hast Thou forsaken Me?"
O agony of mercy and of love!

**Third Point. All these Torments and all this Ig-
nominy Christ suffered for my Sins.**
Alas! I too have often rebelled against my Sovereign Lord, as often as I violated His Holy Law, as
often as I resisted duly constituted authority, as often
as I yielded to my wicked passions, as often as I
committed sin; and for each of these countless acts
of rebellion, Jesus suffered the unspeakable ignominy
and intolerable torments of His Crucifixion. Even if
there had been no other men to be redeemed but me,
He would still have welcomed these horrible pains
and these yet more horrible outrages and this infinitely
horrible dereliction, with the same Divine Avidity,
for me alone. "He loved me and delivered Himself
for me." (Gal. 2:20.) All this, then, He willingly
sustained on account of my sins, to expiate my loathsome sensuality, to atone for my senseless pride, to

blot out my foul rebellion, to free me from everlasting death in the fire of Hell, to bring me to eternal
life, to the bliss and glory of Heaven! All this, then,
He embraced for love of me, a mere nothing, a vile
wretch, a despicable sinner; He, my Creator, my Redeemer, my God! And what have I done for love of
Him? During so many years spent in the world?
during so many more years passed in Religion?
What then must I not do and suffer for Him in the
future? from this very moment till my dying
breath? I have my Vows, I have my Rules, I have
my Resolutions. At the foot of Thy Cross, O my
Jesus, I promise Thee once more to observe them,
henceforth, with the utmost fidelity and generosity,
to seek in all things my greater humiliation and mortification, and to grasp every opportunity of bearing
poverty, contempt, and affliction, simply that I may
become like to Thee, my Crucified Love. O Mary, my
Mother, grant me to share in the anguish and disgrace
of thy Divine Son, grant me to be nailed with Him to
the Cross.

Triple Colloquy with the Blessed Virgin, with our
Adorable Savior, and with the Eternal Father; imploring mainly three graces: first, the grace of ardent
contrition and detestation for my many sins but especially for those against Fraternal Charity; secondly, the grace of doing daily all the penance I can
and of continually advancing in the love of the Cross;
thirdly, the grace of constantly keeping before my
mind and tenderly cherishing in my heart the image
of my Crucified Spouse.

EIGHTH DAY

SPECIAL PATRON : St. Theresa.

MOTTO : " God is charity."— 1 John 4 :16.

SPIRIT : Perfect love of friendship

READING : Imitation; Bk. III, C. 5, 21, 22, 47, 49.
Bk. IV, C. 3, 5, 13, 17.
Fourth Gospel; C. 20.
Apocalypse; C. 21.

Strive, by deeper recollection and greater fervor, to make up for any deficiencies on previous days. Complete and memorize your Resolutions. Keep your heart full of heavenly affection and holy joy.

THE RESURRECTION

Introductory Remarks.— As we now enter upon the Fourth Week, or last period, of the Retreat, St. Ignatius recommends to us three things; first, to think of what is calculated to cause a holy cheerfulness and joy, as for instance, Heaven; secondly, to avail ourselves of the light, the weather, and so forth, in so far as we judge that these things can help us to rejoice in our Creator and Lord; and thirdly, to use moderation in everything instead of practising penance. This, however, does not mean that we should in the least relax in pursuing the object of these Spiritual Exercises. On the contrary, precisely because we are nearing the end of our Retreat, we should redouble our efforts to confirm our determination of walking henceforth in the footsteps of our Holy Founders and Patron Saints, and to express this our determination in a set of practical Resolutions regarding the perfect observance of our Rules and the generous embracing of hardship and contempt.

Subject of this Meditation.— After Christ had expired on the Cross, His blissful Soul, united to the Divinity, descended into Limbo to console the spirits of the Just, while His sacred Body, likewise united to the Divinity, was resting in the sepulcher. But having risen again on the morning of the third day, our Blessed Lord, appeared in body and soul, to His most Holy Mother.

Composition of Place.— The sepulcher, its construction and arrangement; also the dwelling of our Lady and, in particular, the room she occupied.

Petition.—" To be intensely glad, and to rejoice exceedingly in such great glory and bliss of Christ our Lord."— The grace we are directed by St. Ignatius to ask in this Meditation, is nothing less than a most pure, holy, and ardent love of friendship, causing us to look upon the joy and bliss of our Savior as our own, and urging us to immolate ourselves, in continual labor, mortification, and humiliation, for His Greater Glory, since not only the spiritual Improvement of our neighbor, but also our own progress in Perfection, as well as our future reward in Heaven, will serve to complete the everlasting Triumph of Christ our King.

First Point. The Descent of the Soul of Christ into Limbo.

Immediately after the death of our Lord and Savior, while His gory and mangled Body is still hanging on the Cross, His Soul is flooded and overwhelmed with torrents of Heavenly Delights. Now all suffering has ceased for that Soul which only a few moments ago was plunged in an ocean of bitterest desolation. Now also the Divinity, far from concealing Itself, so to speak, as during the Passion, manifests more fully than ever Its intimate presence. Not only does the Soul of Christ enjoy the beatific vision as before, but all limitations to the admirable effects of that vision are now removed.

It is impossible for us even to form a faint idea of this Supreme Happiness and Glory, which most emphatically, in the words of the Apostle, no eye has seen, no ear has heard, and no mind has ever conceived. The only thing we can do is to imagine whatever there is most delightful for the human spirit, and then to say to ourselves, that all this, multiplied and intensified a hundred thousand times, would hardly be more than a feeble shadow or a dim reflection of the blessedness enjoyed by the Soul of Jesus. And what especially renders this beatification and glorification so inconceivably noble, is the fact that it is the reward earned by the hardships and sorrows of the Sacred Humanity, the recompense merited particularly by the anguish, torment, and ignominy of the Passion. I will try to enter into the sentiments of that most Blessed Soul, and to rejoice with it as if its bliss were my own, and then reflecting that a similar Happiness is laid up for me too, if I remain faithful and generous in following my King to Calvary, I will draw additional joy from the hope of thus contributing also my humble share to His Eternal Glory.

Yet what should appeal to us as even more admirable, is that the Sacred Soul of Jesus hastens at once to exercise the office of Consoler. This very moment when Christ enters upon His everlasting Triumph as the Conqueror of Death and Hell, far from resting in the enjoyment of His incomparable bliss and glory, He thinks of nothing but consoling His poor servants, the Just of the Old Law. His Loving Soul, then, hypostatically united to the Person of the Word, immediately descends into Limbo to bring to the Holy Patriarchs the glad tidings of their Redemption, to admit them to the full privileges of Friends and Brothers, and to make them share in Its own Happiness. Does it not seem as if, without their participation, Christ considers His own Bliss and Glory as

imperfect and incomplete? O tenderness of the
Heart of Jesus! Shall I ever again yield to thoughts
of discouragement or despondency? For what He
did then, He still does now, dwelling with us in poverty and obscurity, alas! even in loneliness and oblivion, exposed to insults and profanation, as a Prisoner of Love, in the August Sacrament of the Altar.

Let me figure to myself this Limbo, the abode of
all those who died in the grace of God under the Old
Dispensation. It is not the pit of Hell, therefore,
but a place of profound peace and patient longing.
The imminent death of Jesus has been revealed to
them, and they are all lovingly awaiting His coming.
There He appears suddenly in their midst. What immense joy, what unspeakable gladness, what indescribable scenes of gratitude and love! Limbo is
instantaneously transformed into Paradise; all these
Souls are admitted to the beatific vision, to a share in
the Bliss and Glory of Heaven, a share exactly proportional to their labors and sufferings on earth.
Adam and Eve are there, the first to welcome their
Divine Descendant and Redeemer. What do they
say? How do they feel now about their long penance? Next come the saintly Patriarchs, Abraham,
Isaac, and Jacob; then Moses and Aaron and a host
of Levites; David and several of his successors on
the throne of Israel; the holy prophets that foretold
their Savior's birth, His miracles, His passion, and
His triumph, Isaias, Jeremias, Daniel, Ezechiel; the
noble martyrs of the Old Covenant, Eleazar and the
seven Machabees together with their heroic mother;
then those who immediately preceded our Lord or had
even known Him personally on earth, His grand-
parents Joachim and Anna, the devout old man Sim-
eon, the Innocents of Bethlehem, His beloved pre-

cursor John the Baptist, and, dearest of all, His own Foster-Father Joseph.

I will strive to enter into the feelings of these Souls and to share in their exultation. Now they possess the ample reward for their faith in the Divine Promises, for their fidelity in the accomplishment of the Law, for their patience amid all the trials and hardships of their earthly sojourn. How they congratulate our Lord in terms of the most ardent devotion, how they are filled with heavenly delight with Him, through Him, and in Him; with Him, as their Brother; through Him, as their Redeemer; and in Him, as their God!

Second Point. The Resurrection.

The third day from the death of our Lord is now about to dawn; this is the moment set for the fulfilment of the prophecies. The Soul of Jesus, accompanied by all the Just Souls delivered from Limbo, repairs to the sepulcher, a tomb-chamber hewn out of the solid rock. I contemplate together with them that sacred Body wrapped in cloths and extended on the stone shelf. There It lies cold and livid, but even in death preserving a captivating loveliness and overpowering grandeur. I count with many a tear the terrible lacerations inflicted by the scourge, I kiss with the utmost reverence those cruel wounds in the hands and feet, and then, filled with grief and affection, I dare approach my sinful lips to that wide gash made in the side by the soldier's lance and penetrating even far into the Sacred Heart. But who could describe what sentiments of pity, gratitude, and love animate these Holy Souls, whilst they behold this awful spectacle?

But now the Soul of Jesus unites itself once more

to the Body.   The same instant all is changed.   The
Body rises up, every trace of suffering is gone, It is
erect, full of life and beauty and majesty.   I will contemplate especially the countenance of my Savior, so
expressive of goodness, of meekness, and of love.   I
will look again at those five glorious trophies, and
particularly at the large cleft in His Adorable
Heart, through which now issues a beam of rays of
dazzling brightness.   I will consider the wonderful
qualities of this Risen Body: how It is agile like a
spirit that in one instant can traverse the entire
world; subtile so as to be able to surmount all material
obstacles; impassible, that is, no longer subject to
any corruption or suffering.   What is there left now
of all the torments and ignominy of the Passion?
Only one thing, Everlasting Glory.   This glorification and this blessedness of the Body are the consequences of what It has undergone during Its mortal
existence, as the instrument of our redemption, as the
faithful servant of the Soul.   A similar bliss awaits
also my body, if it is a means of salvation to my soul,
by prayer, humility, mortification, obedience, and
charity.

I should contemplate also the effects of the Resurrection of Christ our Lord on the Saints of the Old
Covenant.   What admiration and what joy!   They
all come to adore this glorified Body of the Son of
God; and with unbounded trust they look forward to
the moment of their own Resurrection; unless we prefer to hold the opinion that they too were, at that same
hour, reunited to their risen bodies.   But, however
this may be, I will strive to take part in their dispositions and to fill my heart with a like confidence,
in order to gather strength and ardor for the remaining combats of life.

Third Point. Jesus Appears to His Beloved Mother.

I will first figure to myself the state of Mary's Heroic Spirit during the time that elapsed after the burial of Jesus, and I will endeavor to realize the sadness of Her Spotless Heart, the Heart of that most Affectionate Mother, as she goes in memory over the painful scenes at which she has assisted. So should I also, after her example, ever revolve in my mind and heart the Passion which my Adorable Master underwent not only for my love but also in consequence of my sins. But meanwhile her faith, her hope, and her love have been growing all along; and as the third day nears, she expects, without perhaps knowing how it will come about, the fulfilment of the predictions made by her Divine Son. Though not present at the Resurrection, she is supernaturally enlightened and consoled while this most glorious miracle is taking place.

But Jesus is coming without delay to His Beloved Mother. We may imagine that Mary first hears the sweet song of Angels: "O Queen of heaven, rejoice." Then a soft radiance fills the apartment where she is praying, and in the midst of this preternatural light appears her Son in all His ineffable Beauty and Majesty. He approaches and greets her as He used to do of old at Nazareth, only with more manifest and tender affection. Mary prostrates herself at His feet to adore Him, but He raises her up and presses her to His Sacred Heart. I will reverently assist at this interview between Jesus and Mary; I will listen to their heavenly conversation in order to realize somewhat the feelings of their Hearts, so desirous of the Glory of God and the Redemption of the World; and I will strive to taste a drop of that unspeakable Happiness which is bursting forth from the Most Loving Heart of Jesus and inundates the Immaculate Heart of Mary. I can also see the Saints whom our Blessed Lord has introduced to her as to their Queen; how lovingly they congratulate the Holy Mother of their Savior; and I can hear Elizabeth exclaim once more with rapturous joy, "Blessed art thou amongst women." Yet all this is only a small instalment of the reward that awaits Mary for the sacrifice she has made of Jesus on Calvary. What an encouragement for me to be generous and persevering in sacrificing all my lower affections for my own sanctification and for the salvation of my neighbor, for the love of my Adorable Spouse, for the sake of the Kingdom of Heaven!

Jesus, after a while, withdraws His visible presence, but leaves the Blessed Virgin wonderfully comforted and sanctified. This fact should remind me never to attach myself even to Spiritual Consolations. What I must seek in my prayer is love of obedience, love of mortification, love of humiliation, love of apostolic toil, love of the Cross, love of Jesus Crucified. What I must look for, above everything else, is real holiness, close union with my Divine Lord, the perfect accomplishment of His Will, through all the trials and hardships of this present world, ever longing to share in His anguish and ignominy, yet ever abounding in gladness on account of His Infinite Bliss and Glory. Far from resting in any consolation as an end, I must use it only as a means to reach the grace I am seeking, which is that of rejoicing so intensely in the Measureless Triumph of my Lord and Master as to make it in a true sense my own, and of promoting it more and more at the sacrifice of everything I have, my energies, my talents, my will, my judgment, my liberty, my health, my limbs, and my very life.

Colloquy.— Rejoicing and exulting with all the Saints in the Ineffable Happiness and Glory of Jesus, as also in the Wonderful Consolations bestowed on Mary, I will beg for grace to follow them generously in suffering and humiliation, that thus I may likewise share in their Everlasting Triumph and Heavenly Bliss.— Our Father.

THE ASCENSION

Subject of this Meditation.— After Christ our Lord had shown Himself for forty days to the Apostles, speaking of the Kingdom of God, He commanded them to await in Jerusalem the coming of the Holy Spirit Whom He had promised them on the eve of His Passion. Then having led them forth to Mount Olivet, He was raised up in their presence, and a cloud received Him out of their sight. While they were still gazing after Him two angels stood by them and said: "Ye men of Galilee, why stand you looking up to heaven? This Jesus Who is taken up from you into heaven, shall so come as you have seen Him going into heaven."— Acts 1 :11.

Composition of Place.— The road leading from Jerusalem through Bethany up to the summit of Mount Olivet.

Petition.— To rejoice intensely in this great glory of Christ our Lord, and to labor strenuously to contribute to it also my share.

First Point. Circumstances Preceding the Ascension.

After the Resurrection, our Adorable Redeemer continued yet for forty days to converse with His Apostles, strengthening them for their future labors and combats, and instructing them more fully about the Kingdom of God, the One, Holy, Catholic Church. Also with us our Divine Lord has deigned to converse intimately during this Retreat, enlightening us as to our failings in the past and inspiring us with holy and practical Resolutions for the future. Like those privileged Disciples, we too have experienced anew how great is His Love and how tender His Solicitude for such as have dedicated themselves entirely to His Service. Now these peaceful days, however, are nearly over, and the time is coming for the contest, for carrying out our good resolves. If we wish to be successful in our efforts and victorious in the fight, we must study the measures and adopt the means best calculated to insure, for ever after, this humble and loving converse of our hearts with God. Jesus, our Heavenly Master, is still with us in the Holy Eucharist. There especially we must keep constantly united to Him. For otherwise we shall infallibly fall back into our former habits of tepidity and sin. It is only by this incessant communication with our Blessed Savior that we can obtain a more and more distinct knowledge of His Holy Will in reference to our personal sanctification, and a proportional increase of grace to correspond to His Adorable Designs. Often, therefore, let us cry out to Him, "Speak, O Lord, for Thy servant listens." And again, "Let Thy voice sound in my ears, O Jesus, for Thy voice is sweet and Thy face comely."

St. Luke also states that our Lord commanded His Disciples not to leave Jerusalem but to await the coming of the Holy Ghost, according as He had promised them on the eve of His Passion. Since Jerusalem is interpreted to mean City of Peace, we may here consider that the only sure way forever to preserve true peace of soul is by manfully resisting our passions, our sensuality, our cowardice, our ambition, our pride; by diligently observing obedience,

silence, and recollection; by never pouring out our
heart on our studies, our occupations, our projects,
our relatives, our acquaintances, our pupils; but by
seeking everywhere opportunities of humiliation and
suffering as so many gems and jewels to offer to our
Heavenly Spouse. Again, to us also our Lord has
made the same promise of the Holy Ghost, and though
we have already received that Divine Spirit particularly in the Sacrament of Confirmation, yet we may
cause Him to dwell in our souls daily with greater
intimacy and efficacy, and to communicate to us in
ever greater abundance His seven gifts: fear, piety,
knowledge, fortitude, counsel, understanding, wisdom. This we can do very effectually by earnest
entreaties and fervent aspirations. Oh! how sorely
we need His Light and His Fire, to dispel our darkness and our pride, to consume our coldness and our
selfishness.

Some of the Disciples asked, " Lord, wilt Thou at
this time restore the kingdom to Israel? " How
worldly-minded these men still were! And such my
Divine Master might also consider me, seeing that,
after so many wonderful proofs of His love, I am still
so strongly attached to the concerns of earth and so
little devoted to the interests of Heaven. Urged on,
then, by a salutary confusion and a holy indignation,
I must beg my Adorable Lord to tear from my heart,
even if it should have to be all bruised and broken,
to tear from it every obstacle to His Glory, every disposition at variance with His Will: my uncharitableness, my impatience, my vanity, my self-complacency,
my precipitation, my meddlesomeness, my inconstancy, my remissness, as well as all national prepossessions and narrow prejudices.

But Jesus answered: " It is not for you to know the

times or moments which the Father hath put in His power. But you shall receive the Holy Ghost coming upon you, and you shall be witnesses unto Me in Jerusalem, and in all Judea and Samaria, and even to the uttermost parts of the earth." This is also our appointed task. Leaving to Divine Providence the time and manner of the final establishment and exaltation of the Heavenly Kingdom, refraining from all useless speculations about the future trials and triumphs of the Church, and setting aside all the cravings and apprehensions of our corrupt nature, of our selfishness and our pride, we must go and render testimony to Jesus our Lord before the whole world, by the Holiness of a life and the efficacy of a Religion that are in perfect accordance with His Teachings, Counsels, and Examples. " In Jerusalem," that is in the midst of my Religious Companions, " in Judea," among the faithful members of the Church, " in Samaria," amongst the partisans of heresy and schism, " even to the uttermost parts of the earth," in the very midst of our modern infidels and civilized pagans. Are we now prepared, or rather determined to give this testimony better than we have done heretofore?

Second Point. The Ascension.

Having thus spoken to enlighten and animate His beloved Disciples, Jesus led them out to Mount Olivet. Our Lord was to enter into the fulness of His Glory from the summit of the hill at the foot of which He had entered upon the agony of His Passion: a very significant fact, in keeping with the words which He had addressed to the two devout men on the road to Emmaus: " Ought not Christ to have suffered these things and so to enter into His Glory?" How de-

lightful this journey to the Mountain of Olives compared with the one made just six weeks before to the
Garden of Gethsemane! Let us, then, constantly bear
in mind this great principle, namely, that if we wish
to triumph with Jesus, we must embrace mortification
and humiliation, suffering and contempt, for His love
and reverence, and in union with His Sacred Heart.

"And lifting up His hands," so we read again, "He
blessed them." How did He bless them? Undoubtedly, with the Holy Sign of the Cross, and ever since
the Cross has been an instrument of Blessing and an
emblem of Victory. The blessing of Jesus meant for
Mary a prolonged exile on this earth for the good of
the faithful and for her own greater sanctity; for
Magdalen, a life of prayer, penance, and charity; for
Peter, the burdensome government of the entire
Church ending in a death by crucifixion; for all the
other Apostles, labors, disappointments, persecution,
and martyrdom. But the blessing of Jesus meant,
besides, an abundant outpouring of heavenly grace, a
notable increase of light and strength.

What is the blessing of Jesus for me at the close of
these Holy Exercises? Surely, some kind of Cross,
some office or trial, under which nature will worry
and chafe and rebel, but accompanied by special helps
and favors. Let me accept it beforehand, with humility, confidence, alacrity, and generosity. And whenever I bless myself, henceforth, with this sacred token
of Man's Redemption and God's Love, I will strive to
remember and to renew my Resolution of being spiritually nailed with Jesus to the Cross. This is to be
the epitome of all my lights, the scope of all my
efforts, the fruit of my whole Retreat; and the very
sign of the Cross or the mere sight of the Crucifix will
be my constant remembrancer, reanimating and con-

firming my determination to embrace every opportunity of self-denial and self-abasement.

"And while they looked on, He was raised up, and a cloud received Him out of their sight." As Jesus, my Lord and Savior, rises up slowly and majestically, by His own power, I will follow Him in thought, I will contemplate the multitudes of Holy Souls and Blissful Angels that surround Him, I will penetrate as far as the eternal gates through which the King of Glory enters into His everlasting realm. How they swing open of their own accord to admit the triumphal procession! Jesus ascends to the highest Heaven and occupies His throne at the right of the Eternal Father. As God, He always possessed infinite Bliss and Glory, as Man He has merited and conquered this universal Sovereignty by His sacred Passion and Death. How I ought to rejoice at this vision! My whole life, from now on, ought to be but one hymn of gladness and exultation, in accord with the rapturous, "Holy! Holy! Holy!" of the Angelic Hosts and the Choirs of the Blessed.

But there is also a throne being prepared for me, and since Jesus, my King, has opened the way, I can and I will merit it by following Him to the Cross, that thus I may complete His Bliss and Glory. Henceforth, I must live only for Him. My heart must ever be with Him in Heaven. It must become more and more detached from all that is earthly, from all that is selfish; more and more purified from every inordinate leaning, from every worldly affection. Suffering and contempt, oh! how welcome these ought to be to me, since they alone can confer on my soul this angelic purity, and make me live only for Jesus, my Adorable Spouse, on the Cross, in the Holy Eucharist, in Heaven.

Third Point.   The Apostles after the Ascension.
" And while they were beholding Him going up to
Heaven," thus we read next, " two men stood by them
in white garments."   The Disciples should have liked
to get one more glimpse of His Adorable Person, to
gather one more word from His Sacred Lips, but this
would not have been conformable to the Providence of
God.   When we receive heavenly consolation, we
must not be so taken up with it as to remain of our
free choice inactive and motionless.   Divine favors
are granted, not to make us rest, but to make us work.
" You men of Galilee, why stand you looking up to
Heaven? "   That is the question which I should put
also to myself at the end of this spiritual Retreat.
Our contemplations must yield practical results, our
Exercises are to bear fruit.   We must go and struggle
and suffer and sacrifice ourselves unreservedly for the
Glory of Jesus our Lord and for the Good of our
Brethren.   In other words, we must begin at once,
with all the energy of our being, to carry out our Resolutions.   For the time is getting short; only a few
years remain, perhaps only a few days, after which
" the night cometh when no man can work."

" This Jesus Who is taken up from you into Heaven,
shall so come as you have seen Him going into
Heaven."   These words are to be fulfilled for each of
us at the close of our life, at the moment of our death,
when of a sudden our soul disengaged from the burden of this corruptible body, will behold, in one intellectual flash, all the favors of God together with all
her own doings, and will thus, indeed, see this Jesus,
her Lord and Savior, how much He has loved her, how
much He has suffered for her, how carefully He has
watched, guided, and protected her all during this
present period of probation, strife, and exile.   Oh! let

us diligently prepare ourselves for that coming of our Divine Lover but also our Sovereign Judge. Let us long for this blessed moment, let us be thankful when our strength is undermined by toil and our body is broken down by sickness, since all this will only serve to hasten the union of our soul with God, her Eternal Spouse.

"They adoring went back to Jerusalem with great joy." But meanwhile,— O consoling thought, O blissful certainty! — Jesus, though enthroned at the right hand of the Father Almighty, above all the hierarchies of Angels and Archangels, of Cherubim and Seraphim, is still thinking of me, His poor servant, with the most tender solicitude; more than this, He stays with me under the same roof in the Holy Eucharist, daily renews for me the sacrifice of the Cross in every Holy Mass, daily deigns to descend into my heart by Holy Communion. Oh! what, then, can I do for Him? Just now I longed to die,— but no, I must long to live, long to labor, long to suffer, long to increase His Glory by my own sanctification, long to be forever the victim of His love.

Colloquy with our Blessed Lord. Adoration, thanksgiving, petition. "Glory to God in the highest. We praise Thee, we bless Thee, we adore Thee, we glorify Thee, we render thanks to Thee, because of Thy great glory, Lord Jesus Christ, Only-Begotten of the Father, Lord God, Lamb of God, King of Heaven; Who livest and reignest with God the Father in the unity of the Holy Ghost, world without end. Amen." — Our Father.

FRATERNAL CHARITY

In What Love Consists.

Love is not sentiment; it consists in deeds more than in feelings and words, in fact, it is all action. Hence God, Who is the infinitely Pure Act, is also the infinitely Perfect Love. Love lies essentially in union of will. Everybody necessarily desires and seeks his own perfection, his own happiness; and therefore, if we love man,. we shall use every means in our power to procure him that perfection, that happiness. This is obviously to love one's neighbor as oneself.

Considered in its motive, the love of our neighbor may be more or less noble. It is sensual, when we love him for the external qualities that please the senses, and it is intellectual, when we love him for his mental and moral endowments. All this is natural love. Our affection, however, should be supernatural; and this is the case when we love him because he reflects in these various gifts of body, mind, and spirit, the Adorable Attributes of the Creator; or because, by sanctifying grace and heavenly bliss, he actually participates in the Sovereign Excellence of God. Hence the love of God and the love of our neighbor are referred to the same virtue of Charity, since they have the same motive, namely the Inexhaustible Goodness, the Infinite Loveliness of the Most High, revealed to us by supernatural faith. It is evident that our love of self should be based on the same considerations, and this gives another and deeper meaning to the precept, "Love thy neighbor as thyself." Even the body may and should be loved for the sake of God, because it is the instrument of the soul in promoting the Divine glory, because it is the temple of the Holy Ghost, sanctified by His presence, and because it is destined to share in the everlasting bliss of Heaven.

We must, then, ardently desire man's real good, his physical welfare, his mental development, his present sanctification, and his eternal beatitude. We must rejoice with him in so far as he attains these blessings and we must compassionate him, suffer with him, in proportion as he is deprived of them. His contentment should be our contentment, his sorrow our sorrow, his glory our glory. Like the Apostle St. Paul, we ought to become weak to the weak, and all things to all. Yes, all things to all; not all things to only a few, especially if this should be because of some sensible attraction or natural sympathy.

But if we sincerely and efficaciously wish our neighbor all true happiness, we shall strive to communicate to him whatever happiness we ourselves may already possess. Our strength will supply his weakness, our knowledge his ignorance, we shall share our food with the hungry, our refreshment with the thirsty, our raiment with the destitute; or at least, availing ourselves of the numerous opportunities daily afforded by Community Life, we shall in all these things leave the better part for those who may stand in greater need than ourselves. In short, we shall render to everybody, whether friend or enemy, every kind of service that it is in our power to give; always, of course, in due subordination of the material and temporal to the spiritual and eternal; for, once more, our love must be supernatural, it must be founded in God, it must be Charity.

It was such Charity as this that impelled St. Peter
Claver to tenderly embrace the poor Negro captives
on their arrival at Cartagena, to nurse them, serve
them, instruct them, and, in one word, to make himself in everything their most abject and most devoted
slave.   Again it was this sincere Charity which animated St. Ignatius Loyola, when he heard that his
faithless countryman and companion, who some time
before had robbed him of a sum of money necessary
for his maintenance at the University of Paris, was
lying dangerously sick, in utter destitution, at Rouen.
At once he hastened, fasting and on foot, to the assistance of this poor wretch, a distance of some sixty
miles, and not only lovingly waited on him all during
his illness, but also procured for him, when restored to
health, the means to return to Spain, and even provided him with letters of recommendation.

This is truly the virtue eulogized by the Great
Apostle: " Charity is patient and obliging; it is not
envious, nor morose, nor arrogant, nor ostentatious;
it is not selfish, nor irascible, nor resentful; it takes
no pleasure in what is evil, but dwells with joy on
what is good; it is ever ready to excuse, to believe, to
hope, and to suffer."   Does our Charity agree with
this brief description?   Does it tally with it exactly
in every point?   Happy, indeed, are we, if it does;
for then, as the Beloved Disciple assures us, God
abideth in our hearts.   But if we still seek our own
satisfaction to the detriment of our brother; if we
have no regard for his comfort and well-being, and
remain unconcerned about his interests; if we are
blind to his good qualities and cannot bear with his
defects; if we neglect to help with due humility towards his correction and prefer to make his faults
the subject of conversation even during time of

silence; surely, we have great reason to fear that our
love is more sentimental than solid, more human than
divine.

Whom to Love.

We must love all those living outside the One True
Church, in original or actual sin: heretics and schismatics, Jews and Mohammedans, unbelievers and idolaters.   How many, many millions, in every division of
the globe, are thus in imminent danger of damnation!
O what heartrending misery! their earthly existence
full of unrest and suffering, and their future condition
one of everlasting anguish and despair.   Can we do
nothing for them?   Can our hearts remain unmoved
and cold, whilst the Sacred Heart of Jesus is consumed with a most ardent longing for their salvation?
Was it not for each one of these wretched souls, that
He so lovingly embraced all the unutterable torment
and infamy of His Passion and Death?   It rests with
us to apply the infinite merits of that Divine Holocaust.   For thus God has decreed in His most Wise
and Loving Providence, that men are to be saved and
sanctified by men.   Glorious task, to be a partner of
the Most High in this wonderful work of mercy; to cooperate with Jesus, the Incarnate Word, in saving
souls; to be the pliant instrument of the Holy Spirit in
the justification of our brethren!

Yet how few busy themselves about the accomplishment of this supreme duty?   What have I done up to
this?   What am I going to do in the future?   Let me
beware lest I too should deserve that withering rebuke
of the Master: " O wicked and slothful servant, thou
oughtest to have committed my money to the banker,
and at my coming I should have received my own with
usury.   Take ye away, therefore, the talent from

him and give it to him that hath ten talents, but the improfitable servant cast ye out into the exterior darkness; there shall be weeping and gnashing of teeth."

On the other hand, how intensely grateful the Adorable Heart of Jesus will feel towards those who bestir themselves to make known to men the fathomless depth and the boundless breadth of His Charity! How He will enrich them with His choicest graces! How His tenderest caresses will be lavished on these His true Disciples! How safe a refuge His most Merciful Heart will prove to them at the hour of death, and how delightful a paradise for all eternity!

But we should love still more all those who belong to Holy Church, those who are living in the state of Sanctifying Grace. These are, of course, much nearer to us than those outside the True Fold, because they are more closely united to Christ our Head; and consequently we ought to love them more. First in our affection among the members of the Church comes the Holy Father, the Reigning Pope, Christ's Supreme Vicar, and with him the College of Cardinals and the entire Catholic Hierarchy, particularly in this our own country. Next; all Priests and Religious. Thirdly; our parents, relatives and benefactors on earth, as well as the Holy Souls in Purgatory. Lastly; all the other Faithful in every clime and nation and social condition. How desirous we should be to promote their sanctification and salvation, to secure their temporary well-being and eternal happiness.

Again, we should be animated with a very tender love for our fellow Religious. We must consider that every member of our holy Institute is truly our brother, much more so, incomparably more so, than those who have the same natural mother. Do we

foster towards each one a truly fraternal affection?
Are we not, on the one hand, lacking in sympathy towards them, without interest in their work, without
concern for their afflictions, attributing their bodily
ailments to a disordered imagination and setting
down their personal views to an unworthy motive?
Do we not, perhaps, speak disparagingly of them to
companions or outsiders, in private or in public, be-
littling their doings, ridiculing their opinions, and
maligning their intentions? and this not merely
through thoughtlessness or levity but even through
envy or resentment? Oh! may there never be found
in this Community any Religious to whom St. Paul
might have referred when he wrote to Timothy,
" But if any man has no care of his own, especially
of those of his house, he hath denied the faith and is
worse than an infidel." On the other hand, are we
not unduly biased by natural qualities, do we not
pay too much attention to outward looks or inward
accomplishments? These commonplace things should
not be allowed to enter into comparison with the sublime qualifications of a chosen disciple of Jesus, a
beloved client of Mary, a fellow soldier for Heaven,
striving together with us, by the same Life and the
same Vows, after the Highest Sanctity, after the
most Perfect Charity, after the Greatest Glory of
God, and who like ourselves, as we firmly hope, will
one day be admitted to share for all eternity in the
Bliss and Triumph of our Adorable Savior. But
even from amongst the members of our own Institute
we should single out all Superiors, cherishing for
them an altogether special love joined to a deep supernatural reverence as the accredited Interpreters of
the Divine Will. And while exercising our Charity
towards the living, let us also be mindful of those

who are still detained in Purgatory. What can we
do to bring them sooner to the inconceivable bliss of
Heaven?

How to Love.

By Fervent Prayer and Personal Sanctification.—
If we can do nothing else, at least let us pray, pray
earnestly, pray continually, especially at Mass and
Communion, pray with that childlike importunity
and holy vehemence which are so pleasing to our
Heavenly Father. Let us be convinced of this, that
if any of these millions of sinners are to save their
souls, it will be owing principally to prayer, humble
prayer, confident prayer, ardent prayer, persevering
prayer. Why can we not take the habit of daily offering ourselves in Meditation, Mass, and Communion,
with the utmost energy of which we are capable, to suffer anything and everything for the good of souls, for
the conversion of sinners, for the sanctification of the
faithful, for the advancement of our Companions and
Superiors? And our prayer will be the more efficacious, the closer we become united to God, by the
practice of mortification and the bearing of humiliation.

Oh! to think that on our own Holiness — on the
Holiness of each one of us — Divine Providence has
made depend the Salvation of some and the Sanctification of others, who, unless we reach the intended
degree of Perfection, will not be saved, will not be
sanctified! And the greater our Holiness, the more
souls we shall help render eternally happy. Our occupations, our infirmities, our age, far from being
insurmountable obstacles on the path of Perfection,
as we fondly fancy, are in reality, every one of them,
powerful aids and indispensable means. Can there

be any consideration more apt to inflame our souls
with an impetuous and insatiable longing after Holiness?

Again, it is by lowly and ardent Supplication and
by diligently gaining the Indulgences attached to
various devotions, that we can give immense assistance to the Holy Souls in Purgatory, abate the fierceness of those cleansing flames, relieve the mortal
sadness of that spiritual prison, and usher them into
the blissful presence of our Heavenly Father. Since
Holy Church is so merciful, so compassionate, and so
prodigal of her supernatural treasures, why can we
not avail ourselves somewhat better of her astounding liberality? It is so easy to gain Indulgences, even
plenary ones; all that is needed on our part is a little
care and a valid intention. Let us frequently and
from our heart renew the so-called "Heroic Act of
Charity for the Souls in Purgatory," and let us make
sure for the future not to lose a single opportunity
of consoling these poor, suffering Brethren of ours,
these dearly beloved Children of God.

By our Labors and Sufferings.— We are busy people, we are working the whole day, and every day of
the year. Now, all this labor, whatever be its character, whether corporal or mental, obscure or conspicuous, should be directed toward one single object,
the Salvation and Sanctification of Souls. But oh!
how often we forget this, how seldom we animate ourselves with this grand thought, this certain truth,
that by our cooking, serving, sewing, and patching,
or by our plowing, planting, harvesting, and pruning,
or by our study, teaching, bookkeeping, and correspondence, we are all cooperating in that most Divine
work of Redemption, all contributing to the Justification and Perfection of Souls, who otherwise would

remain unjustified and imperfect. If we did but think of this, how joyful and light all this toil would become; how little we should mind heat and cold, inconvenience and fatigue, illness and accident; how desirous we should be of achieving real success in our appointed tasks; and how determined to reach in the discharge of our duties the very summit of Holy Obedience! All for the sake of Jesus, and for the good of those souls whom He loves so tenderly.

But, besides, we must always be on the lookout to render everybody all sorts of services, to assist our Religious Companions and our fellow men in a thousand little ways, with sincere humility and unobtrusive kindness; prompt to enlighten and correct the erring with prudent affability and hopeful perseverance; ready to encourage and console the downcast with delicate sweetness and tactful simplicity; and intent, on every occasion and by every lawful means, upon making those round about us as contented and happy as possible. Oh! let us not despise these apparent trifles. They constituted the ordinary practice of the Saints to win souls to God, nor are we to imagine for a moment that our Blessed Lord acted differently. We shall never perform great things unless we first apply ourselves to do these little things. In fact, the greatest thing that most of us, if not all, will ever be called upon to do, is precisely to be constant and diligent and enthusiastic in doing these apparently little things. Each of these trifling actions done in love, though unknown to the rest of mankind, is of inestimable value in the sight of the Most High, while those showy works which for a time call forth so much applause and admiration, are often of no account before the Sovereign Majesty.

Yet especially should we practise Charity by avoid-

ing most carefully whatever might give others pain or
trouble.   The instinct of love is all mildness, for-
bearance, humility; it is averse to everything
haughty, impatient, or harsh.   If we had experienced
only once what it is to love, how clear this would be
to us!   True love, while it enlightens the mind and
makes it discover innumerable ways to do good, at
the same time enchains the heart and robs it of its
liberty to act otherwise.   It really makes us slaves,
but slaves by choice and from joy, not slaves by force
or from fear.   Henceforth, then, no more rash suspicions, no more unfavorable constructions, no more
offensive remarks, no more stinging replies, no more
apathetic silence, and no more selfish complaints.
For we should never add our own to another's burden, each one has enough to bear.   Let us rather
strive to lighten our brother's load, by reminding
him of the cheering aspects of this earthly pilgrim-
age or the solid motives of patience and confidence.

By Word and Example.— Our love, however, must
not stop short at devotedly rendering every kind of
service and at scrupulously avoiding everything that
might cause annoyance or sorrow.   No, we should
also exert ourselves, both by word and by example,
to do positive good, real, lasting, supernatural good.
If only our hearts were animated with a genuine contempt for things perishable and filled with a sincere
esteem for things eternal and inflamed with an ardent
love of God our Lord, how easy it would be to benefit
our neighbor, our brother, by conversation!   It would
flow so spontaneously, so gracefully, that it could not
possibly fail to influence him for the better.   And the
same holds true of our example.   In other words, our
own sanctification, that is, after all, the great means
of doing good, in fact, the only efficacious means.   If

we appear to do good in any other way, it will not
prove solid and durable, but just as superficial and
ephemeral as our varnish of piety. We cannot give
to others what we ourselves do not possess; — a maxim
as plain as daylight, yet apparently very difficult at
times to realize.

Let us, then, lay the ax to the root, and manfully
cut off all earthly attachment; let us strain every
sinew to advance daily, at least a few steps, in poverty,
chastity, and obedience, in the contempt of self and
the imitation of Christ. And while we feel conscious
that as yet we can work but little good either by word
or by example, let us at any rate beware of working
evil, of scandalizing either by word or by example.
This surely we can and must avoid. Should it nevertheless happen that, through human frailty, we give
spiritual offense to our brother, let us not fail to make
for it as soon as possible a suitable reparation. If
we have the excellent habit of asking a penance for
breaking a bit of earthenware or damaging a piece of
furniture, how much more reason we have to ask a
penance if we rend asunder the precious mantle of
Charity! In any case, let us take efficient measures
to undo, as far as lies in us, the harm we may have
caused.

In conclusion; to lead a Life of Love is to live a
life of happiness, a prelude to Life Eternal. It is to
lead the life of a Saint, the life of the Blessed Virgin
Mary, the life of the Sacred Heart of Jesus. May,
then, my entire existence be taken up with love: love
in prayer, love in labor, love in rest, love in recreation, love in health, love in sickness, love in joy, love
in sorrow, love in success, love in failure, love in light,
love in darkness; may I love at every moment of my
life. May I love all men from the least to the greatest,

beginning with those of my own household, the members of my own Community, my own Institute; and for the rest singling out particularly the poor, the ignorant, the rude, the infirm, the suffering, and the dying. May I love all in God and God in all. May I be wholly possessed, may I be wholly consumed by love. May my every thought, my every desire, my every breath, my every pulsation, be an act of the most pure, most tender, and most generous love. May my First and Universal and Supreme Rule be the Law of Love, the Precept of Charity: "Thou shalt love the Lord thy God with thy whole mind, with thy whole heart, with thy whole soul, and with thy whole strength; and thou shalt love thy neighbor as thyself; yea, even so as I have loved thee."

DIVINE LOVE

Introductory Remarks.— Charity is the supernatural love of friendship between God and man. It is a mutual love of benevolence, involving a communication of goods between the Lover and the Beloved. This love of benevolence, on our part, consists in sincerely and effectually wishing Him all the good we can. It comprises, therefore, three kinds of acts. First; Complacency or Joy in the goods God already possesses, His Power, Wisdom, Holiness, and other Attributes, as well as the Glory given Him by His creatures, the spread of His Kingdom, and so forth. To this corresponds Grief on account of our own and other men's sins. Secondly; Benevolence in the strict sense, or the Desire of augmenting, as far as lies in us, the goods possessed by God; which can only be hypothetical with regard to His Intrinsic Perfections, since being Infinite they are incapable of any increase; but should ever be absolute in reference to His Extrinsic Glory. To this corresponds Hatred and Detestation of sin, or the Fear of the Lord. Thirdly; Beneficence, or Zeal for the Glory of God, not only forcibly repelling whatever is contrary or detrimental to the Divine Honor, but also energetically striving to promote it by every possible means; both in ourselves — by the extinction of the guilt, penalty, and effects of sin; by our compliance with God's commandments, counsels, intentions; by the practice of all the virtues; — and in others, by prayer, word, example, service, and suffering. Hence we see that

Love ought to be found in deeds and sacrifices rather than in words and feelings.

Subject of this Meditation.— Charity, or the Love of Benevolence towards God in Himself, which all Christians are enabled to elicit by Sanctifying Grace, and which from the ordinary degrees may gradually rise to the ecstatic union of the contemplatives, the mystics, and the Saints.

Composition of Place.—To see myself standing before God our Creator, seated in light inaccessible above the myriads of glorious Angels and blissful Saints, who are actually interceding for me at the throne of the Most High.—"Standing," that is, ready for any act of service, any proof of love, which the Eternal Lord may be pleased to accept.

Petition.—"An intimate knowledge of the many and great benefits I have received, that, thoroughly grateful I may in all things love and serve His Divine Majesty." There is evidently a close connection between this final grace of the Exercises and the ultimate result of holy Indifference, " Desiring and Choosing only what is most Conducive to the End for which we were created."

First Point. " To Call to Mind the Benefits of my Creation, my Redemption, and Particular Gifts; dwelling with great affection on how much God our Lord has given me of what He has, and consequently how much He desires to give me Himself, in so far as compatible with His Eternal Decree and Infinite Sovereignty."

The Benefits of my Creation.— God in the beginning created for me this beautiful universe, the earth to be my temporary habitation, the plants to feed and clothe me, the animals for my sustenance, assistance, and diversion.   Under this heading, therefore, I should call to mind all physical, moral, and intellectual Gifts; whatever I receive through the senses, through the understanding, or through the will.   To realize the value of each Gift, I may suppose its entire absence or sudden privation.   Besides, after reflecting on what I myself have received and am receiving, I should also think of what others have received, so many millions and millions of men.   For we are all bound together by the bonds of a common origin, we form all one mighty family, we are all brothers, both by Nature and much more by Grace. The goods of each, therefore, are the goods of all; and the goods of all are the goods of each.   If some have been less favored by God in any respect, it is that they may receive more in a better and higher way, and also that others may possess in them an object of Gratitude towards God and of Charity towards their neighbor.

So, then, every breath I draw, every motion I make, every beating of my heart, every thought of my mind, every aspiration of my will, every moment of my life, is a Gift of God.   Every particle of food that nourishes me, every drop of water that refreshes me, every ray of sunshine that warms me, is a Gift of God.   All these Gifts are gratuitous; lavished on me, not only without any antecedent merit, but even in spite of much subsequent demerit.   In every Gift I should consider especially with what measureless Love it is bestowed by God; and from this I should strive to realize how earnestly He longs to give me Himself, in so far as I can become capable of receiving Him.

The Benefits of my Redemption.— Here I should briefly recall the Incarnation, Life, Passion, and Death of Jesus, my Adorable Savior; the Catholic Church and the Sacraments, especially the Blessed Eucharist; Sanctifying Grace, the virtues of Faith, Hope, and Charity, the seven Gifts of the Divine Spirit; my soul made a tabernacle of the Eternal Love, a sanctuary of the most Holy Trinity; the examples of the Saints, the prayers of the Faithful, the constant intercession of the Blessed, the powerful protection of my Guardian Angel, the tender solicitude of the Immaculate Virgin, Mother of God and also my Mother. How sublime, how priceless is every single one of these Supernatural Favors!

Particular Benefits.— Among these I should reckon first, my Religious Vocation, the proof of God's mysterious Predilection, bestowed on me in spite of so many sins and infidelities; then, the innumerable interior graces, conferring light and strength, as well as exterior helps, such as parents, teachers, advisers, books, sermons, incidents, all gradually and gently preparing me for the Divine Call; further, the still more abundant graces and special helps received in this Holy State, ever since I entered the novitiate, particularly the training of an experienced and saintly Master of Novices, the instructions and exhortations of Directors, the counsels and corrections of Superiors, my successive annual Retreats, and these actual Spiritual Exercises.

How wonderful, indeed, that Almighty God should have showered down such beautiful and varied Gifts, in such ceaseless profusion, on one so utterly unworthy! Yet they are only pledges of that Love with which He desires to give me Himself. For, what is infinitely superior to all His Gifts, He longs incessantly, as far as it can be done, to give me Himself. Of all God's Gifts this is the most admirable, His personal Love. Let me then " reflect what I, on my part, ought to offer and give to His Divine Majesty, namely, myself together with whatever is mine." How reasonable it is that I should make the most complete return for so many Gifts, bestowed so gratuitously and so lovingly, by Him, the infinitely Great God, on me a mere nothing, a despicable sinner; and also how just, since He could not possibly have bestowed these Gifts on me for any other purpose than His own Service and Glory! In fact, my human greatness, my royal nobility, my priestly dignity, lies precisely in being privileged to make this return to the Most High.

I must give Him, then, not only all I have, but my very self. This complete donation of self I have already made by the Sacred Vows of Religion; but it remains for me to confirm it daily more and more by the Perfect Observance of these Vows. " My God and my All! " He longs to become mine, as far as this is feasible to the Creator; and I long to be His, wholly, absolutely, forever. With profound humility, therefore, and with tender affection I will say, after St. Ignatius: " Take, O Lord, and receive all my liberty, my memory, my intellect, and my volition; whatever I have and possess. Thou hast given me all these things; to Thee, O Lord, I restore them; and as they are now doubly Thine, I beg Thee, dispose of them according to Thy Good Pleasure." Yes, O Lord, freely dispose of everything, my time, my talents, my body, my senses, my mind, my will, my health, and my very life. Henceforth, my only care, my one absorbing thought shall be how to do Thy most Holy Will, at the merest sign, even in the smallest matter, with all the energy of my being, with the deepest reverence and the greatest eagerness, at the cost of any hardship or ignominy! And this Adorable Will of God is unmistakably made known to me by the dispositions of His Fatherly Providence, by the example of Christ our Lord, by the supreme law of Fraternal Charity, by the prescriptions of my Rules, the duties of my Status, and the arrangements of my Superiors. But, evidently, it is by practising Perfect Obedience that I can best carry out this complete donation of myself to the Ever-Blessed Trinity.

However, I have still something more to give, namely, my Love. This is a "Contemplation for obtaining Love." One way to enkindle Love is intense Gratitude, prompting man to entire Self-Dedication; the other way is ardent Petition, inclining God to boundless Mercy. I must, then, ask for it with the utmost energy and confidence in the words of St. Ignatius. "O Lord, only give me Thy Love and Thy Grace, for this — namely, to love Thee in word and deed — this is all I care for, this alone and nothing else will do."

Total Self-Oblation, made with all possible fervor, is the immediate fruit of this Contemplation, while the remote fruit is Perfect Love. A most precious fruit, indeed, which under the motion of Divine Grace, may be relished in any of the Points; and wherever it is offered, we should concentrate our soul on it alone. This is what St. Ignatius refers to subsequently by the words: "reflecting on myself in the same way as has been said in the First Point, or in any other way that I shall feel to be better."

Second Point. "To Consider how God Dwells in Creatures; in the elements, in the plants, in animals, in men, and so in me; giving me being, life, and feeling; causing me to understand and to will; and making me His very Temple."

A lover not only gives all he has, but also strives to be ever Present to the beloved, at least in thought; and God, through the free act of creation, subjected Himself to this law of Love. God is Present by His essence, by His knowledge, and by His power; in all creatures, animate and inanimate; in the oceans and in the mountains; in the clouds and in the stars; in plants and in beasts, in Angels and in Men. His Presence is manifested by their very existence; by their physical qualities; by their life, strength, and sensation; by their learning, affection, and authority; by their supernatural virtues and heavenly graces. Especially, therefore, is He Present to me in my fellow Religious and in my Superiors. But most intimately is He Present to me in my own Heart.

This universal and immediate Presence of God means an infinitely loving watchfulness, an ineffably tender solicitude,— Divine Providence,— which extends even to the minutest and most trifling details, or in the words of our Blessed Lord, to the very hairs of my head. In fact, my Body is the Temple of the Ever-Blessed Trinity, while the Holy Ghost dwells like a most intimate and devoted Friend in my Soul. I am surrounded by this Loving Presence of God, I am immersed in it, for "in Him we live, and move, and have our being." But God subjected Himself to this law of Love in yet another and, to the human mind, far more striking way. He became Man, He dwelled amongst men in Human Form, He stayed on this earth for a number of years; and He not only remains still with me personally Present, both as God and as Man, in the Adorable Eucharist, but actually descends into my bosom by Holy Communion.

I too, then, if I really love God, if I sincerely desire
to advance in His love, I too must by all means strive
to be ever mindful of Him, to think, speak, and act in
His Sacred Presence. I must keep Present to Jesus in
the Holy Eucharist, by frequent and diligent Visits
from early morning till late at night, and particularly
by daily, fervent Communions made with longing
preparation and humble thanksgiving. Even while
taken up with my usual work, even while passing
through the public streets, my heart must stay at the
foot of the Altar with Jesus, my Divine Lover. I
must also watch over my Body as His Temple, over
my Soul as His Sanctuary, with the greatest care and
reverence, by checking every unguarded movement
and disorderly emotion. Besides, I must be constantly on the alert to see God in all creatures, and
all in Him; I must strive to honor Him in my fellow
men and in my Religious Companions; but I must
especially revere Him in my Superiors, by yielding
them Perfect Obedience.— Oblation and Love.

**Third Point. " To Consider how God Works and
Labors for Me in all Created Things on the Face of
the Earth;** that is, behaves like one that labors, as in
the heavens, elements, plants, fruit, cattle, and so
forth, calling them into being, preserving them, giving
them growth and feeling; and then to reflect on myself."

Love is always Active. Just as a lover is ever laboring for the beloved, so God is, as it were, ever laboring
for me in all creatures. Every change, every movement, every development, every growth, is an effect of
this Divine Labor. Thus He has Labored from the
beginning of the world, directing all His activity
towards my service, my well-being. With Infinite

Wisdom, Power, and Love, He has been arranging
everything for my benefit, for my happiness. God
Labors for me, not only directly, in the elements,
plants, and animals; but also indirectly through men,
my Religious Brethren, my various Superiors, and
through the Heavenly Spirits, especially my Angel
Guardian and Patron Saints. Their service, their
esteem, their affection is all an effect of His Labor.
And how many creatures day after day combine their
exertion,— which is wholly derived from Him and in
which He constantly participates,— in order to provide me with food, clothing, shelter, comfort, pleasure,
and information?

Besides, what is yet far more astounding, Jesus,
true God and true Man, Labored and Suffered for me,
from the moment of His Incarnation till His death on
the Cross. Even now He Labors for me in the Blessed
Eucharist. Also the Holy Ghost Labors in my mind
and will, by continual inspirations and numberless
graces, for my sanctification and perfection. In every
act of supernatural virtue I perform, this Adorable
Spirit Cooperates. Truly, Love and Service are inseparable.

In imitation of this Divine Exemplar and in return
for this Divine Service, I too must always Labor by
using my senses, my faculties, my talents, for the
Glory of God and for the Salvation of His beloved
Children. Giving freely what I have freely received, I
must strive to become all to all. I must ever Labor
for Him by the perfect accomplishment of His Adorable Will. In one word, I must henceforth devote all
my energy to the practice of Perfect Obedience and the
exercise of Fraternal Charity. How, indeed, can we
better correspond to this wondrous manifestation of
Divine Love, how can we more efficiently Labor for

our Heavenly Father than by mutual regard and affection, embracing most eagerly those offices and duties which afford most frequent opportunities for exercising these two virtues, and spending ourselves, according to the directions of our Superiors, in spiritual and corporal works of mercy.— Oblation and Love.

Fourth Point. " **To See how All Good Things and All Gifts Descend from Above;** as my limited power from the Supreme and Infinite Might on high, and in the same way, justice, goodness, pity, mercy, and so forth, just as the rays descend from the sun and waters from the spring. Then to conclude by reflecting on myself, as has been said before."

God is not only most Loving towards each one of us, as shown by His numberless Gifts, by His intimate Presence, by His unceasing Labor, but, besides, He is infinitely Lovable in Himself. To realize somewhat this Divine Loveliness, we must strive to rise gradually from the creatures to the Creator, observing the beauty of nature in the different realms of the physical universe; the beauty of the Human Soul and of the Angelic Spirit; the beauty of Mary the Queen of heaven and earth; the beauty of Jesus in His Sacred Humanity enthroned at the right hand of the Eternal Father; lastly, the Ever-Blessed Trinity, Inexhaustible Source of all beauty, infinitely surpassing even the most exalted creatures.

How interesting is even a tiny grain of sand, a little bit of mineral, when examined and analyzed with scientific instruments! Even after at least six thousand years of study, we barely know something of what lies just on the surface of these physical objects. How is a particle of matter made up? What is the

constitution of an atom? Some time ago, scientists
practically gave up the search by formulating the
atomic theory, but the recent discovery of radium shat-
tered their flimsy hypothesis and emphasized once
more man's prodigious ignorance. What, then, do we
know about this entire globe, about the sun, the plan-
ets, the comets, the nebulæ, and the millions or rather
billions of so-called fixed stars? Yet what grandeur
and beauty is scattered broadcast over the whole
earth, in landscapes, rivers, lakes, meadows, woods,
and mountains!

But passing from the mineral realm to the vegetable kingdom, what inscrutable mysteries do we find
even in a blade of grass! What do we know about
plants, their forces, their qualities? Botany is little
else but a long list of Latin labels. All the ablest students and experimenters of the whole world together,
could not produce one living cell of protoplasm.
And zoology, our knowledge of the animal kingdom,
so immense and so varied, is still more superficial.
Yet how wonderful is even the most common insect,
a fly! Try to make one if you can. How incomparably more perfect any one of these tiny creatures is
than our most improved aeroplane or latest launched
dirigible! Yet all this astounding beauty of min-
erals, plants, and animals is only a most distant imitation, a most dim reflection of the Divine Beauty,
and is entirely due to their absolute dependence on
God, their Infinite Creator.

This physical universe, however, though so magnificent to behold and so interesting to study, is evidently immensely inferior to the world of spirits, even
to a single human soul. Our faculties being so imperfect, we fall far short of the gigantic task of exploring
these loftier and still more mysterious fields of knowl-

edge. But one thing we all do realize; namely, that
the intelligent creation must be immeasurably more
noble, more beautiful, more admirable, than the irrational creation, about which, as we have seen, in spite
of more than six thousand years of constant experience and diligent investigation, we still know next to
nothing.

Lastly, rising once more from the whole natural
creation, rational as well as irrational, mind and matter, to the Supernatural World, the realm of Sanctifying Grace and Heavenly Favors, we stand utterly
helpless before an impassable gulf. About the only
thing we clearly recognize is this, that, in the Supernatural order of things, the wonders of God's workings must be incomparably far above whatever He
does in Nature, in matter or mind, in man or angel.
The few facts that God has deigned to make known
to us by revelation, we apprehend only under very
imperfect figures and images.

And now taking together all these various crea-
tions, the Material and the Spiritual, the Natural
and the Supernatural, with all their untold beauty,
all their countless wonders, gathering all this into
one immense universe of inconceivable excellence, and
multiplying it a hundred-thousandfold, even so I have
nothing but a faint image of the absolutely Infinite
Perfection, Power, Goodness, Loveliness of the Triune
God. And this Supreme Being for my sake became
Man, and on account of my sins died on a Cross. This
Adorable Master still stays with me in the Blessed
Eucharist, continually sacrifices Himself for me in
Holy Mass, daily gives Himself to me in Sacramental
Communion. By Creative Agency I was formed to His
distant likeness and placed in the condition of a serv-
ant. But by Sanctifying Grace I received a true

participation in His Immutable Nature, I became a
child of God the Father, a brother of God the Son, a
spouse of God the Holy Ghost. And all this is yet to
be completed in Heaven, when I shall be actually admitted to the very Family of the Ever-Blessed Trinity,
to the most intimate Society of the three Divine Persons. With what confidence, then, and with what energy, I should strive to become more and more perfect
after the pattern of my Heavenly Father, to become
more and more conformable in my whole conduct to
my Heavenly King, to become more and more docile
and devoted to my Heavenly Spouse!

Colloquy.— Here I will with great fervor renew my
Vows and my Resolutions, I will offer to the Adorable
Trinity all the Affection of devout Christians, of holy
Souls, of blessed Saints and Angels, of the Immaculate Virgin Mary, of the Sacred Heart of Jesus; wishing that I could gather into my own wretched, sinful
heart the Love of all the Children of God and thus
make some return to my most Amiable Creator, Redeemer, and Sanctifier. Oh! could I be wholly consumed with the flames of Divine Love. Oh! how I
long for the day, the hour, when I may be admitted
to see Him, my Eternal Lord, face to face, and to
be inebriated forever with His ineffable Goodness
and Beauty; when there will be no more danger of
losing Him, no more possibility of displeasing Him,
when I shall be irresistibly drawn to Love Him, without any distraction, without any intermission, as He
Himself has deigned to command me, with my whole
heart, with my whole soul, with my whole mind, and
with all my strength. But meanwhile, with the help
of His grace, I will Love Him here on earth, as I have
now learned better and understood more clearly, by

daily sacrificing myself entirely to His most Holy Will in Perfect Obedience, by daily embracing the Cross of Suffering and Contempt, for the Greater Glory of His Divine Majesty and for the Greater Good of His Beloved Children. I will conclude with an Our Father, the most appropriate prayer for a child of God.

THE END

APPENDIX

Of the three meditations contained in this appendix, either the first or the second may be found serviceable for the morning of the day after the Retreat. The third meditation has been added for the convenience of those who wish to follow up the exercises on Sin with the consideration of Death; in which case, by way of compensation, they may omit the meditation on Mary Magdalen. The list of books, which is necessarily very incomplete, may be found helpful to select suitable reading-matter for Community Retreats.

DEVOTION TO THE BLESSED VIRGIN

Introductory Remarks.— Those who by a singular favor of God have been called to be the chosen companions of Jesus, seem with the very grace of their Vocation to receive a spirit of filial reverence and affection for Mary, His most Holy Mother. And as, with increasing years of Religious Life, they come to understand more clearly the perfect union that exists between that Son and that Mother, they also realize more deeply the indispensable relation which their Devotion to Mary bears to their Conformity to Jesus, which is the supreme object of all their thoughts and endeavors, of all their prayers and penances. But what do we really understand by this Devotion to Mary?

By Devotion in general, as all will readily grant, we understand a certain attachment to an object or a person, worthy of our esteem and affection, an attachment not remaining hidden in the depths of our heart but manifesting itself, on suitable occasions, in our words and deeds. Hence it is evident that Devotion is not a mere matter of sentiment. Feeling or sentiment may give rise to Devotion and certainly forms its accidental ornament, but does not constitute its substantial core. A supernatural attachment, such as Devotion to the Blessed Virgin, which should consist merely of sentiment, would be little better than sheer illusion; it would be the outward appearance without the inward essence. On the other

hand, such an attachment solidly founded on motives
of esteem and affection, but without the accidental
finish of human feeling, though surely not an altogether perfect Devotion, would still be a very desirable disposition of the soul and one very pleasing to
our Heavenly Mother. Consequently, let us strive
thoroughly to appreciate the reasons we have for
revering and loving Mary, the Immaculate Virgin,
and for the rest look forward to everlasting bliss as
the condition in which, after the final resurrection,
our Devotion will reach its full maturity, its ultimate
perfection, when the body and all its powers will be
brought into complete and permanent harmony with
all the aspirations of the soul.

Yet mere esteem and affection do not constitute
Devotion. A third factor is wanted. When St. Ignatius, in the Second Week of the Exercises, directs
us to beg for a more intimate knowledge of our Lord,
in order that we may love Him more ardently and follow Him more closely, we realize, even though he
does not use the word, that what he wishes us to
implore is a more intense Devotion to Jesus, our
Adorable King. If so, we shall not be far wrong in
defining Devotion to Mary, a Reverential and Loving
Imitation of our Heavenly Queen and Mother. In
fact, the idea of Devotion contains three distinct elements, namely, veneration, affection, and service; and
though St. Thomas Aquinas makes Devotion to God
consist in a ready will to do whatever may promote
His glory, yet it is clear that this readiness of the
will postulates a mind appreciative of the Divine
Excellence, and an activity directed continually
towards the Divine Service.

Subject of this Meditation.— Our reasons for

revering Mary, our motives for loving Mary, and our means of imitating Mary.

Composition of Place.— The town of Nazareth, the house of the Blessed Virgin, the room of the Annunciation.

Petition.— A more solid, more tender, and more active Devotion to Mary, the Mother of God.

First Point. Our Reasons for Revering Mary.
Since the Blessed Virgin is the most perfect and most exalted of all purely created beings, it cannot be difficult to assign some special claims she has to our Reverence.   The first that naturally offers itself for our consideration is her Sinlessness.   While all other men, in the first instant of their existence are infected by those baneful consequences of the disobedience of Adam, which we comprehend under the term "original sin," Mary, by a marvelous favor conferred on her in view of the merits of her future Son, the Divine Redeemer, was preserved from contracting this hereditary stain.   In other words, she was conceived Immaculate.   At the same time, the Blessed Virgin was completely exempt from concupiscence, that undue inclination towards the goods of earth, towards the pleasures of sense, towards the worship of self, which draws man to evil by forestalling and obscuring his reason.   And what is more, by another most wonderful privilege, Mary ever kept her soul free from the slightest actual sin, nay even from the smallest inordination, that is, she never for a moment swerved in the least from the Adorable Will of God, but corresponded to every indication of it with absolute fidelity and accomplished it with the combined energy of her entire being.

But Sinlessness, after all, is only a negative perfection and, strictly speaking, admits of no degrees.
Let us, therefore, turn our attention to something
positive, namely Grace. "A creature," says St.
Thomas, "receives so much the more Grace as it is
more closely united to God." Now, never was man
or angel admitted to so close a union with God as
Mary enjoyed at the very dawn of her existence, destined as she was from all eternity to become the
Mother of the Incarnate Word; and, hence, we need
not wonder if the Doctors of the Church maintain
that the Grace bestowed on our Blessed Lady in her
first sanctification was more abundant than that
reached by the greatest Saint or the highest Seraph
at the consummation of their merits. Indeed, not a
few Theologians even hold that the Grace lavished
on the Immaculate Virgin in the moment of her Conception, exceeded all the Grace ever to be possessed
by the whole assembly of men and angels arrived at
the summit of their Perfection. Whichever view we
may adopt, we should bear in mind that Grace is not
measured by quantity but by intensity. This initial
wealth of Sanctifying Grace was accompanied by a
proportionate infusion of the theological and moral
Virtues,— faith, hope, charity, prudence, justice,
humility, fortitude,— as well as by a most copious
outpouring of the seven Gifts of the Holy Ghost.
And since the Blessed Virgin had from the outset
the full use of her faculties, she entered immediately
upon that perfect correspondence to all these Divine
Favors which caused them to be multiplied at every
successive instant of her earthly existence. In attempting to gaze at such fulness of Grace, at such
loftiness of Sanctity, our mind is completely dazzled.
    Yet, in addition to her absolute Sinlessness and

surpassing Grace, Mary possesses still another and more powerful title to our Reverence, and that is her inconceivable Dignity of Mother of God. Inconceivable, not only to the human mind and angelic spirit, but even to the Ever-Blessed Virgin herself. God alone knows the true Greatness of Mary, His Mother, because He alone knows His own Infinite Greatness. But for us, just as the Incarnation of the Second Person of the Trinity will forever remain an unfathomable mystery, so will proportionately the Dignity of the Mother of the Incarnate Word. Mary participates in the Divine Excellence not only in a far higher degree than the other Blessed, but also in a mode altogether distinct and unique. Hence, just as the Adoration we give to God, our Sovereign Lord, can never become excessive, so the Reverence we owe to Mary, His favorite creature, can never be exaggerated. This fact, that she is the Mother of God, is the source and the summary of all else, of her absolute Freedom from Sin and her perfect Fulness of Grace. Hail, then, Virgin Immaculate, Mary, Full of Grace, Mother of our Creator and Redeemer!

Second Point.   Our Motives for Loving Mary.

Here again we must limit ourselves to a cursory review of such motives as obtain exclusively in the case of the Blessed Virgin. While all men claim our sincere good-will, because they are made to the image and likeness of God, because they are enabled by grace to enter as children of adoption the very family of God, and also because they are accordingly loved by God Himself; Mary deserves our warmest Affection, because she is the most admirable Masterpiece of the Almighty Father, because she has been admitted to the most intimate Relationship of

Mother of the Eternal Son, and because She is, consequently, the most tenderly cherished Spouse of the Holy Ghost. We ought to love our neighbor because he is really lovable, but the Blessed Virgin is incomparably more lovable than any other creature, while God is infinitely more Lovable than all. Hence, that personal Love of Jesus which we are taught by St. Ignatius to carry to the point of embracing for His sake poverty and pain, contempt and insult, that personal Love can never burn in the heart of a Religious without a correspondingly ardent Affection for Mary.

Again, the Blessed Virgin is also most closely associated with our Adorable Savior, as the Coredemptrix of the human race. It is usual, in explaining the difference between the Sacrifice of the Cross and the Sacrifice of the Mass, to point out that on Calvary Jesus was the only Priest just as He was the only Victim, while on the Altar He is assisted under both these aspects by the faithful present and even by the entire Church. Yet this is true only in so far as Jesus and Mary, in that awful tragedy of Golgotha, constituted practically but one moral agent, one Priest as well as one Victim. Jesus was not absolutely alone in offering Himself on the Cross for our redemption. There stood by the Cross of Christ His Sorrowful Mother. Mary intimately realized the wonderful mystery that was being accomplished on Calvary, and as formerly at the Annunciation she had given her humble consent to the miraculous Incarnation of the Eternal Word, so now at the Crucifixion she generously joined in the fearful Holocaust of her Divine Son. Thus, the share she has in the salvation of the world is not only surpassing great, but also quite indispensable and altogether singular.

Hence, while the mere recollection of the torments and ignominy of the Cross, the sight of a Crucifix or the act of Blessing ourselves, ought to fill our hearts with contrite Love for Jesus, our Adorable Redeemer, it should also animate them with grateful Affection for Mary, our heroic Coredemptrix.

There is still a third motive why we should Love the Blessed Virgin, one which, humanly speaking, appeals to us more forcibly than any other. Mary is also our Heavenly Mother. We are her beloved children,—yes, we in particular, the privileged members of Holy Church, the chosen companions of Christ Jesus. For each one of us she has labored and suffered while on earth, for each one she is now praying and pleading in Heaven. If we could gather up all our experiences of maternal care and realize all our recollections of motherly affection, and could multiply and intensify the resultant to the very borders of the infinite, we should still possess but a very inadequate concept of the profound solicitude and ceaseless concern with which Mary watches over the welfare, the happiness, the salvation of even the least and lowliest descendant of Adam, of even the most reckless and hardened sinner. But who could venture even to give an idea of the tender love which she cherishes for those who strive in all things to do the Perfect Will of her Adorable Lord, to become true followers of her Divine Son, those who seek to be clothed with the same livery and to be spent in the same labors as Jesus Crucified? In return, what should be our Affection for Mary, the supreme Object of the power, wisdom, and love of the Most High, the active Coredemptrix of our fallen race, and our own most devoted Mother?

Third Point.   Our Means of Imitating Mary.

If Reverence may be styled the stem of Devotion and Love its flower, Imitation may well be called its fruit. Surely, those who wish to be truly devoted to the Immaculate Virgin, ought to regulate their conduct after her example. Tender sentiments and burning words are good, provided they are borne out by diligent action. Otherwise they are nothing but illusion and deceit. In what particulars, then, should we strive to Imitate Mary, our Queen and our Mother? Her earthly existence was preeminently a life of Prayer, of Humility, and of Sacrifice. Such, consequently, should be ours also.

A life of Prayer means a life of silence and recollection, of habitual watchfulness over self and constant communion with God. Even amongst those who have long since consecrated themselves entirely to the Divine Service and Glory, there are found some who seem to think an interior life incompatible with exterior activity. But their view, which runs counter to the unanimous teaching of ascetic writers, is based on a misconception, and a simple explanation may suffice to remove their difficulty. It cannot be denied that to form the habit of recollection or to foster the practice of Prayer, we have to lead, for a considerable time, a more or less retired existence, apart from the noise and bustle of the world. But once this inward discipline has been acquired, far from proving a hindrance to outward efficiency, it becomes one of its most powerful and enduring mainsprings. Witness the lives of the Saints, their ceaseless exertions and their astounding achievements. Besides, of what profit will our external labors be to our neighbor, if we are not internally united to God? How can a man pretend to communicate to others what he himself lacks? This is why every Religious Order affords its members constant opportunities for cultivating the spirit of Prayer. Let us strive to avail ourselves of them to the utmost, as loving clients and genuine children of the Blessed Virgin Mary.

Prayer puts the grace and light and energy we need within our reach, but without Humility we would have no capacity for receiving these heavenly treasures. Mary was full of Grace, because she was thoroughly Humble. In fact, among all her marvelous virtues, Humility stands out most conspicuous. It was the Humility of His Handmaid that induced the Most High to become her Son. Humility is at once the most fundamental and the most practicable of all the moral virtues. For it is nothing else than the habit of referring to God everything that is His, namely, whatever good we see in any creature, and to ourselves everything that is ours, namely, our own nothingness and sinfulness. Now, of this fact — that of ourselves we are worse than nothing — we are reminded unceasingly by every object that meets our gaze or falls under our notice: material imperfections and physical drawbacks, bodily ailments, mental defects, and moral shortcomings, trifling mishaps and big disasters, everlastingly repeat to us the same lesson. Hence we can humble ourselves inwardly as well as outwardly, whether alone or with others, at every moment of our conscious existence; the opportunities are never wanting. Humility being only the intelligent and deliberate application of a self-evident truth that happens to be most unpleasant and repugnant to our fallen nature, Self-Humiliation constitutes the best panacea for all our spiritual miseries, the cursed brood of pride. For the sake, therefore, of the Blessed

Virgin, in order to become more like to her, our
Heavenly Mother, and thus more truly her children,
let us gladly welcome every occasion of self-denial,
which is either a Humiliation of the body or a Humiliation of the soul.

But if Humility be sanctity, why not concentrate
our Devotion to Mary on the practice of this one
virtue? Strictly speaking, there would be no objec-
tion, if only we had a perfectly adequate notion of
Humility. But here lies the difficulty. Accordingly,
a few words about Self-Sacrifice as a third means of
Imitating the Immaculate Virgin will not be superfluous. If we study the word Devotion, we recognize
that it is nearly synonymous with Sacrifice. However, since the Mother of God accepts our Devotion
only on behalf of her Divine Son, the desire of Self-
Sacrifice which it necessarily implies, will cause us
to be immolated more and more completely, in union
with her, for the Greater Glory of His Sovereign
Majesty. And this leads us back once more to the
wondrous Sacrifice of the Cross, in which, as we saw,
Mary cooperated so intimately with Jesus, that while
He is truly our sole Redeemer she merited nevertheless
to become our Coredemptrix. Since Holy Mass is the
unbloody reenactment of the bloody Holocaust of
Calvary, it is especially while assisting at the Sacred
Mysteries that we should strive, after the example of
Mary and through her intercession, to unite ourselves
to our Divine Master, both as priests and as victims,
by offering our body and soul, our senses and faculties, our health, our liberty, and our very life, for the
same ends for which He continues to offer Himself
hourly on our altars; namely, adoration, impetration,
and thanksgiving. And that this Self-Immolation in
Holy Mass may become more and more sincere, gen-

erous, and perfect, let us at the same time earnestly beg for abundant grace to carry it out practically, throughout the ensuing day, by eagerly embracing every opportunity of suffering and contempt, especially such as may occur in the observance of our Rules, in the accomplishment of our Duties, in the exercise of Obedience and Charity. By thus Imitating the Holy Mother of God in her Prayer, her Humility, and her Sacrifice, we shall prove our Devotion to consist not merely in Feelings or Words, but in earnest and fruitful Deeds.

Colloquy.— First, with the Blessed Virgin, joining deep confusion to lively confidence. Confusion; because of the immense difference between me and Her: She my Mother, so holy, and I, her child, so wretched; She so rich in grace, and I so destitute; She the Coredemptrix of the world, the Queen of Apostles, and I worse than a useless servant, not only through the grave scandal caused by my past sins, but also by the bad example of my actual worldliness, selfishness, and pride. Confidence; because of her irresistible power with Christ our Savior, assuring me that through her protection I too shall once be admitted, together with many others enlightened and encouraged by my endeavors, to the bliss of Heaven, and thus be united to Her for all eternity in the knowledge, love, and possession of God. After this I will say a Hail Mary. Secondly; with our Divine Lord: for just as fervent Imitation of Mary Immaculate leads necessarily to closer Union with Jesus Crucified, so nowhere better than in the Heart of her Adorable Son can we learn real filial Devotion to our Heavenly Mother. And then I will conclude with an Our Father.

THE BADGE OF PERSEVERANCE

Subject of this Meditation.— The Sacred Heart Badge as a symbol of Religious Perfection and an aid to Perseverance in our good Resolutions.

Composition of Place.— The Chapel in which our Divine Lord appeared to Blessed Margaret Mary Alacoque showing her His Sacred Heart, wounded, inflamed, surmounted by a cross, and encircled by a crown of thorns.

Petition.— That my heart may become daily more and more like to the Sacred Heart of Jesus by the more diligent practice of poverty, chastity, obedience, and regular observance.

First Point. The Wound, a Symbol of Poverty.

The large Wound in the Sacred Heart of Jesus, through which He poured forth even the last drop of His Blood, is an eloquent symbol of that Perfect Poverty which He practised during His entire life, having not even a stone whereon to lay His head and dying in absolute destitution on the Cross.

Surely no self-spoliation could go further than that of our Lord and Savior. I will strive to Imitate Him by embracing the Poverty proper to my Institute, in food, clothing, lodging, and all other details of common life; not admitting any superfluities but rejoicing when things happen to disagree with my personal tastes or even to be insufficient for my actual needs. I will also strive to Imitate Him by keeping myself wholly detached from the very objects that are given me for my present use, with prudent watchfulness lest the enemy should turn them into snares to enslave my heart. I will, moreover, strive to Imitate Him by a childlike and undoubting confidence, an entire and exclusive reliance on the Infinite Goodness of God, never looking for temporal support to any creature, or human favor, or personal exertion, and never indulging in any misgivings or apprehensions about my own future usefulness or the financial condition of the Community. What an insult to the Love of our Heavenly Father and what a disregard for the Doctrine of our Blessed Savior, to entertain any such worldly solicitude! But how doubly shameful and detestable in a Religious, in one that has bound himself by Vow to this complete self-abandonment to Divine Providence!

Second Point.   The Flames, a Symbol of Chastity.
The Flames of love that we see bursting forth from the Sacred Heart of Jesus may very appropriately be taken to symbolize Angelic Chastity. For just as Poverty signifies not only detachment from earthly possessions, which is its negative aspect, but also reliance on Divine Providence, which is its positive side; so Chastity means not only renunciation of sensual affection but also acquisition of spiritual love, by which the human soul is united to her Heavenly Spouse, a supernatural love founded on the same motive as the ardent charity that ever animated our Blessed Lord.

Hence I will strive to Please my Adorable Master by ever keeping strict guard over my senses, particularly my eyes and my touch, and by constantly seeking mortification in cold and heat, in hunger and thirst, in prayer and labor, in fatigue and sickness, in public and private penances. I will also strive to Imitate Him by fostering in my heart, towards all men but especially towards my fellow Religious, genuine and practical Charity. For if the children of an earthly father are bound to mutual affection, how much more the children of our Father in Heaven, particularly such as have voluntarily pledged themselves to live and labor together for His Greater Glory! This Charity I should exercise unceasingly by being kind in all my thoughts, words, and actions; not unconcerned or unsympathetic, but full of delicate attention and tender regard for their needs and troubles, so as to discover and even to anticipate them with industrious simplicity; and, while not expecting or permitting that they should accommodate themselves to my whims or wishes, by seeking on every occasion to satisfy their reasonable desires and to second their lawful aspirations. On the other hand, I should firmly resist and resolutely stifle any tendency to particular friendship, in my conversations or dealings with companions, pupils, or acquaintances. I will, moreover, strive to Imitate the Sacred Heart of Jesus in His Burning Love of God, Father, Son, and Holy Ghost; and this especially by ardent aspirations from morning till night, by frequent visits to my Divine Master in the Adorable Sacrament, by daily sacrificing myself with Him in Holy Mass, and by perseveringly receiving Him in Holy Communion with deep humility and intense fervor. Oh! may this celestial fire purify my heart ever more and more from all earthly dross, and render it more and more similar to the Most Pure and Loving Hearts of Jesus and Mary.

Third Point. The Cross, a Symbol of Obedience.

Since Jesus was Obedient even to the death of the Cross, what else could the Cross that surmounts the Sacred Heart symbolize for a Religious than the virtue of Obedience? Just as Christ consummated the sacrifice of Himself on that Hallowed Wood, so the self-immolation of a Religious is completed by Holy Obedience.

Hence I will strive to Imitate my Adorable Lord, by making the practice of Obedience the chief occupation of every day and every hour of my life, from the moment I arise at the first sound of the bell till the time set for retiring to rest, ever aiming at the utmost promptitude and exactness in execution, at the sincerest joy and love in will, at the greatest simplicity and perspicacity in judgment. I will also strive to Imitate Him by recognizing in the persons of my Superiors, not mere men subject to errors and failings, but the special Representatives of the Most High, and by entertaining towards them, in consequence, deep reverence and warm affection. Thus, Holy Obedience will become for me an ever welcome opportunity of mortification and humiliation, an efficient instrument of immolating my whole self, my body and soul, my senses and faculties, my health and my very life, in union with my Crucified Savior.

Fourth Point. The Crown of Thorns, a Symbol of Regular Observance.

The Crown of Thorns encircling the Sacred Heart will aptly symbolize my fourth Vow either expressed or implied, namely, my further Obligation of devoting my remaining years to this Institute, by the faithful Observance of all its Rules and Constitutions. In some Religious Orders the members take instead a Vow of Enclosure. But, whatever be the particular form of this Obligation by which we have bound ourselves forever to the State of Evangelical Perfection, we must again distinguish the negative aspect from the positive. Taken negatively, this Obligation would only impose separation from the World. But our Divine Lord surely looks for something more than this. The one object why He placed us here in Religion, isolated from the World, is that we might wholly immolate ourselves for the conversion and sanctification of this very World. After the example of the Apostle St. Paul, each one of us is to fill up in himself what is lacking to the Passion of Christ, each one of us is called to contribute his own personal Holocaust towards the wider and fuller application of the infinite merits of the Cross. This is the positive side of this fourth Vow.

Hence I will cherish especially those Rules which are most Disagreeable to nature, and like the Thorns in the Crown of my Adorable Master, I will press them generously into my heart. Besides, I will studiously keep my soul free from all Intercourse with the World, from all temporal interests and secular gossip, attending only to the things of eternity, to the business of my Heavenly Father. In particular, I will abstain from Reading any of the Sensational dailies, weeklies, magazines, or novels of the present day, and not even touch such publications except it be my strict duty to acquaint myself with some of their contents. On the other hand, while carefully observing the Rule of Silence, yet, when Obedience or Charity require me to Speak, I will strive to avail myself of every such opportunity to exhort sinners to contrition and worldlings to penance, to rouse the lukewarm to true fervor and the devout to apostolic

zeal, in short, to fill all hearts with contempt of earth
and forgetfulness of self, and to inflame them with
the love of God and the desire of everlasting Bliss.

Colloquy with the Sacred Heart of Jesus, begging
Him that, through great fidelity in keeping my holy
Vows and good Resolutions, I may steadily advance
in Religious Perfection and daily become more like
to Him, my Supreme Exemplar. But first having
recourse to the Immaculate Heart of Mary, I will
implore her to obtain for me these same graces from
her Divine Son, through her all-powerful intercession.— Hail Mary.   Our Father.

DEATH

Introductory Remarks.— As sin follows from in-ordination, so inordination arises from worldliness. Hence the Apostle St. John exhorts us all in these words: " Love not the world nor the things that are in the world. If any one love the world, the charity of the Father is not in him." For God can-not endure a divided heart. God and the World are two rivals that cannot be served at the same time. Yet even Religious are to some extent infected by the World. We have worldly views, worldly princi-ples, worldly aspirations, worldly manners. One of the best means to cure ourselves of this worldliness is to consider that " the World passes together with its concupiscence, but he that does the Will of God abides forever."

Subject of this Meditation.— The end of all that pertains to the world, Death.

Composition of Place.— The room in which a Reli-gious has just died, the coffin containing the corpse, and the candles lighted on both sides.

Petition.— That I may earnestly resolve to make up for whatever was worldly, inordinate, and sinful in my past life; and that I may apply myself ener-getically to regulate my remaining years in such a way as to insure a happy Death.

First Point. The Meanings of Death.
Death Means the Separation of the Soul from the

Body. How many sufferings this will entail! Not only intense physical pains, but perhaps also violent temptations stirred up by our infernal and implacable enemy, the Devil. Well may we pray with great humility and earnestness, "Holy Mary, pray for us, sinners, now and at the hour of our Death." What will be the fear and anguish of a Christian that has not lived for Heaven, for God, but for this earth, for self; of a Religious that has been neglectful of Prayer and careless in the reception of the Sacraments, has exercised no restraint over his senses and discarded the practice of mortification; in a word, of one who has led a worldly existence?

As soon as the Soul has departed, sometimes even much earlier, the Body becomes an object of loathing and horror; then it turns into a shocking mass of corruption, which serves as food to the worms; and after a few years there is nothing left of it but a heap of dust that will in the course of ages be scattered to the four winds. With what bitter remorse will the lost Soul of the worldling behold this utter humiliation, this complete destruction of his Body! "O fool that I was," he will exclaim, "this, then, is what I have pampered and worshiped at the price of my Eternal Salvation." But it will be too late.

For me, however, it is not yet too late to learn the lesson taught me by the impending dissolution of my Body. So did St. Margaret of Cortona, on seeing the corpse of her murdered lover, with whom she had been living for years in unlawful union, and who one day, on passing through a dark forest, was stabbed to the heart by an enemy. So did St. Francis Borgia, on beholding the ghastly remains of the empress Isabella, the wife of the mighty Charles V, a woman renowned for her beauty and accomplishments.

I too must learn not to devote more time or attention to my Perishable Body, to its comfort, to its clothing, to its lodging, than is demanded by the Service of Almighty God and the Salvation of my Immortal Soul. Oh, the vanity and deception of worldly adornments! as if the rags with which we are obliged to cover ourselves, made of the dead refuse of plants and animals, were not a standing proof of our native misery and personal degradation. How far preferable is the simplicity and uniformity of the Religious habit, fare, cell, and furniture. And shall I still hesitate to mortify my corruptible flesh, to restrain my eyes, my touch, my tongue, to subdue its senseless opposition to my Everlasting Spirit, to my Higher Interests?

Death Means also the Separation from the Goods of this World, earthly possessions, earthly amusements, earthly distinctions, popularity, standing, influence. How frightful an ordeal this will be for the worldling! None of these things can be taken along; others will enjoy what he has gathered with so much anxiety; and soon his very name will be forgotten. How next to impossible it will be for him at the hour of Death to yield up all at once every one of those objects on which his heart has been set for so many years! That is why our Divine Lord tells us, "It is more difficult for a rich man to enter heaven, than for a camel to pass through the eye of a needle."

Oh! what blindness, what folly, to be so solicitous, so eager, so absorbed in the pursuit of these Perishable Goods, these Empty Honors! Yes, and for us too, Religious, though by the grace of God we have given up all worldly advantages and prospects, what a shame to be still so little concerned about the Imperishable Treasures, the Unfading Glory of Heaven.

Let us admire and imitate the practical wisdom and consistent conduct of St. Aloysius, who would often ask himself, " What is this when compared with eternity?" or of St. Stanislaus, who was wont to exclaim, " I was born for something better and nobler."

We ought, then, to labor perseveringly at detaching ourselves from whatever belongs to this earth. In obedience to the loving invitation of Christ our Lord, " If thou wilt be perfect, sell all thou hast and give it to the poor, and come follow Me," we must not only keep our Vow but also earnestly strive to advance in the Virtue of Poverty. Here we see once more how our Religious Profession tends to procure for us a happy Death. But we must make diligent use of the opportunities it offers, we must be eager to give up unnecessary articles and little conveniences, we must strive to be really poor.

Death Means, moreover, the Separation from Relatives and Friends. For loving and generous souls this separation is most painful. Now, those who are drawn towards the Religious Life have usually a loving disposition. Hence they are particularly exposed to temptations that arise from an inordinate love of Relations and Acquaintances. What must we do? Let us anticipate the work of Death, by changing this natural, carnal, selfish affection into one that is unselfish, spiritual, and supernatural. Otherwise we should be unfit for the Religious State; according to the words of Christ: " He who hates not father and mother, yea and his own life also, cannot be My disciple." By thus purifying our affection we do not destroy it; on the contrary, we ennoble and strengthen it.

But to succeed in this we must not be afraid of the cost, and avail ourselves of every opportunity afforded us in Religion. We must not wish or try to see our Relatives, even on the plea of doing them good, which is mostly a self-illusion or a deceit of Satan. We should not allow ourselves to worry about their temporal interests, convinced that we have left them in the care of our most Loving Father in Heaven. If we receive letters, let us mortify our curiosity for a while, a few hours, a day or two, and before reading their communications let us beg our Lord for the grace not to be mastered by our feelings. We must likewise practise moderation in writing letters. It is a good plan for Religious to write to their Relations only at fixed intervals; once, twice, four times, or six times a year, in proportion to the closeness of the kinship.

But what has meanwhile become of the Soul after this Threefold Separation, from the Body, from earthly Goods, and from Friends and Relatives? It has entered upon a new and unchangeable phase of its never-ending existence; it has stood in the presence of the All-Holy, Almighty, Inexorable Judge; it has seen in one intellectual flash all the good omitted and all the evil committed; it has been called to a strict account for every word and action, for its most transient thoughts as well as for its most hidden desires, for the use of every natural gift and every supernatural favor bestowed on it during this earthly period of probation; and it has already heard the Divine, Irrevocable Sentence that will fix its future lot for all Eternity, either in Heaven or in Hell. There will be no room for defense, no call for explanation, just as there will be no plea for mercy, no appeal for pardon. Every sin not atoned for here below shall receive its full measure of punishment, and the whole debt will have to be paid till the last farthing.

Such is the Particular Judgment that will be passed upon us at the very moment of our Death.

Second Point. The Characteristics of Death.

Death is most Certain as to Fact. All men without exception are to die; either in the ordinary way through sickness, or in some unusual way, through accident. Many people nowadays boast that they will not accept anything as a fact unless proved by actual experience; yet, though nobody now living ever had the actual experience of Death, every one holds it for Certain that he is going to die. No man ever dreamed of being kept alive indefinitely by some unknown forces of nature, though these are credited even with the working of miracles. Within a few years, then, the sixteen hundred millions that now inhabit the earth, will all have passed away. Whether rich or poor, learned or ignorant, talented or dull, savage or civilized, good or bad, every one has got to die. Yet many live as if they were by no means convinced of this fact. They have good reason to tremble at the very thought of Death, and hence they try to drown its salutary admonitions in distractions and frivolities.

Let us be more sensible, and daily prepare for Death with the utmost diligence. Every indisposition, every infirmity is a warning of our impending dissolution. The Sentence of Death was passed on Adam and all his descendants by Almighty God. Our own sins too, even our venial sins, have fully deserved this punishment. This is why St. Paul writes to the Corinthians that many sleep, are dead, on account of their irreverent and unbecoming conduct in church. Let us accept Death even now in atonement for our sins, let us humble ourselves be-

neath the chastising hand of God, and let us strive to
conform our Death as closely as possible to that of
our Adorable Lord and Savior.

But Death is most Uncertain as to Circumstances.
Death comes oftenest as a surprise; even very sick
people usually fail to realize that their end is so near.
Hence our Lord tells us that Death will come upon
us as a thief in the night.   The when, the where, and
the how of our death, are completely hidden from our
view.   We do not know anything about the time,
place, and manner of our departure from this world.
How dreadful!   To this truth there is but one exception.   There is one important circumstance which
we can foresee with a fair amount of probability, almost with certainty.   It is whether a person is going
to die in the State of Grace or in the State of Sin.
For, both reason and faith tell us plainly, "As a
man lives so shall he die."   Consequently, if we wish
to die in the friendship of God, we must exert ourselves never for a moment to trifle with a temptation
to grievous sin.   If we want to die with a prayer on
our lips, we should pray often and fervently during our daily occupations.   If we wish to die with
the Sacraments, the surest way is to receive Holy
Communion as far as we can every morning, with the
best possible preparation and thanksgiving.

How grateful, therefore, we should feel for having
been called to Religion, how highly should we esteem
our holy Institute!   How pleasant it is to live in the
convent, and how safe to die!   For there every help
is afforded to persevere in Sanctifying Grace, there
every opportunity is given for the practice of Prayer,
there every facility is found for the frequent and
fervent reception of the Sacraments.   Since we wish
to die in the company of Jesus, Mary, and Joseph,

let us constantly live in their close imitation and loving intimacy. This, indeed, is the essence of the Religious State. How awful it is to die in a doubtful condition, in a lukewarm disposition; and how blessed it is to die in the Lord, in the consciousness of being united with Him on the Cross!

But again, the Moment of Death is most Decisive. We die only once. Death is the great Crisis of our whole existence. On that one moment will depend everything forever after: the salvation or perdition of our Immortal Souls. Our last agony is not so much the beginning of the end, but rather the end of the beginning, the close of the initial period of our existence, the conclusion of our preparation for eternity. A bad Death can never be repaired. Hence, to insure a good Death, it is absolutely necessary to be always ready. Am I ready to die right now? Is there any Task I should prefer to have accomplished, any Resolution I should wish to have taken, any Sacrifice I should like to have made? How would I spend the remaining months or days, if I were to die before the end of this year? With what fervor I would apply myself to Prayer and Penance; with what diligence I would practise Poverty, Modesty, and Obedience; with what energy I would attend to the subject of my Particular Examen. Yet I may die much sooner, even before the end of this month or this week, in fact within the next twenty-four hours.

Third Point. The Preparations for Death.

The most obvious Preparation we can make for a holy Death is habitual Fervor. Even at the best, life is but all too short. Hence we should be watchful not to lose one single instant. We ought never to devote more time to sleep or rest or recreation than really indispensable. From the moment we awake, we should strive to give ourselves entirely to God, in sentiments of adoration, contrition, confidence, and love. Day after day we must exert ourselves by means of the General and Particular Examens to root up all our defects; to purify our heart completely from every venial sin, from every inordinate affection, from every worldly folly; and thus to inflame it more and more with a sincere and ardent love of God and men.

Confession also is an excellent Preparation for Death, provided we labor to make it every time as well as we can, not so much by searching the inmost recesses of our soul — which ought rather to be done in our daily Examinations of Conscience — but especially by conceiving real and deep confusion blended with fervent and practical contrition. While carefully shunning all scrupulosity we should persistently strive to acquire greater delicacy of conscience, which means a more thorough detestation of sin, inordination, and worldliness. To this it will help very much if we earnestly seek to expiate our past faults by every means in our power; not only eagerly accepting the little trials and hardships sent us by God, and gladly embracing the opportunities of penance that come in our Daily Duties and Religious Exercises, but generously adding to the customary acts of mortification some special practices according to the advice or with the permission of our Confessor or Superior.

However, the best Preparation for a happy Death is frequent reception of Holy Communion, since it constitutes a Divine Pledge of Everlasting Life. Unless we are positively prevented by circumstances, we should not allow a single day to pass without partaking of this Heavenly Banquet. However dry, drowsy, or distracted we may feel, we should never hesitate to approach the Holy Table as long as, not conscious of a grievous fault, we are desirous of advancing in the service and love of God. An intense hunger springing from a vivid realization of our manifold shortcomings, and a boundless trust arising from a lively faith in this Adorable Mystery,— these form the chief dispositions with which we should strive to welcome our Heavenly Guest. It is in particular this Divine Sacrament that will enable us to die to ourselves and will render our physical Death more peaceful and more meritorious. " Blessed are they that die in the Lord." These words of Holy Writ will apply literally to us if, every time we prepare for Communion, we take care to do so as though it were to be our Viaticum.

Colloquy: first with St. Joseph, patron of a holy Death in the tender embrace of Jesus and Mary; then with the Blessed Virgin, our Mother, whose Death was the effect of her most ardent love; and lastly with our Adorable Savior on the Cross exclaiming, " Father, into Thy hands I commend My spirit."— Our Father.

CPSIA information can be obtained
at www.ICGtesting.com
Printed in the USA
LVOW10s0226160418
573622LV00020B/563/P